2011 Vol. 67, No. 3

Scaling the Higher Education Pyramid:
Academic and Career Success of Minorities and Women in Science and Engineering

Issue Editors: Moin Syed and Martin M. Chemers

Journal of Social Issues, Vol. 67, No. 3, 2011, pp. 431–434

Foreword: Pursuing Effective Integrated Education

Claude M. Steele*

Columbia University

Pursuing Effective Integrated Education

The American dream of having a truly integrated society in which racial, sexual, and class identities do not obstruct one's life chances, is built on a more specific American dream, that of having a truly integrated educational system, one that, throughout the system from K through 20 or so, affords opportunity to everyone, equal opportunity. It is hard to imagine the larger American dream without the specific American dream, without successfully integrating American schooling. Thus schools are, like it or not, perhaps the major site of America's struggle to integrate itself. We should be proud that as a society we have made a public commitment to these dreams—a commitment signaled most strongly perhaps by the 1954 *Brown v. Board Education* Supreme Court Decision that desegregated American schooling, by the civil rights movement itself, and by the civil rights legislation of the 1960s.

There was great optimism during that era. There was a sense that desegregation—simply opening the doors of previously segregated schools and universities—would be enough; that women and minorities would walk through those doors and fairness of opportunity would be achieved, an integrated society would be achieved.

But soon, and certainly as the years went by, this optimism—and the dreams of integration themselves—began to fray a bit. Two opposing forces quickly emerged: (1) resistance to the very goal of integration in the face of competing priorities; and (2) the gradual recognition that integrated schools and classrooms might not automatically produce equal opportunity, certainly not equal performance and outcomes.

---

*Correspondence concerning this article should be Claude M. Steele.

Woody Allen tells a joke about two Jewish women complaining about the food at a Bar Mitzvah. One says, "Boy, the food is bad." And the other says, "Yeah, and there's not enough of it." Our mood about integration today is similar; "boy, it's not so effective, and yeah, there's not enough of it."

What happened? How did we go from heroic optimism to disenchantment? Sketching an answer to this question gives context for understanding the significance of the articles in this issue of *Journal of Social Issues* (*JSI*). I would point to several factors:

- First, of course, there was always resistance to school integration. A second Brown decision, a year after the first, slowed down the implementation of desegregation court orders with the qualification that they need only proceed "with all deliberate speed."
- Second, the methods for achieving school integration—for example, busing in K through 12 education, and affirmation action in higher education— have been strenuously opposed as infringing on the rights and opportunities of other groups. They are hot-button issues in the American political landscape.
- Third, in schools where numerical integration has been achieved, there has arisen the tenacious problem of minority students not fairing as well as their White counterparts. This phenomenon is manifest in several ways: persistent minority student achievement gaps throughout schooling, and a continuing small number of minorities progressing into higher education and advanced professional training.

It is this part of the integration effort—understanding and fostering minority student achievement and progress into higher education and professional training—on which this issue of *JSI* is focused.

My own research with my colleagues over the years has had a similar goal. Negative stereotypes about the abilities of one's group—say for example, negative stereotypes about women in math, or about minorities in academic, intellectual activities, or about White males in elite basketball—are "threats in the air" that people have to deal with in specific situations because they have a given identity, and these threats can depress performance, especially when one is at the frontier of one's skills, learning new things. Most typically they produce an anxiety and an extra effort to disprove the stereotype that can interfere with learning complex things. We have discovered ways of reducing this effect; things that both individuals and institutions can do to reduce these pressures.

However, of most relevance here is that this research joins a larger effort represented by the research reported in this issue of *JSI*, research aimed at improving minority student performance and participation. If you read the articles in this issue you will be both informed and heartened. You will be heartened by the ability of these investigators to make progress with a problem that is reputedly very difficult to affect. And you will be informed by their discovery of specific ways of achieving that progress.

My hope is that, taken together, these articles and the research they report will help steer our field in the direction of doing more intervention research. Intervention research accomplishes several important things at the same time. It makes a strong causal statement. Interventions are directed at particular causes. So when they work—when they improve the outcome being observed—it constitutes strong evidence that the underlying causal analysis is correct. And, at the same time, the intervention itself offers a practical, usable solution to the problem at hand—something that can actually be done in the real world to have the desired effect. Each of the contributions in this issue is a wonderful example of this double yield. They all deepen our understanding of the factors that influence minority achievement and they show us how to do it.

I am confident that this research, and the movement toward intervention research in this area that I hope it foreshadows, will make great inroads in reducing the achievement and test score gaps that afflict our society, and that weaken our faith in integration.

That will take time. We are, after all, talking about changing fundamental patterns within American society. But in the meantime, this research will also help with the challenge of maintaining faith—faith in the American ideal of an integrated society.

With the Brown decision and the ethos of the civil right era fading farther and farther into the past, with methods for achieving school integration embattled in litigious polarizations, with persistent achievement gaps in integrated schools leading people on both sides of the issue to question the value of integration, the American ideals of integrated schooling and an integrated society have all they can handle to stay alive. In fact, these ideals seem to be losing ground. Gary Orfield and Christopher Edly's Civil Rights Project has documented that American schools are more segregated today than they were 25 years ago. The food is bad—integration is not working that well—and there is not enough of it.

Reading these articles, however, rekindles this important faith. One can see from them that integration can be "good," that is, it can work in the sense of fostering minority achievement. And one can get some really good ideas about how to make it work. Finally, one also sees that what is required to make it work is not beyond our reach. With the understandings this research provides, we see that it is not as far away and hard to realize as we might have thought.

CLAUDE STEELE is Provost and Professor of Psychology at Columbia University. Before joining Columbia he was Lucie Stern Professor in Social Sciences and past chair of the Department of Psychology at Stanford University, and the Director of the Center for Advanced Study in the Behavioral Sciences at Stanford.

He received his BA from Hiram College, and his MA and PhD from Ohio State University. Steele has received the Dean's Teaching Award at Stanford University, the William James Fellow Award from the *American Psychological Society*, the Kurt Lewin Award and the Gordon Allport Prize in Social Psychology from the *Society for the Psychological Study of Social Issues*, the Distinguished Contribution Award and the Senior Award for Distinguished Contributions to Psychology in the Public Interest from the American Psychological Association, and the Cattell Faculty Fellowship. He is a member of the *American Academy of Arts and Sciences*, and he has been awarded honorary doctorates from the University of Michigan, University of Chicago, Yale University, Princeton University, and the University of Maryland, Baltimore County.

Journal of Social Issues, Vol. 67, No. 3, 2011, pp. 435–441

Ethnic Minorities and Women in STEM: Casting a Wide Net to Address a Persistent Social Problem

Moin Syed*
University of Minnesota

Martin M. Chemers
University of California, Santa Cruz

The persistent underrepresentation of Native Americans, African–Americans, Latinos, and women among the annual cohorts of students who complete bachelor's degrees in science and enter and complete graduate training for careers as research scientists has emerged as a societal problem that is resistant to quick solutions (Gándara & Maxwell-Jolly 1999; Treisman, 1992). Despite detailed analyses of the problem by social scientists, educational theorists, science educators, and the design and implementation of a wide variety of proposed solutions, the number of individuals from underrepresented minority (URM) groups who have completed PhDs and secured research positions in academia and industry is increasing more slowly than had been hoped (Tapia & Lanius, 2000). This "problem" set the stage for this issue of the *Journal of Social Issues* (*JSI*). To maintain a reasonably coherent focus, both in terms of the research included and the policy implications of the works, this issue includes articles concerned with underrepresentation in the United States. It is important to understand that other

*Correspondence concerning this article should be addressed to Moin Syed, Department of Psychology, University of Minnesota, 75 East River Road, Minneapolis, MN 55455 [e-mail: moin@umn.edu] and Martin M. Chemers, Department of Psychology, University of California Santa Cruz, 1156 High Street, SS2 Santa Cruz, CA 95064 [e-mail: mchemers@ucsc.edu].

We thank Faye Crosby for planting the seed that became this special issue and Barbara Goza for all of her support, encouragement, and guidance throughout the project. Thanks also to past *Journal of Social Issues* (*JSI*) editor Rick Hoyle for ushering us through the early phases of the project and to current *JSI* editor Sheri Levy and the editorial board for seeing it to completion.

countries, such as Australia, Canada, and the United Kingdom, are facing similar issues (see Phipps, 2007).

The underrepresentation problem in the United States has not been ignored. For example, the National Institutes of Health (NIH) initiated minority-targeted research training programs in 1972 with the creation of the Minority Biomedical Research Support program. Today, NIH supports training opportunities for URMs widely through the Minority Opportunity in Research Division of the National Institute of General Medical Sciences. In the last decade NIH has funded approximately 15,000 trainees per year at a cost of approximately $650 million (Committee for the Assessment of NIH Minority Research Training Programs, 2005). These programs have met with some success (Barlow & Villarejo, 2004; Rochin & Mello, 2007), but not much is known about the specific aspects of the programs that are associated with the greatest success.

Other studies and reports have been clear and strident. A 2005 National Research Council report on the Assessment of NIH Minority Research and Training Programs concluded that although some evidence supported the effectiveness of these programs, the results were equivocal. The report made a strong statement for the necessity of gathering better data on how well and in what manner these programs work. A report summarizing the proceedings from a 1996 Symposium to Develop an Agenda for Research on Diversity and Outcomes in Higher Education (Asera, 1996) called for the development of a stronger evidentiary base of "fine-grained data" on how a variety of practices influence student enrollment, academic performance, and career progress.

It is our contention that important research is being done, and the results of that research needs to be integrated and promulgated. A phenomenon as complex as academic achievement and career success calls for comprehensive and nuanced approaches. The articles in this issue of *JSI* represent high-quality work with broad interdisciplinary and methodological perspectives that have the potential to have an impact on policy and program development.

In conceptualizing this issue of *JSI* and considering the types of article that would be appropriate for the goals of the issue, we felt it was imperative that we embrace four dimensions of diversity in the types of articles included. First, the articles in this issue are not limited to a specific focus on underrepresented groups in science, technology, engineering and math (STEM), per se. It is important to understand the strengths and struggles of students and faculty in all academic disciplines to develop a firm understanding of underrepresented groups in STEM. Similarly, successful policies and practices geared toward individuals not in STEM fields may inform potential reforms and interventions for those who are. This approach is evident in the article by Syed, Azmitia, and Cooper (2011), who provide a broad review of the role of identity for underrepresented ethnic minorities' academic success. In general, the complexity of the problem of underrepresentation in STEM requires a broad and deep understanding of the lives of underrepresented individuals. The collection of articles in this *JSI* is meant to serve this need.

The issue of minorities in STEM is relevant to all levels of the academic pipeline, particularly from high school to the professoriate. Accordingly, the second dimension of diversity that we attended to reflects the multistage nature of the problem. Although several articles focus on college students, we also included articles that discuss the experiences of high school students (Arora, Schneider, Thal, & Meltzer, 2011; Witkow & Fuligni, 2011), graduate students and postdoctoral fellows (Blake-Beard, Bayne, Crosby, & Muller, 2011; Chemers, Zurbriggen, Syed, Goza & Bearman, 2011), and university professors (Smart Richman, vanDellen, & Wood, 2011). Although sampling across the developmental continuum restricts a deep understanding of a single educational period, it does help to highlight how underrepresentation operates at multiple levels along the pipeline.

Complex questions require complex and varied methodologies. Accordingly, the articles in this issue draw upon a number of methodologies. Several of the studies are longitudinal, ranging from 1 year (Hurtado et al., 2011; Phinney, Torres Campos, Kallemeyn, & Kim, 2011) to 4 years (Witkow & Fuligni, 2011). The articles also make use of laboratory (Smart Richman et al., 2011) and field (Phinney et al., 2011) experiments, and two articles describe behavioral sampling methods (Arora et al., 2011; London, Rosenthal, & Gonzalez, 2011). Most of the articles are quantitative based, but Hurtado et al. (2011) include qualitative data generated through interviews and focus groups.

Finally, we sought diversity in the primary level of analysis that researchers chose to focus on. Thus, articles that address both individual (e.g., self-efficacy, identity) and institutional factors (e.g., features of mentoring, support, and training programs) are included in the issue. The differing levels of analysis of the articles ultimately served as the organizational structure of the issue, to which we now turn.

Organization of the Issue

In his foreword to this issue, Claude Steele (2011) discussed the important roles of both individuals and institutions for educational advancement. In advocating for the compelling need for further research on issues of educational equity, he highlights the interplay between psychological factors (particularly personal identity) in minority student success and the powerful role of situational and institutional contexts. It is in this spirit, aligned with important multilevel theorizing in social and developmental psychology (e.g., Bronfenbrenner, 1979; Deaux, 2006; García Coll et al., 1996; Pettigrew, 1997; Rogoff, 1995), that we have structured this issue of *JSI* in three sections, as described below.

The first section, "Individual Reactions: Sources, Mediators, and Outcomes" features articles that primarily focus on the individual-level of analysis. This section addresses the issue of URMs and women's success with a focus on individual psychological and life context variables, such as self-efficacy, identity, and social categorization. The section opens with Syed et al.'s (2011) interdisciplinary review of identity and educational success among underrepresented ethnic minority students. By integrating the literatures of social and developmental psychology, sociology, and educational anthropology, the review by Syed et al. (2011) sets the stage for the remaining articles in the issue. The construct of identity serves as the focal point for the review, but identity is considered within both relational and institutional contexts. Thus, Syed et al. (2011) illustrate how differing levels of analyses can be brought to the foreground, but always operate with the other levels lurking in the background (cf. Rogoff, 1995).

Chemers et al. (2011) propose and test a model of psychological factors (e.g., self-efficacy and personal identity) that mediate the effects of minority science support programs on student motivation and commitment to a career in science. Their study includes both undergraduate students and graduate students/postdoctoral fellows, affording a comparison of how elements of support programs and psychological mediators operate differently at different levels of education. In contrast to the self-report methodology of Chemers et al. (2011), Smart Richman et al. (2011) employ an experimental methodology to explore how "social identity threats" arise for women in male-dominated professions and how various sources of social support (e.g., mentor, family, peers) can help to buffer those threats. Here again we see the inclusion of relational contexts when examining individual-level factors (i.e., perceptions of threat), highlighting the inseparable nature of the different levels of analysis. The final article in the first section, by London et al. (2011) features a discussion of how experience sample methodology may be particularly useful for studying women in STEM fields. The authors review some of their prior work on the topic, and discuss best practices for implementation and implications for the development of new interventions.

The second section of the issue, titled "Institutional Efforts: Barriers and Opportunities," analyzes the ways in which educational institutions can both facilitate and restrict academic success. The first article in this section, by Witkow and Fuligni (2011), examined longitudinally how social support from parents and friends was associated with high school grade point average and college eligibility. Many URM students face barriers to becoming college eligible, and this analysis provides some insights about how some students are able to overcome those barriers to expand their future educational opportunities. The second article, by Hurtado et al. (2011) draws on extensive quantitative and qualitative data to consider the characteristics of supportive and nonsupportive academic environments, including issues of overall commitment to diversity, how students are initiated into the "culture" of science, differential opportunities for gaining relevant information about appropriate avenues to academic advancement including what courses are needed, and what the characteristics of scientific research are.

The final group of articles, assembled under the title, "Intervention Strategies: Aligning Ambitions and Mentoring," will address attempts to bridge the gap between institutional factors and individual experiences through support and mentoring programs. Particular attention is paid to the characteristics of effective mentoring and to issues arising from the personal characteristics of mentors and protégés. This theme is highlighted in Arora et al. (2011), who describe an in vivo study of a program meant to introduce students, who might not otherwise have the opportunity, to develop an accurate and motivating understanding of research careers in medicine. This article makes a unique contribution by detailing the specifics of a theoretically driven intervention program for URM youth. The next article, by Phinney et al. (2011), reports on two longitudinal field experimental studies on peer mentoring with Latino college freshmen. This article highlights how both frequency of contact and quality of mentoring are important for student outcomes, and how peer mentoring is a cost-effective approach to providing support for at-risk students. In the final empirical article, Blake-Beard et al. (2011) analyze an extensive data set of mentoring outcomes to address the question of how mentor–protégé matching with respect to race and gender affects psychological and educational outcomes of protégés. This study is especially valuable, as it addresses the widespread assumptions that URMs and women want to have a matched mentor, and that having a matched mentor matters for key academic outcomes. Finally, Eccles (2011) comments on how the articles in this issue showcase the tremendous progress we have made as researchers over the past 35 years, primarily with respect to the questions asked, theories and methods used, and who is doing the research.

Concluding Thoughts

A proper treatment of the problem of ethnic minorities' and women's underrepresentation in STEM fields would require much more than a single journal issue can provide. Indeed, a whole issue could be devoted to the topics raised in each of the articles contained in this issue. We have attempted to provide a sampling of some of the key issues that future researchers and policymakers should consider. It is our intention that this issue serves as a catalyst for further thinking, as opposed to the final word on the issue. Psychologists and other social sciences have much to contribute to this important social problem, and we are proud of doing our small part by assembling these important articles into this collection.

References

Arora, V., Schneider, B., Thal, R., & Meltzer, D. (2011). Design of an intervention to promote entry of minority youth into clinical research careers by aligning ambition: The TEACH (training early achievers for careers in health) research program. *Journal of Social Issues, 67*(3), 580–598.

Asera, R. (1996). A symposium to develop an agenda for research. In R. Asera (Chair), *Diversity and outcomes in higher education.* Symposium conducted at the U. S. Office of Educational Research and Improvement. Charles Dana Center for Postsecondary Improvement, University of Texas, Austin, TX. Abstract retrieved March 20, 2003, from http://www.ed.gov/offices/OERI/PLLI/proceed.html.

Barlow, A. E. L., & Villarejo, M. (2004). Making a difference for minorities: Evaluation of an educational enrichment program. *Journal of Research in Science Teaching, 41,* 861–881. doi:10.1002/tea.20029.

Blake-Beard, S., Bayne, M. L., Crosby, F. J., & Muller, C. B. (2011). Matching by race and gender in mentoring relationships: Keeping our eyes on the prize. *Journal of Social Issues, 67*(3), 622–643.

Bronfenbrenner, U. (1979). *The ecology of human development.* Cambridge, MA: Harvard University Press.

Deaux, K. (2006). A nation of immigrants: Living our legacy. *Journal of Social Issues, 62*(3), 633–651. doi:10.1111/j.1540–4560.2006.00480.x.

Eccles, J. S. (2011). Understanding educational and occupational choices. *Journal of Social Issues, 67*(3), 644–648.

Gándara, P., & Maxwell-Jolly, J. (1999). *Priming the pump: Strategies for increasing the achievement of underrepresented minority undergraduates.* New York: The College Board.

García Coll, C., Crnic, K., Lamberty, G., Wasik, B. H., Jenkins, R. Vásquez Garcia, H. et al. (1996). An integrative model for the study of developmental competencies in minority children. *Child Development, 67*(5), 1891–1914. doi:10.1111/j.1467–8624.1996.tb01834.x.

Chemers, M. M., Zurbriggen, E. L., Syed, M., Goza, B, K., & Bearman, S. (2011). The role of efficacy and identity in science career commitment among underrepresented minority students. *Journal of Social Issues, 67*(3), 469–491.

Committee for the Assessment of NIH Minority Research Training Programs (2005). *Assessment of NIH Minority Research and Training Programs, Phase 3.* The National Academies Press: Washington, DC.

Hurtado, S., Eagan, M. K., Tran, M. C., Newman, C. B., Chang, M. J., & Velasco, P. (2011) "We do science here": Underrepresented students interactions with faculty in different college contexts. *Journal of Social Issues, 67*(3), 553–579.

London, B., Rosenthal, L., & Gonzalez, A. (2011). Assessing the role of gender rejection sensitivity, identity, and support on the academic engagement of women in non-traditional fields using experience sampling methods. *Journal of Social Issues, 67*(3), 510–530.

Pettigrew, T. F. (1997). Personality and social structure: Social psychological contributions. In R. Hogan, J. A. Johnson, & S. R. Briggs (Eds.), *Handbook of personality psychology* (pp. 417–438). San Diego, CA: Academic Press.

Phinney, J. S., Torres Campos, C. M., Kallemeyn, D. M. P., & Kim, C. (2011). Processes and outcomes of a mentoring program for Latino college freshmen. *Journal of Social Issues, 67*(3), 599–621.

Phipps, A. (2007). Re-inscribing gender binaries: Deconstructing the dominant discourse around women's equality in science, engineering, and technology. *The Sociological Review, 55*(4), 768–787. doi:10.1111/j.1467–954X.2007.00744.x.

Rochin, R. I., & Mello, S. F. (2007). Latinos in science. *Journal of Hispanic Higher Education, 6,* 305–355. doi:10.1177/1538192707306552.

Rogoff, B. (1995). Observing sociocultural activity on three planes: Participatory appropriation, guided participation, and apprenticeship. In. J. V. Wertsch, P. del Rio, & A. Alvarez (Eds.), *Sociocultural studies of mind: Learning in doing: Social, cognitive, and computational aspects,* (pp. 139–164). New York: Cambridge University Press.

Smart Richman, L., vanDellen, M., & Wood, W. (2011). How women cope: Being a numerical minority in a male-dominated profession. *Journal of Social Issues, 67*(3), 492–509.

Steele, C. (2011). Foreword: Pursuing effective integrated education. *Journal of Social Issues, 67*(3), 431–434.

Syed, M., Azmitia, M., & Cooper, C. R. (2011). Identity and academic success among underrepresented ethnic minorities: An interdisciplinary review and integration. *Journal of Social Issues, 67*(3), 442–468.

Tapia, R., & Lanius, C. (2000). *Underrepresented minority achievement and course taking: The kindergarten-graduate continuum.* Paper presented at annual meeting of the National Institute for Science Education Forum, Detroit, MI.

Treisman, U. (1992). Studying students studying calculus: A look at the lives of minority mathematics students in college. *The College Mathematics Journal, 23*, 362–372. doi:10.2307/2686410.

Witkow, M. R., & Fuligni, A. J. (2011). Ethnic and generational differences in the relations between social support and academic achievement across the high school years. *Journal of Social Issues, 67*(3), 531–552.

MOIN SYED is an Assistant Professor of Psychology at the University of Minnesota, Twin Cities. His research is broadly concerned with identity development among ethnically and culturally diverse adolescents and emerging adults, with particular focus on the development of multiple personal and social identities (e.g., ethnicity, social class, and gender) and the implications of identity development for educational experiences and career orientation.

MARTIN M. CHEMERS received a PhD in Social Psychology from the University of Illinois, Urbana. He is presently Professor Emeritus and Research Professor of Psychology at the University of California, Santa Cruz. His current research is supported by the NIH and is focused on understanding and developing the individual and institutional changes needed to increase the number of underrepresented minorities in STEM education and careers.

Journal of Social Issues, Vol. 67, No. 3, 2011, pp. 442–468

Identity and Academic Success among Underrepresented Ethnic Minorities: An Interdisciplinary Review and Integration

Moin Syed[*]
University of Minnesota

Margarita Azmitia and Catherine R. Cooper
University of California, Santa Cruz

A growing body of literature provides insight into the ingredients for academic success for underrepresented ethnic minority students at all points of the academic pipeline. Theory and research in developmental and social psychology, education, and sociology all point to the important role of identity for students' academic success. The purpose of this article is to review some of the major findings across these social science disciplines to identify points of synergy that can inform effective policy recommendations. The review is structured around three points of convergence across disciplines: (1) prejudice and stereotype threat; (2) the role of social support; and (3) the availability of options for identity development. Reviewing these three topics sheds light on how the relation between identity and academic success must be understood on individual, relational, and institutional levels of analysis.

Educational equity for underrepresented ethnic minority students (URMs) in the United States, defined as students from African, Chicano/Latino, and Native American heritages, continues to be elusive despite the many efforts of social scientists and the implementation of policies and programs to increase educational opportunities for URMs. URM students face barriers at every step of the academic

---

[*]Correspondence concerning this article should be addressed to Moin Syed, Department of Psychology, University of Minnesota, 75 East River Road, Minneapolis, MN 55455 [e-mail: moin@umn.edu]; Margarita Azmitia, Department of Psychology, University of California Santa Cruz, 1156 High Street, SS2 Santa Cruz, CA 95064 [e-mail: azmitia@ucsc.edu] and Catherine R. Cooper, Department of Psychology, University of California Santa Cruz, 1156 High Street, SS2 Santa Cruz, CA 95064 [e-mail: ccooper@ucsc.edu].

442

pipeline, from preschool to the professoriate, with an increasingly smaller share of representation that is particularly pronounced in science, technology, engineering, and mathematics (STEM) fields (Cooper & Burciaga, 2011; Eccles, 2005; Gándara & Maxwell-Jolly, 1999).

Nevertheless, a growing body of literature provides insight into the ingredients for academic success for URM students at all points of the academic pipeline. Important work is being conducted across academic disciplines and subdisciplines in psychology, education, sociology, and anthropology. The primary objectives of this article are threefold: (1) to review some of the major findings from these disciplines; (2) to provide an integrated perspective that draws on the strengths of each, identifying points of synergy that can guide future work; and (3) to use this synthesis to make effective policy recommendations.

A common thread that runs through social science disciplines is the importance of identity for students' academic success and persistence throughout the pipeline. Here we construe identity broadly to mean both a sense of collective belonging (Tajfel, 1981) and an emerging sense of clarity about the self and purpose in life (Erikson, 1968). The question of identity is an interdisciplinary one pursued widely in the social sciences, humanities, and arts (Brubaker & Cooper, 2000). In this article, we attempt to provide some structure for the many conceptualizations of identities in the social sciences, how they are constructed, and how they matter for the educational success of ethnic minority youth. In particular, we highlight how identities operate at multiple levels of analysis: identity development is not solely an individual project, but rather, is carried out through important interpersonal relationships in the context of institutional structures (see Cooper, Behrens, & Trinh, 2009).

Our view of the relevant literatures point to three areas of convergence that can help elucidate such a structure: (1) prejudice and stereotype threat; (2) the role of social support; and (3) the availability of options for identity development. These three points are not the only concerns that matter for identity development or academic success, but rather, they are topics that are addressed across multiple disciplines that illustrate the levels of analysis that must be considered when examining the relations between identity and educational achievement. The remainder of this article will be organized around these three broad topics, but first, a brief review of the various disciplinary perspectives that we draw from is in order.

A Theoretical Buffet: Welcome to Research on Identity Development

Inquiry into both identity and education are inherently interdisciplinary, as questions about who people believe they are, what they want to do in life, and how education contributes to these goals can be examined from a variety of perspectives. In this article, we attempt to integrate theory and research among several social science disciplines concerned with identity and education. The utility of considering research from different disciplines lies in their ability to shed unique light on a common problem, as in the well-known Indian fable of the five men examining an elephant in the dark, each with his own understanding of the nature of the elephant.

Psychology is generally concerned with the thoughts and behaviors of individuals, although there are variations by subdiscipline in how this is accomplished. In terms of identity, developmental psychologists draw heavily from Erikson's (1968) psychosocial theory of lifespan development. Erikson specified that forming an identity, which he viewed as a personal sense of coherence across time, context, and multiple identifications, is a formative task emerging in adolescence and continuing throughout adulthood. Subsequently, a large literature pertaining to academic and occupational identities has burgeoned, focusing on topics such as educational and career aspirations, possible selves/future orientations, school engagement, educational and occupational knowledge, and academic pathways. The overarching themes of developmental psychologists' work include documenting change over time, how earlier experiences predict later outcomes, and how at times, specific experiences can alter individuals' developmental pathways.

In contrast to developmental psychology, social psychology focuses predominantly on situational behavior. Tajfel's (1981) social identity theory serves as the basis for many social psychological inquires into identity. Social identity theory posits that identification with social groups—such as race, ethnicity, gender, social class, and religion—is heightened in intergroup situations in which individuals view themselves as the minority and perceive some level of threat. This perceived threat leads to heightened identification with the group and depersonalization of the individual to maximize in-group solidarity and self-worth (Tajfel & Turner, 1986). Because groups wield different amounts of power, members of groups with less power may be subject to prejudice and discrimination, which can lower their self-esteem. In the case of academics, for example, URMs may become aware of negative stereotypes about their achievement potential, leading them to question their abilities and disengage from school.

As illustrated by social identity theory, many social psychologists conceptualize contexts as proximal and immediate, focusing on situations that give rise to increased identification. In contrast, researchers in educational anthropology examine in depth how cultural values and processes—which operate at both proximal and distal levels, contour the diversity and complexity of the school contexts that students inhabit. Much of this work investigates URM students' orientation toward school and features of the school context that shape their academic experiences (e.g., Gibson, Bejínez, Hidalgo, & Rolón, 2004; Ogbu, 1997; Phelan, Yu, & Davidson, 1994). The ethnographic nature of many of these studies provides a rich picture of how the educational context can encourage or discourage students in forming academic identities and holds implications for school reforms at local, state, and national levels.

Sociological research is broadly concerned with how social structures shape behavior and is therefore less focused on the individual than psychology. Oishi, Kesibir, and Snyder (2009) suggested there are two primary facets of sociology that can be understood as macrosociology and microsociology. Macrosociology emphasizes social structures and collectives and de-emphasizes individuals. For example, schooling in the United States is a system that reproduces existing social inequalities, although many teachers and staff working in schools may hold egalitarian beliefs. In contrast, microsociology seeks to link aspects of social structures to how individuals and groups function within them. In other words, these researchers examine social interactions within the context of the cultural and historical forces that shape them and thus consider both structure and agency. Despite their differences, both sociological perspectives emphasize macrolevel influences to a greater degree than do most psychologists.

Returning to the fable of the elephant, after comparing notes about their observations on the elephant, the five men broke into an argument, each feeling that his own version of the truth was the correct representation of reality. This is an apt metaphor for the disciplines that we discuss in this article. Different disciplines, as well as investigations within disciplines, situate their research within different metaphors on the nature of human existence (Pepper, 1942). These metaphors are the basis of scientific theories that can be both incompatible with one another (Cooper, 1987), and are prone to fundamental modifications when translated across disciplines (e.g., a sociological theory can become more individual-centered when adopted by psychologists; see Syed, 2010b). Thus, our intention here is to present pertinent theory and research that may, at times, be resistant to integration, but nonetheless can provide both complementary and distinct insights into the question of how identity is associated with the academic experiences of URM students.

Identifying with School: Stereotype Threat and Academic Identities

There are many negative stereotypes about URM students and their ability to succeed in academics. Although many researchers, educational practitioners, and policy makers have challenged these stereotypes or deficit interpretations of URM students, these interpretations are resistant to change (Good & Aronson, 2008). Indeed, a federal panel of scientific researchers and educators convened in 2008 to seek answers to why URM students are not better represented in science (Schmidt, 2008). Many concluded that the major issue was lack of preparation, rooted in social class and parenting styles, as opposed to attendance in underresourced schools. Most on the panel believed that URM students should not attend rigorous academic institutions, and should choose lower-tier colleges that are better aligned with the preparation they received in high school. Thus, the conclusion was one of deficient ability within a fair and just system, without deep questions about how the system itself might perpetuate the inequalities.

The social psychological literature on prejudice, discrimination, and stereotyping is extensive (for reviews see Stangor, 2009, and edited volumes by Nelson, 2009, and Quintana & McKown, 2008). Within the context of academics, the concept of stereotype threat (Steele, 1997) has emerged as one of the most influential social psychological theories—or psychological theories more broadly—pertaining to academic inequalities. Stereotype threat refers to the phenomenon that negative stereotypes about particular groups can be internalized by individuals in high-stakes situations (e.g., educational testing), thus impairing their performance and confirming the stereotype (Steele, 1997). In the following section, we will discuss some of the major findings on stereotype threat, attempt to delimit situations in which it is appropriate for the theory to be applied, and illustrate how incorporating perspectives outside of social psychology both complicates and clarifies the role of stereotype threat in URMs' academic experiences.

The original stereotype threat research focused on the performance of African Americans on a test of intelligence (Steele & Aronson, 1995). By manipulating instructions, the researchers demonstrated that African Americans underperformed on such tests when they believed them to be diagnostic of their ability, compared with African American students who did not believe the test was diagnostic. No such difference was observed for White students. When African Americans had reason to believe that the negative stereotype did not apply, that stereotype was no longer threatening to them in that situation. These general findings, in various forms, have been replicated many times (see Davis & Simmons, 2009; Smith, 2004; Walton & Cohen, 2003, for reviews and discussion of mediators and moderators) and extended to other groups facing stereotypes about ability, such as women in math and the sciences (Spencer, Steele, & Quinn, 1999). The stereotype threat effect has been robust throughout the experimental literature.

Perhaps the chief criticism of the stereotype threat phenomenon is its ecological validity. Nearly all of the research demonstrating the effect has come from experimental studies conducted in controlled laboratories, prompting questions about whether and how it translates to the real world and thus its relevance to educational policy (Cullen, Hardison, & Sackett, 2004; Sackett, Hardison, & Cullen, 2004; Whaley, 2009). Several studies investigating this question have emerged, with findings still inconclusive (see Danaher & Crandall, 2008; Stricker & Ward, 2004, 2008, for an exchange on this issue). Field experiments are limited by the ethical and logistical constraints of altering the procedures for administering high-stakes tests, making it difficult for findings to translate directly (Cullen et al., 2004, but see Good, Aronson, & Harder, 2008 for an innovative approach with women in math). Despite questions about whether the stereotype threat phenomenon is applicable to the real world, many URM students feel a lack of belonging in classrooms, either from being aware of their underrepresentation or because of stereotypes explicitly or implicitly activated by teachers and classmates (Syed, 2010c; Tinto, 2000). Students' experiences with these stereotypes can threaten their sense of belonging in academic settings, highlighting the importance of identity.

Appropriate Applications and Expanded Perspectives

The stereotype threat phenomenon is most applicable to those students who highly identify with the domain being threatened, such as high-achieving African American students. As a result, in the context of stereotype threat, identity emerges as an important construct for understanding the academic experiences of URM students. Unfortunately, identity has seldom been examined in studies of stereotype threat. Research has examined how the participants identify in terms of gender or racial identity (Cohen & Garcia, 2005; Pronin, Steele, & Ross, 2004), but seldom how much they identify with the academic domain of interest. That is, high math-achieving African American students should be particularly susceptible to stereotype threat because they are highly math-identified. Math identity is typically inferred from students' presence at an elite university or enrollment in honors or advanced placement courses. Although students often identify with domains in which they excel (Brown & Lent, 1996), these factors are neither necessary nor sufficient for identification. One rare study assessed math identity among male and female high school students in Germany (Keller, 2007). Whereas men's performance was not affected by math identity or the threat manipulation, women's performance was. High math-identified women performed worse under the threat condition than did low math-identified women in the threat condition and high math-identified women in the no-threat condition. Thus, domain-specific academic identities play an important role in how students react to stereotypes.

Other research on stereotype threat—although still scant—has examined school or academic identities more broadly, rather than in specific domains. Osborne and Walker (2006) assessed identification with schooling among an ethnically diverse sample of incoming ninth graders. School-identified ethnic minority students were more likely to withdraw from school within 2 years of entering than were low school-identified ethnic minority students. No such association was found for the White students. These findings provide indirect evidence that the URM students most highly identified with academics are at the greatest risk for adverse academic outcomes. Unfortunately, the pervasiveness of these negative stereotypes in schools and society make it difficult to implement policy changes (Good & Aronson, 2008). Still, we know that identities are dynamic and ever-evolving (Erikson, 1968). As a result, if identity is an important aspect of URM educational success, it is crucial to understand how students come to identify and de-identify with school in the first place.

Whether or not students identify with school is not a simple question, and the paths that students take toward school identification are not linear (Cooper,

Domínguez, & Rosas, 2005). The heterogeneity in how and when students create and maintain academic identities calls for theoretical and methodological research strategies that are appreciative of these individual differences. Researchers in educational anthropology and developmental psychology have attempted to chart the variety of paths that students take through school—both successful and not—while providing perspectives on how students negotiate, or succumb to, the academic challenges they face. Germane to the current discussion is the shift away from universal models of what is normative or typical toward more context-dependent models of identity development. This is accomplished somewhat differently in different fields, as described below.

Developmental psychologists are increasingly recognizing that there is not one normative path to positive development that youth follow. Indeed, the developmental concepts of equifinality and multifinality are proving to be compelling, particularly with regard to educational pathways (Cauce, Coronada, & Watson, 1998; Garcia Coll, Akerman, & Cicchetti, 2000). Equifinality refers to how individuals may follow different life paths to the same outcome, whereas multifinality refers to individuals sharing a common starting point yet ending up in different places. Cooper and colleagues have demonstrated these concepts in the context of students' math and language pathways (Cooper, Cooper, Azmitia, Chavira, & Gullatt, 2002; Cooper et al., 2005; see also Garcia Coll, Szalacha, & Palacios, 2005). Looking across the high school years and into college, they found evidence in three longitudinal studies for a group of students who performed consistently high as well as a declining group who started with high grades and then steadily decreased, illustrating multifinality. Equifinality can be seen in the pathways of the decliners and the persistently low-achieving students; both groups were doing poorly in math at the end of high school. Thus, the declining group shared similarities with both the consistently high and low achievers, depending on the point in time in high school considered. The policy implications of this perspective on development are twofold: that "one-size fits all" interventions are not likely to be effective, and that heterogeneity in developmental trajectories must be considered.

A complementary approach is taken by researchers in educational anthropology who take a multidimensional perspective on the nature of the school context. Ogbu's (1997) influential cultural–ecological framework situated educational disparities between Whites and ethnic minorities, particularly African Americans, within broader systems of inequality in the United States. In doing so, he paid particular attention to the heterogeneity within URM populations by examining the interplay between school factors, historical and systemic factors, and what he called community forces, which includes language, culture, social interactions, and identity. As Ogbu described, he approached his study of ethnic minorities' academic experiences as an anthropologist would, considering each group as its own culture and examining all aspects of their experiences. This approach enabled him to understand the similarities and differences among ethnic groups in the role of different factors (e.g., school, historical, community) for school performance. How these factors interact is unique to different schools, giving rise to context-specific opportunities and constraints for identity development.

An example of the approach described by Ogbu can also seen in Gibson's (2005) study of a California high school consisting predominantly of White and Mexican-heritage students, many of the latter being children of migrant farm workers. Gibson described the school environments of these two groups as so different as to practically constitute two different schools. The Mexican-heritage students occupied marginalized positions that compromised their sense of belonging and academic engagement, influencing their choice of classes, their participation in extracurricular activities, and even the physical space they occupied on campus. The school's Migrant Education Program, however, provided a welcoming space and supportive environment for these students. Through their involvement in the program, Mexican-heritage students—whether children of migrant farm workers or not—could find a sense of belonging within the larger context of feeling alienated in the school. Although positive, as Gibson rightly points out, such a program only served a small number of students and did little to alter the structures of the school that promoted lack of belongingness and disengagement.

A notable strength of school-based research is the interconnection between observed behaviors and the school context in which they occurred. This strength gives rise to the opportunity to implement changes to policies at the school level that can then be potentially extrapolated to districts, and perhaps even states. An example of this approach is the Papahana Kaiapuni Hawaiian language immersion program, whose development was documented by Yamauchi, Ceppi, and Lau-Smith (1999), a group of educational psychologists. Due to colonialist policies that banned the use of the native Hawaiian language, by the 1980s the number of native speakers had decreased to such low levels that the language was on the verge of disappearing forever. In response, Hawaiian language immersion preschools were established. Once these children were ready for kindergarten, their parents lobbied to implement an immersion program in the public schools, which was approved for K-1 classes. Through continued parental commitment and tireless lobbying, the immersion program was extended to K-6, and then to K-12. In 2004, there were over 1,500 students enrolled in the program at 19 different sites across the state (Yamauchi, Lau-Smith, & Luning, 2008). What began as a small effort by parents and activists ultimately became a statewide effort to revive the Hawaiian language and culture. As demonstrated in other work (Yamauchi, Billig, Meyer, & Hofschire, 2006), a high school program that integrated aspects of the Hawaiian culture into the curriculum fostered a greater sense of belonging to school and community as well as career identity among its students.

In this section, we have traveled from the controlled laboratory of the social psychologists studying stereotype threat to the sociocultural uprising of Hawaiian-language immersion schools. In doing so, we have attempted to highlight variations in identification and school performance over time and context, and how context-specific research can be effective for translating research to policy. In his critique of stereotype threat research, Whaley (2009) states the policy implications flowing from stereotype threat research "would focus our efforts on minimizing the impact of racial stereotypes instead of promoting a strong ethnic/racial identity and racial socialization" (p. 493). In other words, Whaley argues for the need of proactive rather than reactive policies. Ethnic identity and racial socialization have been shown to have protective effects in a number of life domains, including academic achievement and motivation, well-being, substance use, and the ability to successfully cope with discriminatory experiences (Neblett, Terzian, Harriott, 2010). Indeed, attention to how we can promote strong identities that can serve as resources to overcome a variety of stereotypes may have a wider and more long-lasting impact. We address this issue throughout the remainder of this article by examining identities in the context of interpersonal relationships and institutions.

Supportive Agents: Identity and Education as a Shared Enterprise

Academic achievement and educational advancement do not rest on the shoulders of the students alone. Indeed, research on identity and schooling has consistently highlighted the importance of mentors and the social and instrumental support from families, peers, teachers, and programs for students' academic success throughout the pipeline. These agents provide both instrumental and socioemotional support that students draw on to pursue their career goals and maintain positive mental health. Social support is viewed as directly related to identity development, as different support figures can act as "identity agents" or "cultural brokers"—individuals who have a vested interest and play an active role in the development of youths' identities (Cooper, Denner, & Lopez, 1999; Schachter & Ventura, 2008). Although students from all ethnic backgrounds require and benefit from such support, for URM students the needs are heightened in response to qualitatively different experiences that must be negotiated, such as feelings of isolation and stereotypes about their ability to succeed. In this section, we will describe these experiences and illustrate how URM students draw from multiple sources of support who may act as both resources and challenges (Cooper et al., 2002).

Mentors and Role Models

Research in a variety of disciplines has contributed to understanding how key social support figures can be motivational for success for ethnic minority youth, and how the lack of such figures can act as a barrier to advancement.

For example, some research has pointed to the importance of role models and mentors who come from similar ethnic backgrounds as the students (Zirkel, 2002). These figures are believed to provide prototypes that facilitate students' ability to envision themselves occupying these positions and instill a sense of academic self-efficacy (Markus & Nurius, 1986). In the context of STEM education, the ability to construct such an imagined future is hindered considerably by the very small number of ethnic minority teachers and professors in those fields (Gándara & Maxwell-Jolley, 1999). Thus, the relatively few URM students in STEM, paired with the low availability of same-ethnicity mentors, suggest that having a match may be particularly important for URM adolescents.

The research evidence on the benefit of matched mentors, however, is equivocal (Gándara & Mejorado, 2005). One shortcoming of past research is that much of it was based on the assumption that having a mentor with the same background was important to the student. That is, the fact that there are likely individual differences among URM youth in how important it is for the student to have a matched mentor has been largely overlooked. A study of adolescents participating in a 4-week STEM summer program addressed this limitation by independently assessing how much contact with a matched mentor the adolescents had and how important it was to them have such a mentor (Syed, Goza, Chemers, & Zurbriggen, in press). URM students were less likely to report having contact and more likely to endorse having a matched mentor as important, although there were important individual differences (see also Blake-Beard, Bayne, Crosby & Muller, 2011). Those students who placed importance on having a matched mentor and reported that they received mentoring during the course of the program showed greater increases in feelings of identity and belongingness as a science student, which are essential components of committing to a career in science (Chemers et al., 2010; Chemers, Zurbriggen, Syed, Goza, & Bearman, 2011; see also Erikson, 1968). Thus, the identity-making function of having a matched mentor appears to be most powerful for those students who are yearning for such a relationship, rather than all URM students. Exploring individual differences such as these helps move away from stereotypical assumptions of what URM students want or need to be successful in school.

Beyond Mentors: Broad Conceptions of Social Support

Although academic mentors can be important for URM educational success, they are not the only resources that students draw upon. In particular, research indicates that family members, peers, and teachers can contribute to—yet also restrict—academic success for URM students. Families are often the first to be credited for successes as well as the first to be blamed for problems. In terms of URM academic experiences, the latter has been the norm. Going back to the infamous notion of the "culture of poverty" (Lewis, 1966), URMs' families have been thought of as a hindrance to their success, which can be seen in the 2008 federal report on URMs in science discussed previously. Theories of social and cultural capital advanced by sociologists are aimed at providing a structural rather than dispositional account of the challenges faced by URMs (Bourdieu, 1977; Coleman, 1988). Social capital (e.g., social networks, connections) and cultural capital (e.g., parent education, dominant cultural mores, and knowledge of how systems work) have been viewed as just as important as economic capital in social reproduction, and highlight the role of access and privilege for social mobility. Ostensibly lifting blame from families and placing it within social structures, social and cultural capital theories became quite popular and, in many ways, overextended (see Kao & Rutherford, 2007).

In her critique of the social capital approach, Yosso (2005) describes how social capital has often been used as a deficit model, holding the forms of capital held by the White middle class as the norm to which all others are judged (see also Carter, 2003, but for arguments on the value of social capital models, see Portes & Fernández-Kelly, 2008). Yosso proposes the concept of "community cultural wealth," which addresses the forms of capital that are relevant to different cultural communities, particularly communities of color. For example, Yosso proposes that familial capital can provide a sense of community, belonging, and shared experience that serves as a resource in times of struggle. Yosso sees familial capital as not limited to the immediate family, but can include extended family members (living or dead) and friends (see also Stack & Burton, 1993, on "kinscripts" within African American families and Ebaugh & Curry, 2000, on "fictive kin").

The concepts of community cultural wealth and familial capital are consistent with the work in educational anthropology on "funds of knowledge" (Moll, Amanti, Neff, & Gonzalez, 1992). The funds of knowledge approach seeks to understand how the rich knowledge and skills found in households can be integrated into classroom learning. For example, through knowledge of household practices, a sixth-grade teacher learned of a parent who made Mexican candies. The teacher created a unit that built from this expertise, including having the parent visit the class to share her knowledge. Through carefully crafted curriculum, students were able to explore topics related to math, science, health, consumer education, cross-cultural practices, advertising, and food production, all centered around a topic in which they were interested. Importantly, seeing parents from diverse backgrounds as educational resources helped provide greater integration between home and school life.

Complementary work in other fields has considered the different ways that parents of URM students contribute to, rather than hinder, their academic success. Several studies have documented that parents with low educational attainment have high expectations for their children (Chang, Chen, Greenberger, Dooley, & Heckhausen, 2006; Cooper et al., 1994). Not only does their disadvantaged background serve as inspiration and motivation for their children to succeed, but parents also frequently communicate to their children how their lack of education has limited their options in life and thus, their children should go to college to have a better life (Cooper et al., 1994, 2005; Syed, 2010a). As Tierney and Auerbach (2006) explain, these parents make use of "invisible strategies" such as verbal encouragement and financial sacrifice, rather than the communication with teachers and volunteering practices seen in White middle-class families. Finally, as Hughes et al. (2006) suggest, parents can also discuss stigma and prejudice with their children, thus helping them develop strategies that will help them cope with negative stereotypes at school and society.

Parents can play an important role in youth's academic experiences, but they are not their only source of support. Developmental research on adolescents' "multiple worlds" has examined how ethnic-minority youth coordinate different support systems, or worlds, of friends, families, teachers, and communities, to foster academic success (Cooper et al., 2002; Phelan et al., 1994). Importantly, social support is conceptualized as a dynamic network or system that can be both additive and compensatory (Levitt, Weber, & Guacci, 1993; Reis, Azmitia, Syed, Radmacher, & Gills, 2009). One key finding from this line of research is that different supportive agents seem to play different roles for positive youth development (Azmitia, Cooper, & Brown, 2009). For example, in a school-based sample, while family support and guidance—both emotional and educational— was the strongest predictor of math grades among Latino adolescents, teachers also played an important role by helping with homework. Thus, while families can serve as an important resource for building academic aspirations, teachers provide instrumental support necessary for achievement.

Conceptualizing social support as an evolving constellation of systems re-quires understanding how support is a dynamic process. An important contribution of the developmental literature is the changing nature of these sources of support over time. Research with mostly White youth indicates that, as they move through adolescence and into young adulthood, they increasingly rely on friends for social and emotional support relative to family (Buhrmester & Furman, 1987; Furman & Burhmester, 1992). Even over short time periods, support is dynamic, as research has documented that peers in particular are viewed as both a resource and a challenge for students' academic achievement (Azmitia & Cooper, 2001; Cooper, 2011).

The increasing importance of peers and institutional supports is highlighted in a recent mixed-methods study of young adults' transition to college (Azmitia, Syed, & Radmacher, 2011). Quantitative analyses indicated that family support was not related to mental health trajectories over the first year of college, but friends' support was associated with more positive mental health. Analysis of the interview data generally supported the quantitative findings. In particular, peers and friends stood out as being especially important to the students' transition to college. The students discussed the importance of feeling like they belonged at college and finding a group of peers who shared their interests and helped them feel like they belonged there. In this way, peers served as identity agents that could facilitate social integration through introducing them to new people or inviting them to campus events. Because White students were more likely to attend college with friends from high school and to be familiar with college activities and practices, they typically found creating academic and social niches easier than URMs, who also were more likely to struggle with creating an academic identity that integrated other identity domains, such as ethnicity, race, and social class (see also Azmitia, Syed, & Radmacher, 2008).

The centrality of peers during the transition to college does not suggest that families are not important. Indeed, research that has examined networks or support has found that students with integrated support across multiple domains (i.e., peers, families, teachers) have better mental health than those who have high friend support but are lacking family support (Azmitia et al., 2011; Reis et al., 2009). A further consideration is that the college context that the students inhabit may have an impact on what support systems they draw from. The research described previously was situated in a residential university, meaning that the vast majority of students moved there from other towns and lived on campus their first year. This type of transition experience calls for the development of new support figures that are in the immediate environment, roles that are largely filled by peers. But the reality of contemporary college-going is that most students do not fill the mold of so-called "traditional" college students. Nearly three-quarters all students in United States are considered "nontraditional" (U.S. Department of Education, 2002), meaning that they are older than age 22, work at least part time, live at home, and/or have families of their own. These college students inhabit quite different social and educational contexts than do students who go off to college on their own. Unfortunately, research that examines these students' experiences has been slow to catch up with the changing nature of college-going. Some evidence comes from research with Latino students attending a community college, for whom families remain the most salient sources of support (Cooper, Burciaga, Domínguez, & Su, 2008). That students' social support networks may vary as a function of their college context highlights how institutions can contour the identity development process. In the next section, we discuss the ways in which institutions can restrict access to educational equity for URM students and constrain the identities that URM students can develop.

Institutional Affordances: Availability of Options and Identity Constraints

Given its disciplinary focus on understanding individual behavior and mental processes, it is not surprising that psychology has generally come up short in incorporating macrolevel factors into its theorizing about the individual experience. This perspective has largely been the terrain of education, law, sociology, and anthropology. Despite this disciplinary cleavage, the need for integrating perspectives across disciplines has been advocated by many (Cooper & Denner, 1998; Oishi et al., 2009). In this section, we highlight how such a perspective can contribute to deeper understanding of the academic landscape that URM students must negotiate. In particular, we examine educational options that students ostensibly have available to them, and how institutional structures constrain these options for many URM students.

Tracking Disparities: The Impact of Ability Grouping in Schools

Ability grouping, also called tracking, is a widely implemented educational system that refers to using perceived ability to assign students to instructional groups, with the primary goal of facilitating academic instruction and achievement (Ansalone, 2004). The concept of tracking in high schools in the United States can be traced back to the origins of formal compulsory schooling itself, wherein schooling was founded as a means of preserving and reproducing the existing social order (Bowles & Gintis, 1976). Indeed, long before compulsory schooling was the norm in the United States, Thomas Jefferson proposed a two-track system of schooling, one for the "laborers" and one for the "learned." Contemporary systems of ability grouping take varied forms, can be both formally and informally specified, and can have different structural characteristics (Ansalone, 2004). Regardless of the system, most high schools worldwide employ some form of ability grouping. In Germany, for example, students are tracked at fourth grade by teachers, and immigrant youth are routinely overrepresented in nonacademic tracks (Crul & Schneider, 2009).

In practice, ability grouping segregates ethnic minority and low-income youth from the rest of their peers (Bowles & Gintis, 1976). Youth from ethnic minority and low-income backgrounds are vastly overrepresented in remedial tracks (Mickelson & Heath, 1999; Oakes, 2005). Research suggests that this overrepresentation can have serious consequences for ethnic minority students' academic performance (Mickelson & Heath, 1999) and psychological well-being (Jost, 1999). Furthermore, tracking systems are not limited to students. In critical analyses of the role of teachers, sociologists have documented that teachers themselves become tracked (Finley, 1984; Kelly, 2004; Mehan, 2007; Yonezawa, Stewart, & Serna, 2002). Finley's (1984) school-based study showed that some teachers only taught high-track classes, whereas others taught primarily lower-track classes, even though classes were supposed to be divided evenly. To the teachers who taught the higher-track classes, class assignments were perceived as a meritocratic process, whereas teachers assigned to lower-track classes pointed to the other teachers' political connections as the reason for their assignments. Meanwhile, those who primarily taught in the middle-level tracks felt they were more capable than teachers in the lower tracks but just as able as those teaching higher tracks, who received their assignments via politicking. These ethnographic findings have been supported by quantitative analyses using a national database (Kelly, 2004). In sum, tracking is an institutional problem that requires institutional-level reforms.

Aspects of sociocultural theory (Rogoff, 2003; Vygotsky, 1978) have been particularly influential in guiding reforms aimed at detracking. In particular, the idea that learning is a social and interactional process among individuals of varying capacities is at direct odds with the segregationist model of tracking. Supporters of tracking often feel that students in college-prep tracks will suffer academically if they share a classroom with those of less perceived ability (Ansalone, 2004). This view, however, is at odds with the demonstrated value of teaching and interaction among students of different abilities for their learning (Rogoff, 2003). Thus, movement toward detracking involves a major shift in how we think about school. As Mehan (2007) explained, "detracking is not just a technical or structural change in the academic plan or school calendar. ... It also involves a cultural change in teachers' beliefs, attitudes, and values as well as changes in curriculum and the organization of instruction." (p. 11; see also Oakes, Wells, Datnow, & Jones, 1997). The need for this change is evident in light of Yonezawa et al.'s (2002) analysis of six high schools that underwent voluntary detracking. The detracking mechanism used in the schools was one of "freedom of choice" in which students could choose whatever classes they wanted to take. Although this approach removed restrictions on course choice, it altered neither the structures that enabled and maintained tracks nor the environments students inhabited. For example, students from low and middle tracks felt high-track classes were not for students "like them," opting for the familiar spaces and faces. All in all, the freedom of choice model preserved underlying tracking structures and was therefore not a successful reform.

In contrast to the choice-based reform described by Yonezawa et al. (2002), a major component of the cultural change needed in schools involves creating a "college-going culture" to support the development of college-going identities among all students (Mehan, 2007; Oakes, 2005; Oakes et al., 1997). Tracking sends a clear message to students in lower tracks that college is not for them. Although most formal tracking systems in the United States are not introduced until middle or high school, ability grouping starts in elementary school (Mehan, 2007). Thus, messages about whether or not college is likely to be in a student's future is communicated at an early age, and these have implications for students' identities. Indeed, some have documented academic disengagement among URM elementary students (Stambler & Weinstein, 2010). Accordingly, researchers have discussed and implemented a variety of reforms aimed at providing all students with opportunities to develop college-going identities.

Oyserman and her colleagues have conducted studies with ethnically diverse youth aimed at facilitating the development of college-going identities

(Oyserman, Bybee, & Terry, 2006). Their work seeks to align both proximal and distal identities with children's current academic efforts. In one study, the researchers experimentally manipulated whether seventh-grade students were presented with either information that explicitly linked education with earnings or information that displayed the high earnings associated with successful athletes, actors, and musicians (Destin & Oyserman, 2010). Students in the education–earnings condition reported higher plans to invest time and effort into their schooling and were eight times more likely to turn in an extra credit assignment the next day than were students in the noneducation condition. The researchers argued that congruence between identities, in this case current academic identities and future career identities, are a key ingredient for academic success (Oyserman & Destin, 2010). Thus, interventions geared toward fostering identity congruence are especially needed.

College Eligibility

A direct outgrowth of ability grouping is the gap between URMs and Whites in college eligibility. In California, for example, to be eligible to attend the University of California (UC) or California State University (CSU) systems, students must complete a set of high school courses, including 3 years of specific math classes and 2 years of a foreign language (see Witkow & Fuligni, 2011). Notably, these requirements are generally not aligned with those for high school graduation, and represent a breadth of coursework not expected of students in lower tracks. Indeed, research indicates that students in lower tracks are not aware of this misalignment between graduation and eligibility requirements; those who do become aware of it tend to realize when it is too late, as they are contemplating college for the first time as a senior. Thus, the decision to attend 4-year colleges and universities or not is essentially made for these students at an early age. A clear indicator of eligibility for college and future success in college is whether and when the student took and passed Algebra I (Cooper et al., 2005). In a longitudinal study of Latino youth, the earlier the students took Algebra the more likely they were to receive a passing grade, and students who passed Algebra by ninth grade had higher math grades in the sixth grade and were more likely to attend a 4-year university.

In their longitudinal analysis, Witkow and Fuligni (2011) demonstrated that divergent paths toward college eligibility were apparent in the ninth grade. Students who went on to be UC/CSU eligible reported greater encouragement from parents and peers at the beginning of high school than those who were not ultimately eligible. Further, they clearly linked eligibility and enrollment: 2 years postgraduation 93% of students who were UC/CSU eligible had enrolled in a 4-year college, compared with only 40% of noneligible students. A notable finding is that, once again, math course completion was an important indicator of 4-year college enrollment; 75% of students who had completed Algebra I, geometry, and Algebra II enrolled in a 4-year college, whereas only 19% of students who did not complete these courses were enrolled.

Although the requirements for college-going are frequently assumed to be common knowledge, an example of an attempt to be more explicit about the requirements for college is a school that promotes a "college-going culture," in which a poster on the wall titled "How to Get to College" clearly indicates these requirements (Mehan, 2007). Greater communication to both students and families about requirements for college are clearly needed. One promising reform has been to align the requirements for graduation and college eligibility, as was done by the San Jose (CA) Unified School district in 2002. Although this policy change was controversial, critics' fears that it would increase the dropout rates were not substantiated. Following the success of this policy change in San Jose, the San Francisco Unified School District and Los Angeles Unified School District recently made this change (Kane, 2010). In addition to extensive staff development, administrators made extra efforts to communicate with students and families about their detracking change with the intent of making college-going opportunities and identities available to all students. Taken together, these policy changes provide students and families of all backgrounds with important educational capital, thus contributing to efforts toward equity and altering institutional structures that promote the reproduction of social class to increase opportunities for social mobility.

But attending 4-year colleges is not the only marker of success, and success is defined in different ways by different people. Paraphrasing Ogbu (1997), whether schools succeed depends on where people locate schooling in their folk theories about what it means to be successful. For example, the staff and funders of a community college outreach program had broad ideas about what constitutes student success, be it 4-year college, 2-year college, trade school, military service, or graduating from high school (Cooper, 2011; Cooper et al., 2005). This broad definition of success must be reconciled with the realities of what these different pathways entail. A detailed discussion of each choice is beyond the scope of this article, but we will briefly discuss the implications of enrolling in 4-year versus 2-year colleges. Although the requirements for a 4-year university exclude many students who lack the opportunities to complete the necessary coursework or pay for college, community college is in principle open to all students. However, Fry's influential (2002) report on Latinos documented the worrisome statistics that most Latinos who attend community college do not transfer to 4-year institutions. Similarly, Gándara and Orfield (2006) reported that only between 3% and 8% of Latinos and African Americans attending 2-year colleges in California transferred to 4-year universities. This shockingly low rate suggests that for many URM students, community college is not a realistic pathway to a 4-year college. Given the disproportionate number of URMs who attend 2-year colleges, these patterns contribute to low representation of URMs in STEM fields and other high-status professions.

The Myth of Free Choice: How Students Choose their College Major

Of course, getting to college does not signal that URM students have overcome all barriers to education. URM students are more likely than White and Asian students to leave college after (or during) their first year and take longer to graduate (Tierney, Colyar, & Corwin, 2005). Much of the research on leaving college draws on Tinto's (1993) model of college student retention. Central to Tinto's model is the concept of belongingness, or developing a sense of attachment and purpose to the college environment. Although Tinto's model includes both academic and social integration, empirical support is strongest for the role of social integration for retention (Kuh, Kinzie, Buckly, Bridges, & Hayek, 2006). Indeed, others have highlighted how the ability of URMs to develop feelings of belongingness is moderated by indicators of campus climate, including the diversity of the student body, perceptions of the prevalence of racism and discrimination by students, staff, and professors, and positive attitudes toward multiculturalism (e.g., Hurtado, Griffin, Arellano, & Cuellar, 2008; Hurtado et al., 2011).

Comprehensive reviews of research on college retention and campus climate are available elsewhere (see Gurin, Dey, Hurtado, & Gurin, 2002; Hurtado et al., 2008; Pascarella & Terenzini, 2005; Tinto, 1993). Here we would like to highlight an overlooked issue regarding URM college experiences: how they select a college major. There are two distinct factors to consider when investigating the process of arriving at a major: (1) the initial selection of a major and (2) how and why students change their major. We now consider each of these issues.

When students enter college, they have a seemingly infinite number of options for their academic major. Research on college major choice has been mostly conducted with White samples and examined how personal interests and personality characteristics influence the majors students choose (e.g., Leaper & Van, 2008; Sullivan & Hansen, 2004). However, the availability of options may not be the same for URM students as for White students. In a longitudinal analysis, Syed (2010a) found that only 16% of first-year students who were sampled did not have some idea about what they wanted to major in, and those who did have an idea were fairly committed to it. Thus, this study suggests that by the time they arrive to college, most students have already decided their major.

This conclusion is reinforced by the finding that students who came to college intending to major in STEM fields were quite clear about that from the beginning, with their aspirations having roots in earlier experiences. As a result, ethnic disparities in access to science education in high school directly translate to disparities at the college level. URM students, who are more likely to experience lower-quality high school education, may not have been granted the opportunities to develop an interest in STEM that they could carry forward to college. Furthermore, they face barriers in their opportunities to acquire sufficient academic preparation and have less access to the knowledge of how to obtain academic advising (Eccles, 2005).

Entering college, however, is just the first step in the academic major selection process. A question that has received very little attention in the psychological literature is how and why students change their major. The study by Syed (2010a) provides some insights on this issue. In his sample, no student, either URM or majority, who came to college interested in a humanities or social sciences major switched to a STEM major. Moreover, most of the students who were undecided at the beginning of college ultimately majored in humanities of social sciences. Thus, as argued above, the decision to major in a STEM field is generally undertaken before college.

For those students in Syed's sample who had made the decision to major in STEM at the beginning of college there was a striking pattern: all of the White students stayed with STEM, whereas nearly all of the URM students eventually switched their major to the humanities or social sciences. Why would this be? These were students who held strong aspirations to go into STEM and had adequate support in high school to facilitate their interests. The answer, as described in Syed (2010a), was a matter of identity. URM students attending college are in the process of developing their ethnic identities as well as their career identities (Azmitia et al., 2008; Syed & Azmitia, 2008, 2009), and many see their college experiences as facilitating the attaining of these identities (Santos, Ortiz, Morales, & Rosales, 2007). Majors in the humanities and social sciences, which tend to address issues of culture, ethnicity, and diversity, are seen by many URM students as more attractive than STEM majors. Humanities and social science majors afford an opportunity for URM students to learn about themselves and their cultures while attaining their goal of a college degree. As most high schools do not offer substantial content outside of the White American and European context, for URM students, college courses can be the first time they see themselves in the course material. As a result, they tend to be attracted toward certain majors and away from STEM fields.

The implications of this research on identity and college major choice are that STEM fields would do well to incorporate diversity into their curriculum. For example, making students aware of significant ethnic minority figures in the field, surfacing the historical and cultural context in which STEM research is situated, and highlighting different ways of knowing used around the world are a few of the possible topics that could be integrated into college STEM courses. Future research still needs to determine what form and content of STEM curriculum will meet URM students' identity-related needs, but as Yamauchi et al. (2006) have shown in their work with native Hawaiian youth, there is tremendous benefit in acknowledging, appreciating, and integrating cultural considerations into students' educations.

Conclusions

The lack of educational equity for URM students, both within STEM and more broadly, is a complex problem that requires interdisciplinary perspectives to generate feasible solutions. In this article, we highlighted key research across the social sciences that is both useful for understanding the role of identity development for URM educational experiences and a starting point for where and how reforms can occur. Taking an interdisciplinary approach fuels analyses that move beyond a focus on the individual to incorporate relational, contextual, historical, and societal factors that influence students' experiences.

We identified three points of convergence across disciplines that illustrate the different levels of analysis that should be considered when examining the relation between identities and educational achievement. Research on prejudice and stereotype threat raised the crucial issue of how identities interact with educational environments in which negative stereotypes may be held. From this work and other research on identity and school contexts, polices are especially needed that are aimed at altering school environments in ways that can facilitate identities that are resistant to such stereotypes. As argued by Whaley (2009), studies of ethnic identity and ethnic/racial socialization are good starting points, as they can serve as protective factors against the negative impact of discrimination and have been linked to academic achievement. We would also do well to change our thinking about how relationships with important figures can provide needed support. In particular, educators must rethink how they value different forms of families' contributions to their children's education, rather than holding all families to a White, middle-class standard. Finally, policies that attempt to create a college-going culture for all students would allow more students to have the opportunity to attend college. As part of this college-going culture, high schools need to align graduation requirements with college eligibility requirements and have more frank discussions with high school students about selecting their college major. Particularly if students are interested in STEM, research suggests that if they wait until college to make that decision, it is already too late because they lack the necessary foundational knowledge.

Rather than advise that more research is needed on these topics to make effective and well-targeted policy recommendations (it is), we suggest that different research is needed. In particular, theoretically based, interdisciplinary research that is policy-oriented in its conceptualization, design, analysis, and dissemination is needed most. There does seem to be movement, particularly in developmental science, toward such interdisciplinary policy-oriented collaborations. For example, the Human Capital Research Collaborative, a partnership between the University of Minnesota and the Federal Reserve Bank of Minneapolis, is concerned with the intersections of social policy, economic development, and educational policy and practice from birth through college (Reynolds, Rolnick, Englund, & Temple,

2010). The collaboration between developmental psychologists and economists led to a cost-benefit analysis of early childhood educational interventions, which indicated a net benefit to society associated with children participating in the program due to increased earnings and staying out of the criminal justice system (Reynolds, Temple, White, Ou, & Robertson, 2011).

Another example can be seen in work with the Bridging Multiple Worlds Theory (Cooper, 2011; Cooper et al., 2002). Building on Erikson's (1968) writings on identity development, the Bridging Multiple Worlds Theory is designed to integrate research, policy, and practice pertaining to the academic pipeline problem. The theory consists of five inter-related dimensions: (1) demographics along the pipeline; (2) developing college going identities; (3) math and language pathways; (4) resources and challenges across multiple worlds of families, peers, schools, and communities; and (5) cultural research partnerships. What is particularly useful about this theory in the context of the current article is that the research and policy are intricately connected; each informs the other through the progression of the work. This is evident in the fifth dimension, cultural research partnerships, which are collaborations among researchers, educators, policy makers, students, and others who have a stake in student success. Thus, partnership, collaboration, and a reciprocal relationship between research and policy are built directly into the model, as opposed to being an outgrowth of the model.

We return once more to the fable of the five men investigating the elephant in the dark. The motivating force in their investigations was to inspect the elephant to arrive at the truth about its nature. With respect to the questions of this article, we would like to suggest a modification to the story, where the motivation for the investigation is to understand the nature of this elephant so as to help it function better. Perhaps this is a more suitable metaphor for how to conduct research on the educational experiences of URM youth.

References

Ansalone, G. (2004). Getting our school on track: Is detracking really the answer? *Radical Pedogogy,* *6*(2). Retrieved November 10, 2005, from http://radicalpedagogy.icaap.org/content/issue6_2/.

Azmitia, M., & Cooper, C. (2001). Good or bad? Peer influences on Latino and European American adolescents' pathways through school. *Journal of Education for Students Placed at Risk,* *6*(1–2), 45–71. doi:10.1207/S15327671ESPR0601–2_4.

Azmitia, M., Cooper, C. R., & Brown, J. R. (2009). Support and guidance from families, friends, and teachers in Latino early adolescents' math pathways. *Journal of Early Adolescence, 29(1),* 142–169.

Azmitia, M., Syed, M., & Radmacher, K. (2008). On the intersection of personal and social identities: Introduction and evidence from a longitudinal study of emerging adults. In M. Azmitia, M. Syed, & K. Radmacher (Eds.), *The intersections of personal and social identities. New directions for child and adolescent development* (Vol.120, pp. 1–16). San Francisco, CA: Jossey-Bass.

Azmitia, M., Syed, M., & Radmacher, K. (2011). *Finding your niche: How ethnically and socioeconomically diverse emerging adults transition to college.* Manuscript submitted for publication.

Blake-Beard, S., Bayne, M., Crosby, F., & Muller, C. (2011). Matching by race and gender in mentoring relationships: Keeping our eyes on the prize. *Journal of Social Issues, 67*(3), 622-643.

Bowles, S., & Gintis, H. (1976). *Schooling in capitalist America.* New York: Basic Books.

Bourdieu, P. (1977). *Outline of a theory of practice.* Cambridge, UK: Cambridge University Press.

Brown, S. D., & Lent, R. W. (1996). A social cognitive framework for career choice counseling. *The Career Development Quarterly, 44,* 354–366.

Brubaker, R., & Cooper, F. (2000). Beyond "identity." *Theory and Society, 29*(1), 1–47. doi:10.1023/A:1007068714468.

Buhrmester, D., & Furman, W. (1987). The development of companionship and intimacy. *Child Development, 58*(4), 1101–1113. doi:10.2307/1130550.

Carter, P. L. (2003). "Black" cultural capital, status positioning, and schooling conflicts for low-income African American youth. *Social Problems, 50*(1). 136–155. doi:10.1525/sp.2003.50.1.136.

Cauce, A. M., Coronado, N., & Watson, J. (1998). Conceptual, methodological, and statistical issues in culturally competent research. In M. Hernandez & R. Mareasa (Eds.), *Promoting cultural competence in children's mental health services* (pp. 305–329). Baltimore, MD: Paul Brooks Publishing.

Chang, E. S., Chen, C., Greenberger, E., Dooley, D., & Heckhausen, J. (2006). What do they want in life? The life goals of a multi-ethnic, multi-generational sample of high school seniors. *Journal of Youth and Adolescence, 35*(3), 321–332.

Chemers, M. M., Syed, M., Goza, B. K., Zurbriggen, E., Bearman, S., Crosby, F., et al. (2010). *The role of self-efficacy and identity in mediating the effects of science enrichment programs for under-represented minority students.* Manuscript submitted for publication.

Chemers, M. M., Zurbriggen, E., Syed, M., Goza, B. K., & Bearman, S. (2011). The role of efficacy and identity in science career commitment among underrepresented minority students. *Journal of Social Issues, 67*(3), 469-491.

Cohen, G. L., & Garcia, J. (2005). "I am us": Negative stereotypes as collective threats. *Journal of Personality and Social Psychology, 89*(4), 566–582. doi:10.1037/0022–3514.89.4.566.

Coleman, J. (1988). Social capital in the creation of human capital. *American Journal of Sociology, 94*(suppl.), 95–120. doi:10.1086/228943.

Cooper, C. R. (1987). Conceptualizing research on adolescent development in the family: Four root metaphors. *Journal of Adolescent Research, 2*(3), 321–330. doi:10.1177/074355488723010.

Cooper, C. R. (2011). *Bridging multiple worlds: Cultures, identities, and pathways to college.* New York: Oxford University Press.

Cooper, C. R., & Burciaga, R. (2011). Pathways to college, to the professoriate, and to a green card: Linking research, policy, and practice on immigrant Latino youth. In T. N. Maloney & K. Korinek (Eds.), *Migration in the 21st century: Rights, outcomes, and policy* (pp. 177–191). London, UK: Routledge Kegan Paul.

Cooper, C. R., & Denner, J. (1998). Theories linking culture and psychology: Universal and community-specific processes. *Annual Review of Psychology, 49,* 559–584. doi:10.1146/annurev.psych.49.1.559.

Cooper, C. R., Azmitia, M., Garcia, E. E., Ittel, A., Lopez, E., Rivera, L., et al. (1994). Aspirations of low-income Mexican American and European American parents for their children and adolescents. In F. A. Villarruel, & R. M. Lerner (Eds.), *Promoting community-based programs for socialization and learning* (pp. 65–81). San Francisco, CA: Jossey-Bass.

Cooper, C. R., Denner, J., & Lopez, E. M. (1999). Cultural brokers: Helping Latino children on pathways toward success. *The Future of Children, 9*(2), 51–57. doi:10.2307/1602705.

Cooper, C. R., Cooper, R. G., Jr., Azmitia, M., Chavira, G., & Gullatt, Y. (2002). Bridging multiple worlds: How African American and Latino youth in academic outreach programs navigate math pathways to college. *Applied Developmental Science, 6*(2), 73–87. doi:10.1207/S1532480XADS0602_3.

Cooper, C. R., Domínguez, E., & Rosas, S. (2005). Soledad's dream: How immigrant children bridge their multiple worlds and build pathways to college. In C. R. Cooper, C. García Coll, T. Bartko, H. Davis & C. Chatman (Eds.), *Developmental pathways through middle childhood: Rethinking contexts and diversity as resources* (pp. 235–260). Mahwah, NJ: Erlbaum.

Cooper, C. R., Cooper, R. G., Burciaga, R, Dominguez, E., & Su, D. (2008). *Capital and challenge: Bridging cultural worlds on pathways to college and the professoriate by Latino immigrant youth*. Paper presented at the meetings of the Society for Research in Child Development, Denver, CO.

Cooper, C. R., Behrens, R., & Trinh, N. (2009). Identity. In R. A. Shweder, T. R. Bidell, A. C. Dailey, S. D. Dixon, P. J. Miller, & J. Modell. (Eds.) *The Chicago companion to the child* (pp. 474–477). Chicago, IL: University of Chicago Press.

Crul, M., & Schneider, J. (2009). *TIES Policy Brief: The second generation in Europe: Education and the transition to the labour market*. Amsterdam, The Netherlands: TIES. Retrieved June 10, 2010, from www.tiesproject.eu/component/option,com_docman/task,cat_view/gid,45/Itemid,142/.

Cullen, M. J., Hardison, C. M., & Sackett, P. R. (2004). Using SAT-grade and ability-job performance relationships to test predictions derived from stereotype threat theory. *Journal of Applied Psychology, 89*(2), 220–230. doi:10.1016/j.jesp.2010.04.004.

Danaher, K., & Crandall, C. S. (2008). Stereotype threat in applied settings re-examined. *Journal of Applied Social Psychology, 38*(6), 1639–1655. doi:10.1111/j.1559–1816.2008.00362.x.

Davis, C., & Simmons, C. (2009). Stereotype threat: A review, critique, and implications. In H. A. Neville, B. M. Tynes, & S. O. Utsey (Eds.), *Handbook of African American psychology* (pp. 211–222). Thousand Oaks, CA: Sage.

Destin, M., & Oyserman, D. (2010). Incentivizing education: Seeing schoolwork as an investment, not a chore. *Journal of Experimental Social Psychology, 46*(5), 846–849. doi:10.1016/j.jesp.2010.04.004.

Ebaugh, H. R., & Curry, M. (2000). Fictive kin as social capital in new immigrant communities. *Sociological Perspectives, 43*(2), 189–209.

Eccles, J. S. (2005). Studying gender and ethnic differences in participation in math, physical science, and information technology. *New Directions for Child and Adolescent Development, 110*, 7–14. doi:10.1002/cd.146.

Erikson, E. H. (1968). *Identity: Youth and crisis*. New York: Norton.

Finley, M. K. (1984). Teachers and tracking in a comprehensive high school. *Sociology of Education, 57*, 233–243. doi:10.2307/2112427.

Fry, R. (2002). *Latinos in higher education: Many enroll, two few graduate*. Washington, DC: Pew Hispanic Center. Retrieved August 4, 2010, from http://pewhispanic.org/reports/report.php?ReportID=3.

Furman, W., & Buhrmester, D. (1992). Age and sex differences in perceptions of networks of personal relationships. *Child Development, 63*(1), 103–115. doi:10.2307/1130905.

Gándara, P., & Maxwell-Jolly, J. (1999). *Priming the pump: Strategies for increasing the achievement of underrepresented minority undergraduates*. New York: The College Board.

Gándara, P. & Mejorado, M. (2005). Putting your money where your mouth is: Mentoring as a strategy to increase access to higher education. In W. G. Tierney, Z. B. Corwin, & J. E. Colyar. (Eds.), *Preparing for college: Nine elements of effective outreach* (pp. 89–110). Albany, NY: State University of New York Press.

Gándara, P., & Orfield, G. (2006). Introduction: Creating a 21st-century vision of access and equity in higher education. In P. Gándara, G. Orfield, & C. L. Horn (Eds.), *Expanding opportunity in higher education: Leveraging promise* (pp. 1–16). Albany, NY: State University of New York.

García-Coll, C. T., Akerman, A., & Cicchetti, D. (2000). Cultural influences on developmental processes and outcomes: Implications for the study of development and psychopathology. *Development and Psychopathology, 12*, 333–356. doi:10.1017/S0954579400003059.

García-Coll, C. T., Szalacha, L. A., & Palacios, N. (2005). Children of Dominican, Portuguese, and Cambodian immigrant families: Academic attitudes and pathways during middle childhood. In C. R. Cooper, C. T. García Coll, W. T. Bartko, H. Davis, & C. Chatman (Eds.), *Developmental pathways through middle childhood: Rethinking contexts and diversity as resources* (pp. 207–233). Mahwah, NJ: Erlbaum.

Gibson, M. A. (2005). Promoting academic engagement among minority youth: Implications from John Ogbu's Shaker Heights ethnography. *International Journal of Qualitative Studies in Education, 18*(5), 581–603. doi:10.1080/09518390500224853.

Gibson, M. A., Bejínez, L. F., Hidalgo, N., & Rolón, C. (2004) Belonging and school participation: Lessons from a migrant student club. In M. Gibson, P. Gándara, & J. P. Koyama (Eds.), *School connections: U.S. Mexican youth, peers, and school achievement* (pp. 129–149). New York: Teachers College Press.

Good, C., & Aronson, J. (2008). The development of stereotype threat: Consequences for educational and social equality. In C. Wainryb, J. G. Smetana, & E. Turiel (Eds.), *Social development, social inequalities, and social justice* (pp. 155–184). New York: Erlbaum.

Good, C., Aronson, J., & Harder, J. A. (2008). Problems in the pipeline: Stereotype threat and women's achievement in high-level math courses. *Journal of Applied Developmental Psychology, 29*(1), 17–28. doi:10.1016/j.appdev.2007.10.004.

Gurin, P., Dey, E. L., Hurtado, S., & Gurin, G. (2002). Diversity and higher education: Theory and impact on educational outcomes. *Harvard Educational Review, 72*(3), 330–366.

Hughes, D., Rodriguez, J., Smith, E. P., Johnson, D. J., Stevenson, H. C., & Spicer, P. (2006). Parents' racial/ethnic socialization practices: A review of research and agenda for future study. *Developmental Psychology, 42*, 747–770. doi:10.1037/0012–1649.42.5.747.

Hurtado, S., Griffin, K. A., Arellano, L., & Cuellar, M. (2008). Assessing the value of climate assessments: Progress and future directions. *Journal of Diversity in Higher Education, 1*(4), 204–221. doi:10.1037/a0014009.

Hurtado, S., Eagan, M. K., Tran, M. C., Newman, C. B., Chang, M. J., & Velasco, P. (2011) "We do science here": Underrepresented students interactions with faculty in different college contexts. *Journal of Social Issues, 67*(3), 553-579.

Jost, J. (1999). Outgroup favoritism and the theory of system justification: A paradigm for investigating the effects of socioeconomic success on stereotype content. In G. Moskowitz (Eds.), *Cognitive social psychology: On the future of social cognition* (pp. 89–102). Hillsdale, NJ: Erlbaum.

Kane, W. (2010, August 17). New requirements for high schoolers to graduate. *San Francisco Chronicle*, p. C-1.

Kao, G., & Rutherford, L. T. (2007). Does social capital still matter? Immigrant minority disadvantage in school-specific social capital and its effects on academic achievement. *Sociological Perspectives, 50*(1), 27–52.

Keller, J. (2007). Stereotype threat in classroom settings: The interactive effect of domain identification, task difficulty and stereotype threat on female students' maths performance. *British Journal of Educational Psychology, 77*(2), 323–338. doi:10.1348/000709906×113662.

Kelly, S. (2004). Are teachers tracked? On what basis and with what consequences. *Social Psychology of Education, 7*, 55–72. doi: 10.1023/B:SPOE.0000010673.78910.f1.

Kuh, G. D., Kinzie, J. Buckley, J. A., Bridges, B. K., & Hayek, J. C. (2006). What matters to student success: A review of the literature. *Commissioned Report for the National Symposium on Postsecondary Student Success: Spearheading a Dialog on Student Success*. Washington, DC: National Postsecondary Education Cooperative.

Leaper, C., & Van, S. R. (2008). Masculinity ideology, covert sexism, and perceived gender typicality in relation to young men's academic motivation and choices in college. *Psychology of Men & Masculinity, 9*(3), 139–153. doi:10.1037/1524–9220.9.3.139.

Levitt, M. J., Weber, R. A., & Guacci, N. (1993). Convoys of social support: An intergenerational analysis. *Psychology and Aging, 8*(3), 323–326. doi:10.1037/0882–7974.8.3.323.

Lewis, O. (1966). The culture of poverty. *Scientific American, 215*, 19–25. doi:10.1038/scientificamerican1066–19.

Markus, H., & Nurius, P. (1986). Possible selves. *American Psychologist, 41*(9), 954–969.

Mehan, H. (2007). *Restructuring and reculturing schools to provide students with multiple pathways to college and career* (paper mp-rr006–0207). Los Angeles, CA: UCLA Institute for Democracy, Education, and Access.

Mickelson, R. A., & Heath, D. (1999). The effects of segregation on African American high school seniors' academic achievement. *Journal of Negro Education, 68*(4), 566–586.

Moll, L. C., Amanti, C., Neff, D., & Gonzalez, N. (1992). Funds of knowledge for teaching: Using a qualitative approach to connect homes and classrooms. *Theory into Practice, 31*(1), 132–141.

Neblett, E. W., Jr., Terzian, M., & Harriott V. (2010). From racial discrimination to substance use: The buffering effects of racial socialization. *Child Development Perspectives, 4*(2), 131–137.

Nelson, T. D. (Eds.). (2009). *Handbook of prejudice, stereotyping, and discrimination*. New York: Psychology Press.

Oakes, J. (2005). *Keeping track. How schools structure inequality* (2nd ed.). New Haven, CT: Yale University Press.

Oakes, J., Wells, A. S., Jones, M., & Datnow, A. (1997). Detracking: The social construction of ability, cultural politics, and resistance to reform. *Teachers College Record, 98*(3), 482–510.

Ogbu, J. U. (1997). Understanding the school performance of urban blacks: Some essential background knowledge. In H. J. Walberg, O. Reyes, & R. P. Weissberg (Eds.), *Children and youth: Interdisciplinary perspectives* (pp. 190–222). Thousand Oaks, CA: Sage.

Oishi, S., Kesebir, S., & Snyder, B. H. (2009). Sociology: A lost connection in social psychology. *Personality and Social Psychology Review, 13*(4), 334–353.

Osborne, J. W., & Walker, C. (2006). Stereotype threat, identification with academics, and withdrawal from school: Why the most successful students of colour might be most likely to withdraw. *Educational Psychology, 26*(4), 563–577.

Oyserman, D. & Destin, M. (2010). Identity-based motivation: Implications for intervention. *The Counseling Psychologist, 38*, 1001–1043. doi:10.1177/0011000010374775.

Oyserman, D., Bybee, D., & Terry, D. (2006). Possible selves and academic outcomes: How and when possible selves impel action. *Journal of Personality and Social Psychology, 91*, 188–204. doi:10.1037/0022–3514.91.1.188.

Pascarella, E. T., & Terenzini, P. T. (2005). *How college affects students: A third decade of research* (Vol. 2). Indianapolis, IN: Jossey-Bass.

Pepper, S. P. (1942). *World hypotheses*. Berkeley, CA: University of California Press.

Phelan, P., Yu, H. C., & Davidson, A. L. (1994). Navigating the psychological pressures of adolescence: The voices and experiences of high school youth. *American Educational Research Journal, 31*(2), 415–447.

Portes, A., & Fernández-Kelly, P. (2008). No margin for error: Educational and occupational achievement among disadvantaged children of immigrants. *Annals of the American Academy of Political and Social Science, 620*, 12–36. doi:10.1177/0002716208322577.

Pronin, E., Steele, C. M., & Ross, L. (2004). Identity bifurcation in response to stereotype threat: Women and mathematics. *Journal of Experimental Social Psychology, 40*(2), 152–168. doi:10.1016/S0022–1031(03)00088-X.

Quintana, S. M., & McKown, C. (Eds.). (2008). *Handbook of race, racism, and the developing child*. Hoboken, NJ: John Wiley & Sons.

Reis, O., Azmitia, M., Syed, M., Radmacher, K., & Gills, J. (2009). Patterns of social support and mental health among ethnically-diverse adolescents during school transitions. *European Journal of Developmental Science, 3*(1), 39–50.

Reynolds, A. J., Rolnick, A. J., Englund, M., & Temple, J. (Eds.). (2010). *Childhood programs and practices in the first decade of life: A human capital integration*. New York: Cambridge University Press.

Reynolds, A. J., Temple, J. A., White, B., Ou, S. & Robertson, D. L. (2011). Age-26 cost-benefit analysis of the Child-Parent Center Early Education Program. *Child Development, 82*(1), 379–404. doi:10.1111/j.1467–8624.2010.01563.x.

Rogoff, B. (2003). *The cultural nature of human development*. New York: Oxford University Press.

Sackett, P. R., Hardison, C. M., & Cullen, M. J. (2004). On interpreting stereotype threat as accounting for African American-White differences on cognitive tests. *American Psychologist, 59*(1), 7–13. doi:10.1037/0003–066X.59.1.7.

Santos, S. J., Ortiz, A. M., Morales, A., & Rosales, M. (2007). The relationship between campus diversity, students' ethnic identity and college adjustment: A qualitative study. *Cultural Diversity and Ethnic Minority Psychology, 13*(2), 104–114. doi:10.1037/1099–9809.13.2.104.

Schachter, E. P., & Ventura, J. J. (2008). Identity agents: Parents as active and reflective participants in their children's identity formation. *Journal of Research on Adolescence, 18*(3), 449–476. doi:10.1111/j.1532–7795.2008.00567.x.

Schmidt, P. (2008, September 15). Federal panel seeks cause of minority students' poor science performance. *Chronicle of Higher Education*.

Smith, J. L. (2004). Understanding the process of stereotype threat: A review of mediational variables and new performance goal directions. *Educational Psychology Review, 16*(3), 177–206. doi:10.1023/B:EDPR.0000034020.20317.89.

Spencer, S., Steele, C. M., & Quinn, D. (1999). Stereotype threat and women's math performance. *Journal of Experimental Social Psychology, 35*(1), 4–28. doi:10.1006/jesp.1998.1373.

Stack, C. B., & Burton, L. M. (1993). Kinscripts. *Journal of Comparative Family Studies, 24*(2), 157–170.

Stambler, M. J., & Weinstein, R. S. (2010). Psychological disengagement in elementary school among ethnic minority students. *Journal of Applied Developmental Psychology, 31*, 755–765.

Stangor, C. (2009). The study of stereotyping, prejudice, and discrimination within social psychology: A quick history of theory and research. In T. D. Nelson (Eds.), *Handbook of prejudice, stereotyping, and discrimination*. (pp. 1–22). New York: Psychology Press.

Steele, C. M. (1997). A threat in the air: How stereotypes shape intellectual identity and performance. *American Psychologist, 52*(6), 613–629. doi:10.1037/0003–066X.52.6.613.

Steele, C. M., & Aronson, J. (1995). Stereotype threat and the intellectual test performance of African Americans. *Journal of Personality and Social Psychology, 69*, 797–811. doi:10.1037/0022–3514.69.5.797.

Stricker, L. J., & Ward, W. C. (2004). Stereotype threat, inquiring about test takers' ethnicity and gender, and standardized test performance. *Journal of Applied Social Psychology, 34*(4), 665–693. doi:10.1111/j.1559–1816.2004.tb02564.x.

Stricker, L. J., & Ward, W. C. (2008). Stereotype threat in applied settings re-examined: A reply. *Journal of Applied Social Psychology, 38*(6), 1656–1663. doi:10.1111/j.1559–1816.2008.00363.x.

Sullivan, B. A., & Hansen, J. C. (2004). Mapping associations between interests and personality: Toward a conceptual understanding of individual differences in vocational behavior. *Journal of Counseling Psychology, 51*(3), 287–298. doi:10.1037/0022–0167.51.3.287.

Syed, M. (2010a). Developing an integrated self: Academic and ethnic identities among ethnically-diverse college students. *Developmental Psychology, 46*(6), 1590–1604. doi:10.1037/a0020738.

Syed, M. (2010b). Disciplinarity and methodology in intersectionality theory and research. *American Psychologist, 65*(1), 61–62. doi:10.1037/a0017495

Syed, M. (2010c). Memorable everyday events in college: Narratives of the intersection of ethnicity and academia. *Journal of Diversity in Higher Education, 3*(1), 56–69. doi:10.1037/a0018503.

Syed, M., & Azmitia, M. (2008). A narrative approach to ethnic identity in emerging adulthood: Bringing life to the identity status model. *Developmental Psychology, 44*(4), 1012–1027. doi:10.1037/0012–1649.44.4.1012.

Syed, M., & Azmitia, M. (2009). Longitudinal trajectories of ethnic identity during the college years. *Journal of Research on Adolescence, 19*(4), 601–624. doi:10.1111/j.1532–7795.2009.00609.x.

Syed, M., Goza, B. K., Chemers, M. M., & Zurbriggen, E. (in press). Individual differences in preferences for matched-ethnic mentors among high-achieving ethnically-diverse adolescents in STEM. *Child Development.*

Tajfel, H. (1981). *Human groups and social categories.* Cambridge, England: Cambridge University Press.

Tajfel, H., & Turner, J. C. (1986). The social identity theory of intergroup behavior. In S. Worchel & W. Austin (Eds.), *Psychology of intergroup relations* (pp. 7–24). Chicago, IL: Nelson-Hall.

Tierney, W., & Auerbach, S. (2006) Toward developing an untapped resource: The role of families in college preparation. In W. Tierney, Z. B. Corwin, & J. E. Colyar (Eds.), *Preparing for college: Nine elements of effective outreach* (pp. 29–48). Albany, NY: State University of New York Press.

Tierney, W., Colyar, J. E., & Corwin, Z. B. (2005). *Preparing for college: Nine elements of effective outreach.* Albany, NY: State University of New York Press.

Tinto, V. (1993). *Leaving college: Rethinking the cases and cures of student attrition* (2nd ed.). Chicago, IL: University of Chicago Press.

Tinto, V. (2000). Linking learning and leaving: Exploring the role of the college classroom in student departure. In J. M. Braxton (Eds.), *Reworking the student departure puzzle* (pp. 81–94). Nashville, TN: Vanderbilt University Press.

U.S. Department of Education, National Center for Education Statistics (2002) *Nontraditional undergraduates, NCES 2002–012.* Washington, DC: U.S. Department of Education.

Vygotsky, L. S. (1978), *Mind in society: The development of higher mental processes*. Cambridge, MA: Harvard University Press.

Walton, G. M., & Cohen, G. L. (2003). Stereotype lift. *Journal of Experimental Social Psychology, 39*(5), 456–467. doi:10.1016/S0022–1031(03)00019–2.

Whaley, A. L. (2009). Stereotype threat paradigm in search of a phenomenon: A comment on Kellow and Jones's (2008) study. *Journal of Black Psychology, 35*(4), 485–494. doi:10.1177/0095798408329986.

Witkow, M. R., & Fuligni, A. J. (2011). Ethnic and generational differences in the relations between social support and academic achievement across the high school years. *Journal of Social Issues, 67*(3), 531-552.

Yamauchi, L. A., Ceppi, A. K., & Lau-Smith, J. (1999). Sociohistorical influences on the development of Papahana Kaiapuni, the Hawaiian language immersion program. *Journal of Education for Students Placed at Risk, 4*(1), 27–46. doi:10.1207/s15327671espr0401_3.

Yamauchi, L. A., Billig, S. H., Meyer, S., & Hofschire, L. (2006). Student outcomes associated with service-learning in a culturally relevant high school program. *Journal of Prevention & Intervention in the Community, 32*(1–2), 149–164. doi:10.1300/J005v32n01_10.

Yamauchi, L. A., Lau-Smith, J., & Luning, R. J. I. (2008). Family involvement in a Hawaiian language immersion program. *The School Community Journal, 18*(1), 39–60.

Yonezawa, S., Wells, A. S., & Serna, I. (2002). Choosing tracks: "Freedom of choice" in detracking schools. *American Educational Research Journal, 39*, 37–67. doi:10.3102/00028312039001037.

Yosso, T. J. (2005). Whose culture has capital? A critical race theory discussion of community cultural wealth. *Race Ethnicity and Education, 8*(1), 69–91. doi:10.1080/1361332052000341006.

Zirkel, S. (2002). Is there a place for me? Role models and academic identity among white students and students of color. *Teachers College Record, 104*(2), 357–376. doi:10.1111/1467–9620.00166.

MOIN SYED is an Assistant Professor of Psychology at the University of Minnesota, Twin Cities. His research is broadly concerned with identity development among ethnically and culturally diverse adolescents and emerging adults, with particular focus on the development of multiple personal and social identities (e.g., ethnicity, social class, and gender) and the implications of identity development for educational experiences and career orientation.

MARGARITA AZMITIA is a Professor of Developmental Psychology at the University of California at Santa Cruz. Her research focuses on how children and adolescents from diverse backgrounds manage developmental and school transitions. She is especially interested in the roles of family, peers, and school in adolescents' adjustment to these transitions and in the roles of gender, ethnicity, and social class in adolescents' and young adults' identity development and educational trajectories.

CATHERINE R. COOPER is Professor of Psychology and founding director of the doctoral program in Developmental Psychology at the University of California, Santa Cruz. She developed the Bridging Multiple Worlds Theory to trace how youth forge identity pathways to college, careers, and adult roles without giving up ties to their families and cultural communities. Cooper is director of the Bridging Multiple Worlds Alliance, a network of researchers, educators, and policymakers working to open educational opportunities from preschool through graduate and professional school (P-20).

Journal of Social Issues, Vol. 67, No. 3, 2011, pp. 469–491

The Role of Efficacy and Identity in Science Career Commitment Among Underrepresented Minority Students

Martin M. Chemers,* **Eileen L. Zurbriggen, Moin Syed, Barbara K. Goza, and Steve Bearman**
University of California, Santa Cruz

A web-based survey of members of the Society for the Advancement of Chicanos and Native Americans in Science tested a model that proposed that the effects of science support experiences on commitment to science careers would be mediated by science self-efficacy and identity as a scientist. A sample of 327 undergraduates and 338 graduate students and postdoctoral fellows described their science support experiences (research experience, mentoring, and community involvement); psychological variables (science self-efficacy, leadership/teamwork self-efficacy, and identity as a scientist); and commitment to pursue a career in scientific research. Structural equation model analyses supported our predictions. Among the undergraduates, science (but not leadership/teamwork), self-efficacy, and identity as a scientist fully mediated the effects of science support experiences and were strong predictors of commitment. Results for the graduate/postdoctoral sample revealed a very similar pattern of results, with the added finding that all three psychological mediators, including leadership/teamwork self-efficacy, predicted commitment.

*Correspondence concerning this article should be addressed to Martin Chemers, Department of Psychology, University of California Santa Cruz, 1156 High Street, Santa Cruz, CA 95064 [e-mail: mchemers@ucsc.edu].

This research was supported by Grant Number R01GM071935 from the National Institute of General Medical Sciences. The content is solely the responsibility of the authors and does not necessarily represent the official views of the National Institute of General Medical Sciences, or the National Institutes of Health. We are grateful for the support of research team members Faye Crosby, Elizabeth Espinosa, Lisa Hunter, Beth Jaworski, Deborah Kogan, Carrol Moran, Elizabeth Morgan, Jerome Shaw, and Julie Shattuck, as well as the leadership and members of the *SACNAS* .

At the time the study was conducted, all authors were in the Department of Psychology at the University of California, Santa Cruz (UCSC), with the exception of Barbara K. Goza, who was at the Educational Partnership Center at UCSC. Moin Syed is now in the Department of Psychology at the University of Minnesota, and Barbara K. Goza is now in the Department of Psychology at UCSC.

Despite much discussion and many efforts at change, the representation of Native Americans, African–Americans, and Latino Americans in science fields is still quite low. This is true at all points in the academic pipeline, including completing of bachelor's degrees, entering graduate programs, and completing graduate programs in science. Over the last 15–20 years, change has occurred, but not at a sufficient level (Gándara & Maxwell-Jolly, 1999; Treisman, 1992). Equity in science education is of concern internationally (Baker, 1998; Smith, 2010); however, the current article addresses the issue with respect to education in the United States.

Attempts to redress these inequities have most often involved the development of "science support" programs, in which underrepresented students or young professionals receive guidance and encouragement to pursue a career in scientific research. The typical program model and components embedded in these programs were highlighted by Gándara and Maxwell-Jolly (1999), and include professional experiences such as research, mentoring, as well as academic, financial, and psychosocial support. Specific programs that have been lauded as achieving notable successes in enhancing minority undergraduate performance in the sciences and promoting subsequent graduate school attendance and success include the Meyerhoff Scholars Program at University of Maryland, Baltimore County (Maton, Hrabowski, & Schmitt, 2000) and the Biology Undergraduate Scholars Program (BUSP) at University of California, Davis (Barlow & Villarejo, 2004; see also Hurtado et al., 2011, for a fuller discussion of programmatic and institutional features affecting student outcomes).

Although some programs have been effective in helping some students, an empirical basis for a nuanced understanding about how and why the "better" programs are effective has been lacking. Without targeted theory and empirically established findings, new programs and programs seeking to improve results have only intuitive and anecdotal guides. In recent years, there has been a call for more intensive, theory-based research on the underlying processes that affect underrepresented minority (URM) students' commitment and success.

The design of the present research is based on our belief that the most powerful tool for building better science support programs is a deep understanding of the processes that underlie student decision-making and performance. In the current research, we are not so much interested in programs per se, as in the experiences and opportunities they provide, which could occur outside the programs as well. We examine how psychological factors, such as self-efficacy and personal identity, mediate the relationships between science support experiences (such as research experience, mentoring, and community involvement) and desirable outcomes (such as commitment to and effort expended toward a career in scientific research). We present, here, a "mediation model" of how these program and psychological variables are predicted to combine to produce greater commitment to a scientific career (Figure 1).

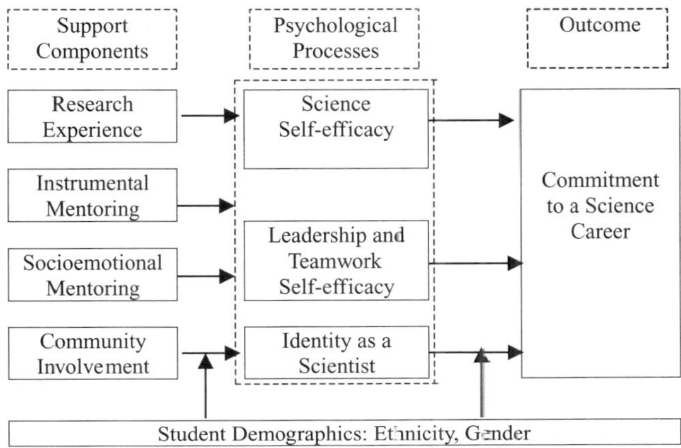

Fig. 1. Mediation model of the effects of science support experiences, adapted from Chemers et al. (2010).

The Mediation Model of the Effects of Science Support Experiences

The model that we propose is one in which science support experiences affect relevant psychological processes, which in turn lead to commitment and involvement in a scientific career. We focused on several important science support experiences: research experience, mentor influences, and community involvement. Three key mediators are tested: science self-efficacy, leadership and team work self-efficacy, and identity as a scientist.

Research experience. A growing body of evidence supports the assumption that involving students in doing research promotes learning outcomes. Sadler, Burgin, McKinney, and Punjuan (2010) synthesized 53 studies of research apprenticeships. Research experiences were found to enhance attitudes such as interest in science careers and self-efficacy regarding research skills, and students who were engaged in the more complex aspects of the research process, such as analysis, showed gains in scientific reasoning (e.g., Charney et al., 2007; Ryder & Leach, 1999). In addition to those reported by Sadler et al. (2010), a number of studies have addressed the effectiveness of science support programs that include a research component. Merna Villarejo and her colleagues reported the evaluation of the BUSP, an educational enrichment program for underrepresented biology students at the University of California Davis (Barlow & Villarejo, 2004; Villarejo & Barlow, 2007). They found BUSP students outperformed others in general chemistry and calculus and in persisting to graduation with a biology major. Their analyses suggested that this persistence may be due to BUSP students' high rates of research participation. In a related survey of high-achieving BUSP alumni, Villarejo, Barlow, Kogan, Veazey, and Sweeney (2008) found that among those who pursued PhDs in biomedical research, over half indicated that their experience in undergraduate research was transformative.

Similarly, Maton et al. (2000) analyzed the effect of the Meyerhoff Scholars Program for African–American students at the University of Maryland, Baltimore County. Compared with multiple relevant samples, Meyerhoff students achieved higher grade point averages, graduated from science and engineering majors at higher rates, and had higher rates of admittance to graduate school. Students reported that research internships and mentors were among the experiences responsible for their success. A follow-up study found that participation in on-campus, academic year research was associated with substantial increases in science, technology, engineering, and mathematics (i.e., STEM) PhD pursuit (Carter, Mandell, & Maton, 2009).

Mentor influences. Among the program components empirically identified as elements of effective science support programs are mentor relationships between science faculty and undergraduate and graduate protégés. High school students also have opportunities to experience research apprenticeships, which usually include a mentoring component. Investigations are exploring the nature of mentoring, and how mentoring influences students in high school, undergraduate, and graduate work (Linnehan, 2001; Tenenbaum, Crosby, & Gliner, 2001). These studies have shown that mentored students demonstrate higher academic performance, attendance, and satisfaction. For example, Witkow and Fuligni (2011) describe how failure to get good advice about career and educational planning for some high school students influences their future educational trajectories. Similarly, Phinney, Torres Campos, Kallemeyn, and Kim (2011) discuss the critical role of effective mentoring for first-year college students. A study by Foertsch, Alexander, and Penberthy (2000) compared program design features with outcomes for participants in summer research programs at 15 midwestern research universities. The study found that the pivotal factor in determining summer interns' success was the quality of the relationship with the faculty mentor, even when the actual number of contact hours with the faculty member was limited.

Community involvement. We use the term community involvement to reflect opportunities that might be available for a student to develop a sense of being part of the scientific community, one aspect of the psychosocial support element identified by Gándara and Maxwell-Jolly (1999). Work contact that goes beyond formal lectures or assignments might allow a student to get to know better the faculty, postdoctoral fellows, graduate students, and undergraduate peers who have chosen scientific research as a major or a career. Additionally, social events (such as pizza parties, picnics, etc.) that are part of many programs provide an alternative context for developing a network. At a national level, many organizations with the goal of broadening participation in science offer conferences that bring students, faculty, and professional scientists together.

It has been assumed that these science support program components (i.e., research experience, mentoring, and community involvement) contribute to success, but the psychological processes involved are not well understood. From both a policy and a practice perspective, understanding the underlying psychological mechanisms provides guidance to select new programs for funding and to improve the effectiveness of existing programs. A serious question, then, is what are the pathways by which mentoring and other science support activities affect student commitment and performance in science education contexts? In this study we focused on three relevant constructs: science self-efficacy, leadership and teamwork self-efficacy (LTSE), and identity as a scientist.

Science self-efficacy. Based on an extensive literature on commitment and achievement in academic performance environments, academic self-efficacy is a good candidate as a probable mediator of the effects of science support activities. A vast program of research on self-efficacy (Bandura, 1997) indicates that confidence in one's ability to perform a specific behavior or accomplish a specific task is predictive of performance above and beyond predictions based on objective measures of ability alone. Self-efficacy has been related to persistence, tenacity, and achievement in both educational and experimental settings (Bandura, 1986; Zimmerman, 1989). Chemers, Hu, and Garcia (2001) applied efficacy theory to predict academic success and personal adjustment of first-year university students. Based on assessments near the beginning and end of the academic year, the findings indicated that, above and beyond any effects of previous ability, academic self-efficacy was a strong and significant predictor of academic goals, academic performance, personal adjustment, and health.

Most programs designed to increase minority student representation and academic performance in the sciences place a great deal of emphasis on an authentic research experience. As indicated above, some studies have examined how research apprenticeships affect the knowledge and skills of science learners at the high school and undergraduate levels (Barab & Hay, 2000; Bell, Blair, Crawford, & Lederman, 2003; Kardash, 2000; Richmond & Kurth, 1999; Seymour, Hunter, Laursen & Deantoni, 2004). These studies found that engagement in authentic science offers the opportunity for students to use scientific and technical language, communicate about the problems of science, and appreciate the actual work of science. Our hypothesis is that a significant contributor to successful academic (and professional) work in science depends on the possession of high self-efficacy for science skills, and that science self-efficacy will fully mediate the effects of science experiences on student commitment and performance.

Leadership and teamwork self-efficacy. We argue for the inclusion of leadership and teamwork efficacy as an important mediator on the grounds that most research, particularly in the STEM fields, is conducted by teams (i.e., lab groups) rather than individuals working alone.

Almost 50 years ago, Hagstrom (1964) argued that "teamwork is necessary in science" (p. 242), due to the collection of skills necessary to solve a problem and/or the need for faster, more efficient problem solving than individuals can accomplish. Over this 50-year period, the proportion of team-produced scientific publications and patents has increased dramatically (Wuchty, Jones, & Uzzi, 2007). Practical advice for managing scientific teamwork is now available in print (see, e.g., Barker, 2002; Boss & Eckert, 2003; Harmening, 2003) and from many professional associations (see websites of the American Psychological Association, *American Chemical Society*, and the *Society for the Advancement of Chicanos and Native Americans in Science [SACNAS]* for examples). A budding field called the science of team science aims to enhance the productivity of large-scale collaborative research and training programs. However, little research has been done regarding the impact of interpersonal processes such as leadership and teamwork on scientific collaboration (Stokols, Hall, Taylor, & Moser, 2008). When a student is exposed to the importance of leadership, as modeled by mentors, and teamwork, as modeled by peers, s/he may come to recognize that to be a good scientist also involves being a good team member.

As science self-efficacy is critical to sustaining students' success in science, so too is leadership/teamwork self-efficacy. A series of studies by Chemers and his associates indicates that leadership efficacy has effects, similar to those observed in the academic domain, on leader and team performance (Chemers, Watson, & May, 2000; Watson, Chemers, & Preiser, 2001). If leadership efficacy promotes successful performance in scientific endeavors, it is reasonable to expect that positive beliefs about one's leadership self-efficacy should contribute to students' expectations of success in a science career. Those expectations should in turn contribute to commitment to such a career.

Identity as a scientist. Erikson (1968) and Arnett (2004) proposed that the optimal developmental outcome for adolescents and emerging adults is to achieve a sense of coherence that integrates their multiple identities across time and contexts. Azmitia, Syed, and Radmacher (2008) further argued that developing an identity can be confusing and stressful, because of the multiple worlds and identities to which a college student is exposed. "One source of confusion is whether a person's unique, or personal, self develops in connection with his or her sense of identity and belonging to a group or collective (i.e., a social identity)" (p. 3) (see also Syed, Azmitia & Cooper, 2011, for extensive coverage of identity and academic integration).

The empirical literature on student persistence and success in academic settings reports that identification is related to a sense of fit with other academics and the academic world in general (Dovidio, Gartner, Niemann, & Snider, 2001). A number of studies have found that identification with context relevant identities (e.g., student, scientist, etc.) provides better prediction of academic performance and persistence than racial or ethnic identity (Boncus-Hammarth, 2000; Eccles & Barber, 1999; Osborne & Walker, 2006). Eccles and Barber (1999) found that underrepresented minorities who identify strongly with academic role identities have greater persistence to degree completion than do underrepresented students who identify more strongly with their social identities (e.g., ethnic/racial, gender, socioeconomic status). Franco-Zamudio (2010) reported that a large proportion of the successful graduate students that she studied belonged to some organization that combined their academic and personal identities (e.g., Women in Engineering Society, Hispanic Scientists).

The foregoing interpretation of the relevant literature led to the proposed model of research experience, i.e., that the experiences of research participation, mentoring, and involvement in a community of science will enhance commitment to a career in science, but only if they positively affect science self-efficacy, LTSE, and science identity; in other words, a model of full mediation by self-relevant attitudes.

Previous Research with the Mediation Model of the Effects of Science Support Experiences

Chemers et al. (2010) reported the findings of two studies of undergraduate students enrolled in research support programs at the University of California, Santa Cruz. The first study involved a retrospective survey of past participants in science support programs as well as students enrolled in science and engineering majors during the same time period, but who did not participate in programs. Following the model outlined in Figure 1 and described above, the researchers predicted that science and leadership/teamwork self-efficacy and identity as a scientist would mediate the effects of science support activities on commitment to continue as a scientist. The science support activities that were significant predictors included research experience, community involvement, and instrumental mentoring, but not academic support, financial support, or the socioemotional aspect of mentoring. Among the psychological mediators, science self-efficacy and identity as a scientist, but not leadership/teamwork self-efficacy had effects strong enough to be included in the final path model. The second study conducted by Chemers et al. (2010) tested the same model using a prospective design and yielded similar findings. The analyses indicated a plausible chain of effects in which research experience and instrumental mentoring lead to higher levels of science self-efficacy, which leads to enhanced identity as a scientist, which leads to stronger commitment to a science career.

These studies provided strong support for the role of science self-efficacy and identity as a scientist as psychological mediators of science support activities on commitment to a career in science. They also supported the value of research experience and at least some aspects of mentoring. Despite this general support for the mediation model, some hypothesized relationships (e.g., the effect of leadership/teamwork self-efficacy) were not found. In addition, the sample was limited to undergraduates studying at one university, and the sample size in Study 2 was small. Thus, it would be useful to conduct additional research involving broader, nationally distributed samples of undergraduates and post-baccalaureates, from a diverse group of colleges, universities, and graduate schools.

The current study is a replication and extension of the earlier studies reported in Chemers et al. (2010), designed to build on those findings. Through the auspices of the *SACNAS* we were able to survey a large sample of underrepresented participants at the undergraduate, graduate, and postdoctoral levels. *SACNAS* was founded in 1973, dedicated to helping Hispanic/Chicano and Native American scientists succeed in obtaining the advanced degrees necessary for science research, leadership, and teaching careers at all levels. The centerpiece of *SACNAS* programming is the annual conference that brings together over 2000 participants in scientific symposia, keynote speakers, career advancement workshops, exhibits, student research presentations, and mentoring. In addition, *SACNAS* supports about 45 local chapters on college and university campuses across the country. The *SACNAS News* publishes mentoring and science information for 17,000 readers nationally. Targets of these interventions include undergraduate and graduate students, postdoctoral scholars, and science educators at K-12, community college, and university levels.

Based on Chemers et al.'s (2010) earlier studies, we employed the mediation model (Figure 1) to predict that the psychological variables of science self-efficacy, LTSE, and identity as a scientist will mediate the effects of science support experiences (research experience, mentoring, and community involvement) on commitment to a science career. We expect to replicate the findings of the earlier research. We are also interested in whether, with a sample that is more diverse in several ways, including age/stage of science education, we would find effects of leadership/teamwork self-efficacy, and of socioemotional mentoring. For example, it seems plausible that because graduate students and postdoctoral fellows have more experience than undergraduate students in working as part of a scientific team, LTSE might emerge as a significant mediator for those students and fellows.

Method

Participants

Participants were recruited from the *SACNAS*. In December 2006, *SACNAS* staff members sent e-mail invitations on behalf of the *SACNAS* Board, describing their collaboration on a research project to "help us learn about the 'active ingredients' that support science students most effectively." The invitation indicated that the survey is for anyone connected with *SACNAS* who is currently an undergraduate, graduate student, or postdoctoral fellow, or anyone who has graduated from college or university in the last 3 years. Two reminder invitations were sent over the following month. All individuals in the *SACNAS* database received the invitation, although the available information in the database suggested that there were 4,101 members who met the survey eligibility criteria, of whom 1,944 had updated their e-mail addresses since the beginning of 2006. Participants completing the entire survey included 242 current undergraduates, 85 who had earned bachelor's degrees within the last 3 years, 278 graduate students, and 60 postdoctoral fellows. These 665 participants represent a response rate of 16.22% of eligible participants and 34.21% of those with likely current addresses. For purposes of this study, recent graduates were grouped with undergraduates because many faculty and graduate programs recommend that students delay graduate admissions 2 or 3 years post-baccalaureate, so that students gain work experience and assess continuing science interests. Postdoctoral fellows were grouped with graduate students.

Among the 327 undergraduates/recent graduates who completed the entire survey, there were 67% females, with a mean age of 24.06 years ($SD = 5.67$). Ethnicity was quite diverse, with 160 (49%) reporting Latino/Hispanic heritage, 28 (9%) Black/African–American, 14 (4%) Native American, 38 (12%) mixed URMs (Latin, Black, Native American), 47 (15%) Asian American or Pacific Islander, and 36 (11%) White. Although 231 (71%) were born in the United States, only 163 (50%) spoke English as their first language.

Of the 338 graduates and postdoctoral fellows who completed the entire survey, 63% were female, with a mean age of 29.83 years ($SD = 6.61$). Reported ethnic background was 192 (57%) Latino, 24 (7%) Black/African–American, 16 (5%) Native American, and 60 (18%) mixed URMs; 23 (7%) Asian American or Pacific Islander, and 20 (6%) White. Most (240 or 71%) were born in the United States, and 194 (57%) spoke English as their first language.

Measures

The surveys included numerous constructs. Those reported in this article were adaptations of the scales used in Chemers et al. (2010). Most of the constructs and items were the same across undergraduate and graduate/postdoctoral versions, with variations described below. Initial analyses were conducted to ensure that each construct was a single factor, and items not loading on the construct were deleted from further analysis.

Science support experiences.   To isolate the effects of student engagement in extracurricular activities such as science support program interventions, items requested students to consider how active they were as undergraduates (or graduate students/postdoctoral fellows) outside regular coursework. Students reported their involvement using a 5-point scale, ranging from 1 (*not at all*) to 5 (*a lot*).

Research experience.   For undergraduates, 10 items measured students' involvement in professional science activities of varying levels of complexity. Sample items include "I learned scientific language and terminology" and "I created my own explanation for the results of a study/research project." Cronbach's alpha was .93. For graduate students, we added 11 items of a more advanced nature, such as "I was sole or first author on a paper or poster presentation on scientific content at a meeting of a professional organization" and "I supervised and trained undergraduate or graduate students." The resulting two-factor structure included a 6-item basic research construct ($\alpha=.92$) and a 14-item advanced research construct ($\alpha=.85$).

Community involvement.   Community involvement was measured for undergraduates with a four-item scale including items such as "I networked with fellow students," and I participated in social events with faculty or staff members, and/or fellow students." For graduate students and postdoctoral scholars, one of these items did not load with community involvement resulting in three-item scale. In both cases, Cronbach's alpha coefficients were sufficiently high (.80 for undergraduates and .76 for graduates/postdocs).

Socioemotional and instrumental mentoring.   The Chemers et al. (2010) measures were built on earlier work by Tenenbaum et al. (2001) and Kram (1985). We assessed two functions of mentoring: socioemotional mentoring that supports students' emotional development, and instrumental mentoring that helps students learn essential tasks of science career development. Mentors were defined as "anyone more experienced than you who has given you individual support related to your development as a science student." Students were invited to think back to possible mentoring from faculty members, program staff, graduate students, or peers, including people who were not formally designated as mentors, and describe the extent to which their mentor(s) provided them with opportunities. Students responded on a 5-point Likert-type response scale, with higher values indicating greater opportunities.

The undergraduate and graduate student versions of the socioemotional mentoring scale were exactly the same, consisting of seven stems such as "given you the impression that they believed in you" and "earned your trust" (Cronbach's alphas = .94 for undergraduates and .95 for graduates). For the instrumental mentoring scale, six items included stems such as "taught you specific research or analysis skills" and "helped you figure out for yourself how to answer a research question." For graduate students, five stems were added to assess more advanced professional activities, such as "helped you with job searches (by reviewing your application materials, watching practice talks, providing feedback, etc.)" and "gave you advice about good conferences to attend" (Cronbach's alphas = .90 for undergraduates and .92 for graduates).

Psychological processes.

Science self-efficacy. Building on the work of Bandura (1997), Chemers et al. (2010), and Kardash (2000), the science self-efficacy scale assessed students' confidence in their abilities to function as a scientist. Students indicated the "extent to which you are confident you can successfully complete the following tasks." For undergraduates, a 10-item scale parallels the research experience scale, including "use scientific language and terminology" and "create explanations for the results of a study." For graduate students and postdoctoral fellows, these 10 items were augmented with three more advanced items such as "publish research in peer-review outlets." Students responded on a 5-point scale that ranged from 1 (*not at all confident*) to 5 (*absolutely confident*), resulting in Cronbach's alphas of .94 and .95 for undergraduates and graduates, respectively.

Leadership/teamwork self-efficacy. This scale, adapted from Chemers' program of research (Chemers et al., 2000, 2010; Watson et al., 2001), invited students to report on their confidence in leading and working on a research team. Leadership was defined as "getting people to work together effectively to answer a question or solve a problem (e.g., motivating good performance, dealing with conflict, etc.)." Teamwork was described as including communication and collaboration, such as "I know how to cooperate effectively as a member of a team." Students responded on a 5-point scale ranging from 1 (*strongly disagree*) to 5 (*strongly agree*), with a Cronbach's alpha of .90 for both undergraduates and graduates.

Identity as a scientist. The Chemers et al. (2010) scale was based on the work of Sellers (see, e.g., Sellers, Smith, Shelton, Rowley, & Chavous, 1998) and Luhtanen and Crocker (1992) as well as interviews. Students were asked to think about themselves and their personal identity, to help us "understand how much you think that being a scientist is part of who you are." On a 5-point scale ranging from 1 (*strongly disagree*) to 5 (*strongly agree*), students indicated their agreement to six items such as "In general, being a scientist is an important part of my self-image," and "I am a scientist" (α=.89 for undergraduates and .90 for graduates).

Outcome: Commitment to a science career. The outcome variable in this survey was developed to measure students' intentions to work in the field of science. Both undergraduates and graduate students responded to seven items on a

5-point scale ranging from 1 (*strongly disagree*) to 5 (*strongly agree*). Items included "I intend to work in a field of scientific research" ($\alpha=.96$ for undergraduates and .94 for graduates).

Results

Analysis Strategy

The conceptual model was tested through a series of path analyses using maximum likelihood estimation in EQS 6.1 (Bentler, 2004). Several fit statistics were used to assess how adequately the model represented the covariance matrix. The chi-square goodness-of-fit test was used because it is helpful for comparing nested models. However, because the chi-square statistic is greatly affected by sample size, we also present the normed chi-square (NC), which is the chi-square divided by the number of parameters. The chi-square statistic should be nonsignificant and the NC less than 2.0. The remaining fit indices were a mix of incremental, absolute, and residual-based indices. Incremental indices included the comparative fit index (CFI) and nonnormal fit index (NNFI), which compare the model being tested to an independence model. The additional advantage of the NNFI over the CFI is that it corrects for the number of parameters in the model (Hu & Bentler, 1995). The goodness of fit index (GFI) is an absolute-fit index that represents the proportion of variance in the covariance matrix that is accounted for by the model. Higher values of the CFI, NNFI, and GFI are indicative of better fit, with values above .90 generally preferred. Last, we consulted the root mean square error of approximation (RMSEA) as a residual-based index. Lower values of the RMSEA reflect better model fit, with values less than .08 considered acceptable (Kline, 2005).

The base model tested was the conceptual model (Figure 1), which specifies that psychological processes (i.e., identity, science self-efficacy, and leadership/teamwork self-efficacy) mediate the association between program components (i.e., research experience, instrumental mentoring, socioemotional mentoring, community involvement) and commitment to a science career. This model was tested first, rather than a model that included direct effects from program components to commitment, due to the previously established support for the mediational model (Chemers et al., 2010). To maximize statistical power, we first ran a series of regression analyses to determine whether any variables could be removed from the analysis (see below). Once we moved to the path analyses, all nonsignificant paths were dropped based on the results of the base model, and the Lagrange multiplier tests and standardized residuals were consulted regarding the need for adding unspecified paths.

Table 1. Means, Standard Deviations, and Bivariate Correlations for Undergraduate Sample

	M	SD	1	2	3	4	5	6	7
1. Research experience	3.57	1.02	–						
2. Instrumental mentoring	3.70	0.95	.55	–					
3. Socioemotional mentoring	3.84	0.99	.34	.70	–				
4. Community involvement	3.37	1.02	.32	.30	.25	–			
5. Science self-efficacy	3.89	0.74	.48	.44	.31	.19	–		
6. Leadership and teamwork self-efficacy	4.42	0.52	.23	.24	.23	.28	.30	–	
7. Identity as a scientist	4.01	0.75	.24	.35	.27	.14	.34	.18	–
8. Commitment to a science career	4.53	0.74	.15	.28	.23	.11	.30	.20	.55

Note. $rs > .11, p < .05; rs > .14, p < .01; rs > .18, p < .001.$

Undergraduate Sample

Descriptive statistics and intercorrelations are presented in Table 1.The preliminary multiple regression analyses indicated that socioemotional mentoring did not predict commitment or any of the three mediators, so it was dropped from further analysis. Thus, the base model tested for the undergraduate sample was the conceptual model without socioemotional mentoring as an exogenous predictor. Fit indices for the mediation model indicated a good fit, $\chi^2(5) = 16.11, p = .007$, NC $= 3.22$, CFI $= .98$, NNFI $= .90$, GFI $= .97$, RMSEA $= .08$ (90% C.I. $= .04, .13$). The modification indices did not indicate that fit would be improved by adding direct paths from program components to commitment. However, there were several nonsignificant paths in the full mediation model. Accordingly, the next model we tested was a trimmed mediation model that removed all nonsignificant paths. The fit for this model was excellent, $\chi^2(10) = 22.20, p = .01$, NC $= 2.22$, CFI $= .97$, NNFI $= .94$, GFI $= .97$, RMSEA $= .06$ (90% C.I. $= .03, .10$). Furthermore, this model did not have significantly worse fit than the previous full mediation model, $\Delta\chi^2(5) = 6.09, p = .30$, yet is more parsimonious.

This final trimmed model (Figure 2) indicated that science self-efficacy fully mediated the association between two of the program components (research experience and instrumental mentoring) and commitment. Identity was also a mediator of the association between instrumental mentoring and commitment. Further, although science self-efficacy had a modest direct path to commitment ($\beta=.10$), identity also acted as a partial mediator of this association. Last, both research experience and community involvement predicted leadership/teamwork self-efficacy, but because the latter did not have a direct path to commitment there was no association to mediate.

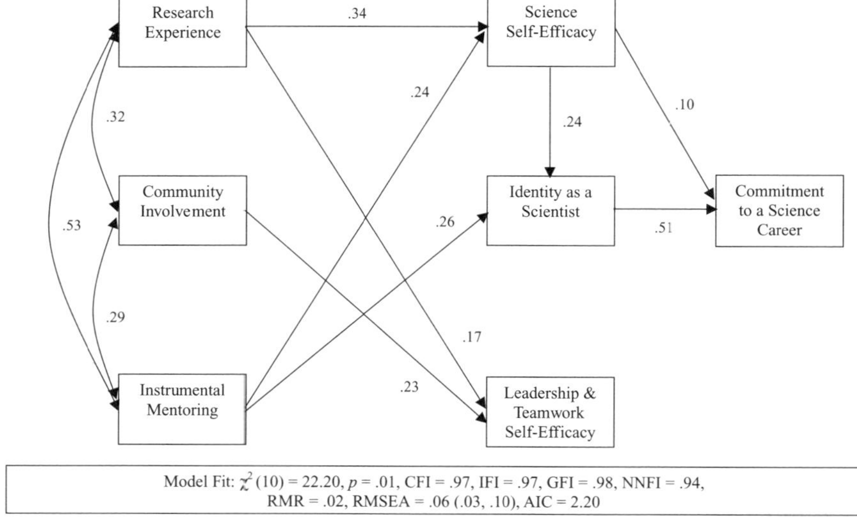

Fig. 2. Results for the undergraduate sample. All paths are significant at $p < .05$.

Table 2. Means, Standard Deviations, and Bivariate Correlations; Graduate Student/ Postdoctoral Fellow Sample

	M	SD	1	2	3	4	5	6	7	8
1. Research experience	4.09	0.95	–							
2. Advanced research experience	2.61	0.85	.53	–						
3. Instrumental mentoring	3.23	0.97	.41	.47	–					
4. Socioemotional mentoring	3.47	1.18	.22	.16	.67	–				
5. Community involvement	3.58	0.97	.23	.40	.32	.23	–			
6. Science self-efficacy	3.97	0.74	.50	.48	.44	.23	.29	–		
7. Leadership and teamwork self-efficacy	4.40	0.53	.28	.29	.34	.33	.28	.46	–	
8. Identity as a scientist	3.97	0.79	.18	.29	.30	.28	.24	.38	.34	–
9. Commitment to a science career	4.38	0.74	.12	.18	.30	.23	.22	.37	.35	.58

Note. $rs > .11$, $p < .05$; $rs > .14$, $p < .01$; $rs > .18$, $p < .001$.

Graduate Student/Postdoctoral Fellow Sample

Descriptive statistics and intercorrelations are presented in Table 2. The models for the graduate/postdoc sample were tested using the same procedures as for the undergraduate sample. One difference between the two models was that the "research experience" predictor was separated into two new predictors, "basic research experience" and "advanced research experience" to reflect the wider variety of experiences and skills needed at the graduate/postdoctoral level.

Preliminary regression analyses indicated that all variables should be retained, so the base model is the conceptual model illustrated in Figure 1 (although with the addition of the advanced research experience variable). The test of the mediation model suggested acceptable fit, $\chi^2(7) = 53.95$, $p < .001$, NC $= 7.71$, CFI $= .95$, NNFI $= .95$, GFI $= .97$, RMSEA $= .14$ (90% C.I. $= .11, .18$). The modification indices did not indicate that fit would be improved by adding direct paths from program components to commitment.

The next model we tested dropped all nonsignificant paths from the previous full mediation model. This model had good fit, $\chi^2(13) = 62.26$, $p < .001$, NC $= 4.79$, CFI $= .95$, NNFI $= .86$, GFI $= .96$, RMSEA $= .10$ (90% C.I. $= .08, .13$), and was not significantly worse than the previous model despite its relative parsimony, $\Delta\chi^2(6) = 8.31$, $p = .21$. Examination of the standardized residuals indicated two major sources of poor fit. One was the lack of a path between leadership/teamwork self-efficacy and identity, suggesting that, like science self-efficacy, identity at least partially mediates the association between leadership/teamwork self-efficacy and commitment. Adding this path was a significant improvement in fit over the previous model, $\Delta\chi^2(1) = 7.72$, $p = .006$. However, the RMSEA was still high ($.10$, 90% C.I. $= .08, .13$), and the NNFI was a bit low ($.87$). Reexamining the standardized residuals indicated that there was only one source of poor fit: the unmodeled association between science self-efficacy and leadership/teamwork self-efficacy, for which we have no a priori expectations about causal flow. Although it is important to use caution when correlating error terms, in this case it may be reasonable to do so as both constructs tap into efficacious beliefs and share similar item structure and content. Adding the path between the errors improved fit dramatically, $\Delta\chi^2(1) = 36.41$, $p < .001$, for a final model fit of $\chi^2(11) = 18.02$, $p = .08$, NC $= 1.64$, CFI $= .99$, NNFI $= .98$, GFI $= .99$, RMSEA $= .04$ (90% C.I. $= .00, .08$).

The final model (Figure 3) contains a set of findings that very closely approximate the conceptual model. The effects of program elements on commitment were fully mediated by the psychological variables: science self-efficacy mediated the paths from basic research experience, advanced research experience, and instrumental mentoring; identity mediated the paths from advanced research experience and socioemotional mentoring; and leadership/teamwork self-efficacy mediated the paths from basic and advanced research experience, community involvement, and socioemotional mentoring. Moreover, the three psychological mediators of science self-efficacy, leadership/teamwork self-efficacy, and identity each independently predicted commitment. However, identity also partially mediated the association between both domains of self-efficacy and commitment.

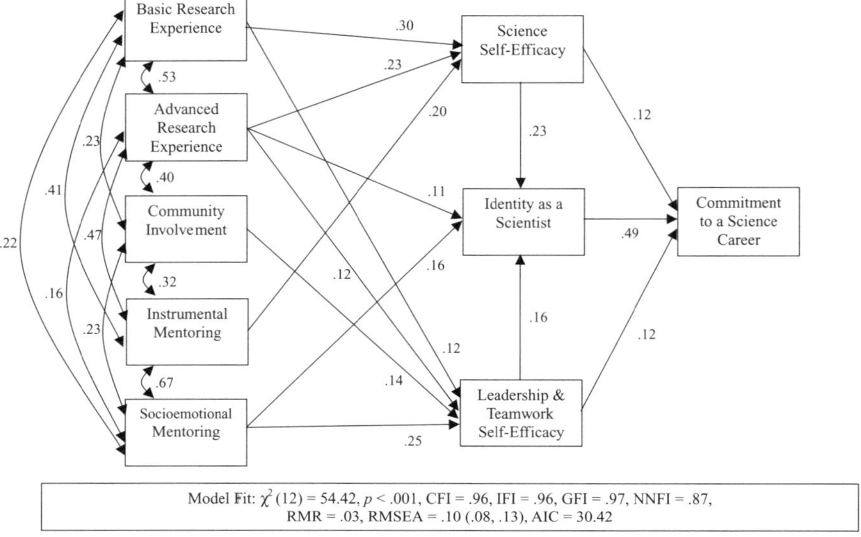

Model Fit: $\chi^2(12) = 54.42$, $p < .001$, CFI = .96, IFI = .96, GFI = .97, NNFI = .87, RMR = .03, RMSEA = .10 (.08, .13), AIC = 30.42

Fig. 3. Results for the graduate/postdoc sample. All paths are significant at $p < .05$.

Discussion

The current study offered an extension and refinement of a mediation model that is suggestive of possible causal effects in underrepresented students' science career commitment. The model includes the effects of various support structures and processes designed to prepare students for research careers in science, such as hands-on research experience, mentoring, and community involvement (i.e., interactions with professionals and peers who are involved in research and/or in scientific education). The model proposes that the effects of these support mechanisms are fully mediated by students' psychological reactions to the mechanisms in terms of self-efficacy and identity.

Initial tests of the model were reported in an earlier study by Chemers et al. (2010). Chemers et al. conducted retrospective and prospective studies of undergraduates, surveying students who had either majored in science or engineering and/or were participants in science support programs during the period 1999–2004. As reported in the introduction to this article, the Chemers et al. (2010) study provided strong support for the model.

In the present research, we sought to replicate the Chemers et al. (2010) findings and to extend the model beyond undergraduates to more advanced members of the science education community, i.e., graduate students and postdoctoral fellows. Our findings provide strong support for the mediation model for both groups of students, but especially for the more advanced students. The path analyses shown in Figure 2 (for undergraduates) and Figure 3 (for the graduate students and post-doctoral fellows, combined) again demonstrate that the effects of science support activities on commitment to a career in science are fully mediated by science self-efficacy and identity as a scientist. Even more striking are the results for the more advanced sample, which are remarkably similar to the predicted model, including significant pathways for the effects of leadership/teamwork self-efficacy that were not seen earlier.

In the current study, LTSE enters the model for both undergraduate and graduate/postdoc samples. For the undergraduates, higher levels of research experience and mentoring are associated with higher levels of LTSE, but LTSE has no direct or indirect connections to commitment. On the other hand, for the graduate post/doctoral sample, these variables, as well as community involvement, are associated with LTSE, and LTSE has both a direct and an indirect (through science identity) connection to commitment. Why might this be so?

Chemers et al. (2010) posited that the reason they failed to obtained effects of LTSE, even though predicted, was that the undergraduates they studied may not have had sufficient experience with team-based research to recognize and value the effects of teamwork. That explanation is consistent with our finding of partial mediation effects for LTSE in the more advanced sample. The undergraduate sample evidences a connection between their science support experiences and their own LTSE, though those connections do not extend to enhancement of commitment. One possible line of reasoning might be that the *SACNAS* membership, the majority of which is Latino and Native American, might be more oriented toward and sensitive to social relations (i.e., teamwork) in research teams, because of the greater focus on social relations in more collectivist cultural communities (Markus & Kitayama, 1991). Much more extensive research will be needed to understand fully these distinctions.

The strength and coherence of the replications and extensions in this study dramatically increase our certainty of the productive research value of self-efficacy and personal identity in studies of motivation, commitment, and performance of underrepresented students, and all students, in the science education pipeline.

Future Research

Our findings point to some important directions for future research. One complex, but fascinating, set of questions relates to whether or not ethnic differences might have important moderating effects on these findings. Chemers et al. (2010) compared White and URM students in their analyses and found very few differences. Nonetheless, there are many theoretical perspectives that might predict such differences (Chemers & Murphy, 1995; Markus & Kitayama, 1991).

One perspective highlights the potential role of cultural differences that might make communication and understanding more difficult. Markus and Kitayama (1991) have examined differences and similarities between individuals who have been raised in individualistic and collectivist societies. They report difference between these groups in cognitive, emotional, and motivational domains. In her model of the multicultural organization Mai-Dalton (1993) addresses these same difficulties and concludes that the degree of assimilation into the dominant culture is related to the strength of negative experiences. URM students in the United States occupy a range of levels of cultural assimilation.

Another perspective is concerned with the obstacles and barriers that face some individuals in educational and organizational settings. A large and growing body of work on "stereotype threat" has shown that negative stereotypes and expectations for one's social group or category (e.g., URM or gender) can engender anxiety, poor performance, and withdrawal from situations and endeavors that make the threat salient (Steele & Aronson, 1995). Chemers and Murphy (1995) reviewed the literature relating to organizational leadership of American ethnic minorities and found that while actual differences between minority and dominant group members are small, stereotypes and negative expectations often create obstacles and difficulties for minority employees in U.S. organizations. Both perspectives (cultural differences and barriers/threats) might affect both a sense of competency and personal identity, which our research finds to be critical aspects of career commitment (see also Syed et al., 2011).

In all of the data reported thus far, the effects of mentoring are strong, with instrumental mentoring having stronger effects than socioemotional mentoring. Aside from this distinction, however, we know very little about the specific behaviors, paths, and contexts of successful mentoring (see also Blake-Beard, Bayne, Crosby, & Muller, 2011). A better understanding of mentoring could help program faculty and staff provide training to improve the effects of mentoring. Mentoring, of one kind or another, was a strong predictor in all four studies, but the effects for instrumental mentoring were generally stronger. We want to understand more about why this is, and when each type of mentoring is helpful.

Some research directions could go a long way to enhancing both the internal and external validity of research findings. Internal validity could be addressed powerfully by the use of true experiments with random assignment of participants to various science support experiences. We recognize that such a suggestion is controversial. Program directors have expressed concern about turning away any student who might benefit from the experience. However, our colleagues in mental health research employ the "waiting list control group" design. Because mental health programs are chronically understaffed relative to the demand for services, some clients must be put on a waiting list for treatment when resources permit. If assignment to the waiting list were random, it could serve as a valid control group.

One such study (Nagda, Gregerman, Jonides, von Hippel, & Lerner, 1998) of programmatic support for students was conducted at the University of Michigan where the cohort of African–American students was relatively large. More students requested admission into the program than could be accommodated, so among all students whose credentials reached threshold for inclusion in the program, participants were chosen at random. Their methodology allowed them to draw strong conclusions about student persistence and to determine which students benefitted most from program support (i.e., second-year African–Americans whose academic performance was lower than their African–American peers).

Long-range follow ups of study participants could be a contributor to greater external validity. The demonstration of long-range effects on important outcomes (e.g., progress through the pipeline, performance in terms of grades, presentation, and publications) would help to authenticate the role of psychological variables in prediction of such effects.

The close replication of the Chemers et al. (2010) study in the current study creates more certainty about the importance of the targeted mediators (self-efficacy and identity), which should lead to greater attention to and greater targeted efforts at producing these effects by program faculty and staff. As in many studies of student performance, mentoring played an important role. However, we have not identified the particular aspects or behaviors that mentors should follow. Further research in this area will add substantive practical value to the mediation model.

Our study also has implications for policy level decisions. This is a productive research area with even greater potential for helping to broaden participation of underrepresented populations in scientific careers. On this basis, we would argue for maintaining high levels of research funding to encourage subsequent research. If further study supports our findings, science support funding agencies might begin to mandate attention to psychological mediators in program proposals.

References

Arnett, J. J. (2004). *Emerging adulthood: The winding road from the late teens through the twenties*. New York: Oxford University Press.

Azmitia, M., Syed, M., & Radamacher, K. (2008). On the intersection of personal and social identities: Introduction and evidence from a longitudinal study of emerging adults. In M. Azmitia, M. Syed, & K. Radmacher (Eds.), *The intersections of personal and social identities. New directions for child and adolescent development* (Vol. 120, pp. 1–16). San Francisco, CA: Jossey-Bass. doi:10.1002/cd.212.

Baker, D. R. (1998). Equity issues in science education. In B. J. Fraser & K. G. Tobin (Eds.). *International handbook of science education* (pp. 869–896). Boston, MA: Kluwer.

Bandura, A. (1986). The explanatory and predictive scope of self-efficacy theory. *Journal of Clinical and Social Psychology, 4*, 359–373. doi:10.1521.

Bandura, A. (1997). *Self-efficacy: The exercise of control*. New York: Freeman. ISBN 0716726262.

Barab, S. A., & Hay, K. E. (2000). Doing science at the elbows of experts: Issues related to the science apprenticeship camp. *Journal of Research in Science Teaching, 38*, 70–102. doi: 10.1002/1.

Barker, K. (2002). *At the helm: A laboratory navigator.* New York: Cold Springs Laboratory Press.

Barlow, A. E. L., & Villarejo, M. (2004). Making a difference for minorities: Evaluation of an educational enrichment program. *Journal of Research in Science Teaching, 41*(9), 861–881. doi:10.1002/tea.20029.

Bell, R. L., Blair, L. M., Crawford, B. A., & Lederman, N. G. (2003). Just do it? Impact of a science apprenticeship program on high school students' understandings of the nature of science and scientific inquiry. *Journal of Research in Science Teaching, 40*, 487–509. doi:10.1002/tea. 10086.

Bentler, P. M. (2004). *EQS structural equations modeling software (Version 6.1).*[Computer software.] Encino, CA: Multivariate Software.

Blake-Beard, S., Bayne, M. L., Crosby, F. J., & Muller, C. B. (2011). Matching by race and gender in mentoring relationships: Keeping our eyes on the prize. *Journal of Social Issues, 67*(3), 622-643.

Bonous-Hammarth, M. (2000). Pathways to success: Affirming opportunities for science, mathematics, and engineering majors. *Journal of Negro Education, 69*, 92–111. doi and iid: 10.2307/i326903.

Boss, J. M., & Eckert, S. H. (2003). *Academic scientists at work: Navigating the biomedical research career.* New York: Kluwer Academic/Plenum Publishers.

Carter, F. D., Mandell, M., & Maton, K. I. (2009). The influence of on-campus, academic year undergraduate research on STEM Ph.D. outcomes: Evidence from the Meyerhoff Scholarship Program. *Educational Evaluation and Policy Analysis, 31*, 441–462. doi:10.3102/0162373709348584.

Charney, J., Hmelo-Silver, C. E., Sofer, W., Neigeborn, L., Coletta, S., & Nemeroff, M. (2007). Cognitive apprenticeship in science through immersion in laboratory practices. *International Journal of Science Education, 29*, 195–213. doi:10.1080/09500690600560985.

Chemers, M. M. & Murphy, S. E. (1995). Leadership and diversity in groups and organizations. In M. M. Chemers, S. Oskamp, & M. A. Costanzo (Eds.), *Diversity in organizations* (pp. 157–188). Thousand Oaks, CA: Sage.

Chemers, M. M., Watson, C. B., & May, S. T. (2000). Dispositional affect and leadership effectiveness: A comparison of self-esteem, optimism, and efficacy. *Personality and Social Psychology Bulletin, 26*, 267–277. doi:10.1177/01461672002265001.

Chemers, M. M., Hu, L., & Garcia, B. F. (2001). Academic self-efficacy and first-year college student performance and adjustment. *Journal of Educational Psychology 2001, 93*(I), 55–64. doi:10.1037/0022–0663.93.1.55.

Chemers, M. M., Syed, M., Goza, B. K., Zurbriggen, E. L., Bearman, S., Crosby, F. J., et al. (2010). *The role of self-efficacy and identity in mediating the effects of science support programs.* Technical Report No. 5 (under review). Santa Cruz, CA: University of California.

Dovidio, J. F., Gaertner, S. L., Niemann, Y. F., & Snider, K. (2001). Racial, ethnic, and cultural differences in responding to distinctiveness and discrimination on campus: Stigma and common group identity. *Journal of Social Issues, 57*, 167–188. doi:10.1111/0022–4537.00207.

Eccles, J. S., & Barber, B. L. (1999). Student council, volunteering, basketball, marching band: What kind of extracurricular involvement matters? *Journal of Adolescent Research, 14*, 10–43. doi:10.1177/0743558499141003.

Erikson, E. H. (1968). *Identity: Youth and crisis.* New York: Norton.

Foertsch, J., Alexander, B. B., & Penberthy, D. (2000). Summer Research Opportunity Programs (SROPs) for minority undergraduates. A longitudinal study of program outcomes 1986–1996. *Council for Undergraduate Research Quarterly, 20*, 114–119.

Franco-Zamudio, J. L. (2010). The impact of social and role identity on student retention. In M. Tsethlikai (Chair), *From mice to mentors to media: Technology and diversity in psychology.* Symposium conducted at the meeting of the Society for the Advancement of Chicanos and Native Americans in Science, Anaheim, CA.

Gándara, P. & Maxwell-Jolly, J. (1999). *Priming the pump: Strategies for increasing the achievement of underrepresented minority undergraduates.* New York: The College Board Publications.

Hagstrom, W. O. (1964). Traditional and modern forms of scientific teamwork. *Administrative Science Quarterly, 9*, 241–263. doi:10.2307/2391440.

Harmening, D. M. (2003). *Laboratory management: Principles and processes.* Englewood Cliffs, NJ: Prentice Hall.

Hu, L., & Bentler, P. M. (1995). Evaluating model fit. In R. H. Hoyle (Eds.), *Structural equation modeling: Issues, concepts, and applications* (pp. 76–99). Newbury Park, CA: Sage.

Hurtado, S., Eagan, M. K., Tran, M. C., Newman, C. B., Chang, M. J., & Velasco, P. (2011) "We do science here": Underrepresented students interactions with faculty in different college contexts. *Journal of Social Issues, 67*(3), 553-579.

Kardash, C. M. (2000). Evaluation of an undergraduate research experience: Perceptions of undergraduate interns and their faculty mentors. *Journal of Educational Psychology, 92*, 191–201. doi:10.1037//0022–0663.92.1.191.

Kline, R. B. (2005). *Principles and practices of structural equation modeling* (2nd ed.). New York: Guilford Press.

Kram, K. E. (1985). *Mentoring at work.* Glenview, IL Scott Foresman.

Linnehan, F. (2001). The relation of a work-based mentoring program to the academic performance and behavior of African American students. *Journal of Vocational Behavior, 59*, 310–325. doi:10.1006/jvbe.2001.1810.

Luhtanen, R., & Crocker, J. (1992). A collective self-esteem scale: Self-evaluation of one's social identity. *Personality and Social Psychology Bulletin, 18*, 302–318. doi: 10.1177/0146167292183006.

Mai-Dalton, R. (1993). Managing cultural diversity on the individual, group, and organizational levels. In M. Chemers & R, Ayman (Eds.), *Leadership research and theory: Perspectives and directions.* : San Diego, CA: Academic Press.

Markus, H. & Kitayama, S. (1991). Culture and self: Implications for cognition, emotion, and motivation. *Psychological Review, 98*, 224–253. doi:10.1037/0033–295X.98.2.224.

Maton, K. I, Hrabowski F. A. III, & Schmitt, C. L. (2000). African American college students excelling in the sciences: College and postcollege outcomes in the Meyerhoff Scholars Program. *Journal of Research in Science Teaching, 37*, 629–654.

Nagda, B. A., Gregerman, S. R., Jonides, J., von Hippel, W., & Lerner, J. S. (1998). Undergraduate student-faculty research partnerships affect student retention. *Review of Higher Education, 22*, 55–72.

Osborne, J. W., & Walker, C. (2006). Stereotype threat, identification with academics, and withdrawal from school: Why the most successful students of colour might be most likely to withdraw. *Educational Psychology, 26*, 563–577. doi:10.1080/01443410500342518.

Phinney, J. S., Torres Campos, C. M., Kallemeyn, D. M. P., & Kim, C. (2011). Processes and outcomes of a mentoring program for Latino college freshmen. *Journal of Social Issues, 67*(3), 599-621.

Richmond, G. & Kurth, L. A. (1999). Moving from outside to inside: High school students' use of apprenticeships as vehicles for entering the culture and practice of science. *Journal of Research in Science Teaching, 36*, 677–697. doi:10.1002/(SICI)1098–2736(199908)36:6<677::AID-TEA6>3.0.CO;2-#.

Ryder, J., & Leach, J. (1999). University science students' experiences of investigative project work and their images of science. *International Journal of Science Education, 21*, 945–956. doi:10.1080/095006999290246.

Sadler, T. D., Burgin, S., McKinney, L., & Punjuan, L. (2010). Learning science through research apprenticeships: A critical review of the literature. *Journal of Research in Science Teaching, 47*, 235–256. doi:10.1002/tea.20326.

Schunk, D. H. (1981). Modeling and attributional effects on children's achievement: A self-efficacy analysis. *Journal of Educational Psychology, 73*, 93–105. doi:10.1037//0022–0663.73.1.93.

Sellers, R. M., Smith, M. A., Shelton, J. N., Rowley, S. A. J., & Chavous, T. M. (1998). Multidimensional model of racial identity: A reconceptualization of African American racial identity. *Personality and Social Psychology Review, 2*, 18–39. doi:10.1207/s15327957pspr0201_2.

Seymour, E., Hunter, A., Laursen, S. A., & Deantoni, T. (2004). Establishing the benefits of research experiences for undergraduates in the sciences: First findings from a three-year study. *Science Education, 88*, 493–534.

Smith, E. (2010). Do we need more scientists? A long-term view of patterns of participation in UK undergraduate science programmes. *Cambridge Journal of Education, 40*, 281–298.

Steele, C. M., & Aronson, J. (1995). Stereotype threat and the intellectual test performance of African Americans. *Journal of Personality and Social Psychology, 69*, 797–811. doi:10.1037//0022–3514.69.5.797.

Stokols, D., Hall, K. L., Taylor, B. K., & Moser, R. P. (2008). The science of team science: Overview of the field and introduction to the supplement. *American Journal of Preventive Medicine, 35*(2S), S77–S89.

Syed, M., Azmitia, M., & Cooper, C. R. (2011). Identity and academic success among under-represented ethnic minorities: An interdisciplinary review and integration. *Journal of Social Issues, 67*(3), 442–468.

Tenenbaum, H. R., Crosby, F. J., & Gliner, M. D. (2001). Mentoring relationships in graduate school. *Journal of Vocational Behavior, 59*, 326–341. doi:10.1006/jvbe.2001.1804.

Treisman, U. (1992). Studying students studying calculus: A look at the lives of minority mathematics students in college. *The College Mathematics Journal, 23*, 362–372. doi:10.2307/2686410.

Villarejo, M. & Barlow, A. E. L. (2007). Evolution and evaluation of a biology enrichment program for minorities. *Journal of Women and Minorities in Science and Engineering, 13*, 119–144. doi:10.1615/JWomenMinorScienEng.v13.i2.20.

Villarejo, M., Barlow, A. E. L., Kogan, D., Veazey, B. D., & Sweeney, J. K. (2008). Encouraging minority undergraduates to choose science careers: Career paths survey results. *CBE Life Sciences Education, 7*, 394–409. doi:10.1187/cbe.08–04-0018.

Watson, C. B., Chemers, M. M., & Preiser, N. (2001). Collective efficacy: A multilevel analysis. *Personality and Social Psychology Bulletin, 27*, 1057–1068. doi:10.1177/0146167201278012.

Witkow, M. R., & Fuligni, A. J. (2011). Ethnic and generational differences in the relations between social support and academic achievement across the high school years. *Journal of Social Issues, 67*(3), 531-552

Wuchty, S., Jones, B. F., & Uzzi, B. (2007). The increasing dominance of teams in production of knowledge. *Science, 316*, 1036–1039. doi:10.1126/science.1136099.

Zimmerman, B. J. (1989). A social cognitive view of self-regulated academic learning. *Journal of Educational Psychology, 81*, 329–339. doi:10.1037//0022-0663.81.3.329.

MARTIN M. CHEMERS received a PhD in Social Psychology from the University of Illinois, Urbana. He is presently Professor Emeritus and Research Professor of Psychology at the University of California, Santa Cruz. His current research is supported by the National Institutes of Health and is focused on understanding and developing the individual and institutional changes needed to increase the number of underrepresented minorities in STEM education and careers.

EILEEN L. ZURBRIGGEN is currently Professor of Psychology at the University of California, Santa Cruz. Her program of research focuses on connections between power and sexuality, adolescent sexual development, sexual objectification, and sexual aggression and abuse. She served as chair of the American Psychological Association's Task Force on the Sexualization of Girls, and is interested in how sexualization and objectification hamper girls' career aspirations and educational achievement.

MOIN SYED is an Assistant Professor of Psychology at the University of Minnesota, Twin Cities. His research is broadly concerned with identity development among ethnically and culturally diverse adolescents and emerging adults, with particular focus on the development of multiple personal and social identities (e.g., ethnicity, social class, and gender) and the implications of identity development for educational experiences and career orientation.

BARBARA K. GOZA completed her PhD in social/organizational psychology at the University of Utah. For over 30 years, she has specialized in program evaluation of educational and mental health programs. She has directed and taught program evaluation and applied research at the University of Utah, California State Polytechnic University Pomona, and the University of California, Santa Cruz.

STEVE BEARMAN received his PhD in social psychology from the University of California, Santa Cruz. His work integrates the perspective that people are not self-contained entities, but rather are distributed across networks of interactions, with research on interventions to diminish racism and other forms of oppression. Bearman is also a counselor and the founder of Interchange Counseling, a training program in San Francisco based on the idea that everyone can learn to skillfully support others to heal, grow, and get free of unnecessary limitations.

Journal of Social Issues, Vol. 67, No. 3, 2011, pp. 492–509

How Women Cope: Being a Numerical Minority in a Male-Dominated Profession

Laura Smart Richman and **Michelle vanDellen**
Duke University

Wendy Wood
University of Southern California

Women who have academic careers in engineering have successfully navigated the social identity threats that prevent many other women from feeling that they belong in science, technology, engineering, and math fields. In this research, we examined what factors may be related to resilience in these academic environments. Female academics in engineering and nonengineering fields watched a fictitious conference video depicting either an unbalanced ratio of men to women or a balanced ratio. Subjective measures of identity threat were collected. Past experience with discrimination, positive experience with female role models, family support, and general social support were associated with a greater sense of belonging to or desire to participate in the conference. These variables all buffered negative responding to social identity threat. Implications are discussed for understanding resilience to social identity threat, particularly among women in engineering.

Women in the United States and other industrialized nations increasingly are entering traditionally male fields of study, employment, and athletic competition (Wood & Eagly, in press). This remarkable social change is evident especially in engineering and math-intensive science fields. For example, women in 1958 earned less than 1% of the doctorates in engineering, but in 2006 they earned 20% of those doctorates (National Science Foundation, 2008). Women also increasingly are assuming academic faculty positions in engineering. Although women comprised

---

*Correspondence concerning this article should be addressed to Laura Smart Richman, Department of Psychology and Neuroscience, Duke University, Durham, NC 27708 [e-mail: lrichman@duke.edu].

This research was supported by a NSF Advance Program Award (SBE-05–48323). Many thanks to Michelle Patriquin for her technical assistance with data collection.*

492

less than 1% of tenure-track or tenured engineering faculty through 1979, they increased to 11% of engineering faculty in 2006 (National Science Foundation, 2008). Yet, these gains are smaller at the higher levels of the academy, with women making up only 5% of the full professors in engineering in 2006. This overall pattern typifies women's inroads into math-intensive science fields: Despite the substantial increase over the past half century, women are still a distinct minority, especially in higher status positions.

The changing role of women in science thus has several faces. On the downside, women continue to be in the minority. On the upside, women's increasingly greater entry and success indicates that some women are coping effectively with their minority status in math-intensive science and engineering fields. How do they do it? What are the factors that enable some women to be relatively impervious to the threats of being a minority in a traditionally male-dominated field?

In the present article, we address these questions by identifying sources of resilience for women academics, including freedom from discrimination, helpful female role models, and social support outside of work. Thus, our focus is not on whether identity threat occurs—this already has been well documented. Instead, we are trying to understand how some women succeed despite this threat. Specifically, we report the results of an experimental study testing the buffering factors that help women academics to cope with exposure to the identity threat of being in a numerical minority in a professional setting. By examining how successful women academics thrive despite their minority status, we highlight ways to develop measures and methods to promote women's success under such circumstances.

Challenges for Women in Science and Engineering

The challenges that women experience in science and engineering fields have fascinated college presidents and researchers alike (Ceci & Williams, 2007; Halpern et al., 2007). These challenges include men's possibly greater aptitude for certain math skills (Hedges & Nowell, 1995, although see Hyde, Lindberg, Linn, Ellis, & Williams, 2008) and women's preference to study people as opposed to men's preference to study things (Lippa, 2005).

Other challenges women face stem from structural features in science and engineering fields, especially the low numerical representation of women. Being a numerical minority in work settings can activate gender stereotypes. Sex is one of the most visible social categories at work (Eagly & Carli, 2008), and it becomes perceptually salient and is used in social categorization especially when one sex is in the numerical minority in a group (Kanter, 1977; Taylor & Fiske, 1978).

A numerical minority position, by activating gender stereotypes, poses a particular threat to the identity of women scientists and engineers because it highlights expectations of men's performance advantage in a culturally masculine domain

(Eagly & Carli, 2008). Women scientists and engineers, in trying to grapple with the negative stereotype about their social identity, experience a situational burden that interferes with their performance. In fact, numerical distinctiveness is a common manipulation in experiments to activate stereotypic performance expectations and thus stereotype threat (Steele, 1997). For example, women performed worse at a difficult math test when they were the solo female in a group of men (Ben-Zeev, Fein, Inzlicht, 2005; Chatman, Boisnier, Spataro, Anderson, & Berdahl, 2008; Inzlicht & Ben-Zeev, 2000). This performance deficit was not found when sex ratios were more favorable to women or when the test assessed verbal skills (Chatman et al., 2008; Inzlicht & Ben-Zeev, 2000). Even anticipating being a token woman in a work group can induce negative expectations about the experience (Cohen & Swim, 1995).

At essence, the threat to self-integrity experienced by many women engineers stems from a state of cognitive imbalance in which women's concept of self and expectations for success conflict with primed social stereotypes of low competence at relevant tasks (Schmader, Johns, & Forbes, 2008). That is, women scientists and engineers are faced with the cognitive imbalance from the following propositions: Women generally are not skilled at math and science; I am a woman; I am skilled at math and science. This state of imbalance is a stressor that impairs performance by activating physiological markers of stress, cognitive deficits, negative affect, and efforts to cope with these aversive experiences (e.g., Lord & Saenz, 1985).

Thus, women's numerical minority status in traditionally masculine fields is a structural barrier that activates gender stereotypes and thereby poses a social identity threat. Some women resolve this imbalance by accepting that they are not skilled and do not belong in the relevant work setting. That is, women could limit their participation in these fields, especially in settings that precipitate threat. For example, female undergraduate math, science, and engineering majors expressed less desire to attend a professional conference depicted with more men than women than a conference with an equal sex ratio (Murphy, Steele, & Gross, 2007). Nonetheless, some women become successful in these fields. These individuals are the focus of the present research. We seek to understand how these successful women reduce the experience of social identity threat.

Resilience to Being a Numerical Minority

Women scientists and engineers have several potential avenues to resolve the identity threat sparked by their numerical minority status in a traditionally masculine field. One way to resolve this threat is to focus on experiences that imply belongingness. Specifically, women engineers who have professional experiences indicating that they are valued and accepted in the engineering profession are likely to believe that, regardless of the stereotypes, they belong in the field. As we explain below, the experience of not being discriminated against and receiving fair treatment in comparison with others, having a positive female role model, and having social support is likely to establish such beliefs. These experiences might thus be the key to buffering the social identity threat faced by women in masculine fields.

Experience of Discrimination

Personal experiences of fair treatment and the absence of discrimination might increase women's sense of belonging in a field. Most of the relevant evidence has focused on the debilitating effects of discrimination and unfair treatment. Illustrating this negative impact, the mere suggestion of sexism caused women to feel less comfortable and to perform worse on a logic test than when sexism was not implied (Adams, Garcia, Purdie-Vaughns, & Steele, 2006). Additional evidence of the debilitating effects of discrimination comes from the experience of racial and ethnic minorities. For example, minority adolescents' exposure to discrimination from teachers and friends at school was associated with lower grades and academic self-concept (Wong, Eccles, & Sameroff, 2003) and discrimination also predicts broader effects on self-regulation capacity (Pascoe & Richman, 2011). Although this research has focused on the debilitating effects of discrimination, it is possible also that fair treatment and the absence of discrimination have positive effects by heightening feelings of belonging.

Female Role Models

Female role models who demonstrate that women can be successful and who support other women's success also contribute to feelings of belongingness. In an illustration of the importance of female role models in academic settings, female junior faculty members who received mentoring from senior women had stronger academic self-concepts and higher rates of retention, grant funding, and promotion than those who did not receive such mentoring (Gardiner, Tiggemann, Kearns, & Marshall, 2007). A female role model is particularly influential in performance domains where negative gender stereotypes exist. For example, when female students who were skilled in math took a difficult math test, the salience of female role models who were competent at math reduced the experience of social identity threat and bolstered women's self-appraised math ability (Marx & Roman, 2002). Additionally, women who reported being influenced positively by role models in their training had higher career aspirations in science, technology, engineering, and math fields (Nauta, Epperson, & Kahn, 1998).

Social Support

The social support provided by others is a general protective factor that may promote self-worth in conditions of social identity threat. When such threats occur, social support can provide a sense of belonging and access to emotional and tangible benefits such as people whom they feel close to and can turn to for guidance and assistance when needed. Social support is related to better achievement outcomes among minority groups (Walton & Cohen, 2007), and evidence suggests that family encouragement and the perceived availability of social support influences the educational and occupational choices women make (Eccles, 1994; see also Syed, Azmitia, & Cooper, 2011).

The Present Research

The present research examined how successful female engineering faculty cope with the social identity threat of being a numerical minority in this traditionally masculine field. To activate the experience of identity threat, participants watched a slide presentation describing an upcoming professional conference supposedly in their field based on Murphy et al. (2007). In the predominantly male (*gender-imbalanced*) condition, most of the conference attendees were male, and other cues indicated that the conference was designed for men (e.g., extracurricular activities were baseball and golf). The gender equal (*gender-balanced*) condition provided a more balanced representation of women and men, and cues to the conference were not strongly gender typed (e.g., extracurricular activities were an art museum and golf). We compared women engineers' responses to this stereotype threat experience with a control group of similar academic women from more gender-balanced academic fields (e.g., sociology, psychology).

Successful women academics in engineering are likely to have developed a certain level of resilience to social identity threat, as evidenced by their presence in this traditionally masculine field. Thus, we predicted that successful academic women engineers would be less sensitive to social identity threat than women from more gender-balanced fields and would be less likely to resolve the inconsistency of a male-dominated conference by deciding not to attend. Thus, our central prediction was a significant interaction between type of conference and disciplinary field on ratings of belonging at, and interest in the conference. This resilience to threat among engineers is likely to arise from personal experiences that suggest that they, personally, belong in the field. Thus, in predicting belongingness and interest, we anticipated significant interactions between gender balance of conference, disciplinary field, and buffering factors of lack of discrimination and positive female role models. This interaction should reflect that female engineers with these experiences have a stronger sense of belonging at, and are more interested in attending the predominantly male conference than engineers without these experiences. Additionally, social support is a general protective factor that may promote a sense of belongingness and self-worth for both engineers and nonengineers. Thus, we anticipated a significant interaction between extent of social support and gender balance of conference that held across disciplines.

Method

Participants

Participants were female academics in the field of engineering ($N = 31$) or in control, nonengineering fields ($N = 27$) selected to have relatively gender-balanced faculty ratios (i.e., psychology, sociology, anthropology, nursing, history, English). Recruitment was done via e-mails, advertisements placed in academic buildings, and during an engineering conference. Participants received $20 for their time.

Procedure

Prior to the experimental session, participants completed an online survey assessing background characteristics. They reported on their past discrimination, experience with female role models, and extent of social support.

During the laboratory session, participants watched a 5-minute video (adapted from Murphy et al., 2007) advertising a fictitious upcoming academic conference describing where the conference would be held, procedures for admission, and professional activities. The specific discipline of the conference was ambiguous so that all participants could identify with the video. In the gender-balanced condition, the video portrayed equal numbers of males and females, and the social activities included golfing and a tour of art museums. In the gender-imbalanced condition, males outnumbered females 5:1, and the social activities included golfing and a tour of a local baseball stadium. Participants gave their reactions to the video (see below).

Measures

Past discrimination. On the Everyday Discrimination Scale (Williams, Yu, Jackson, & Anderson, 1997), participants indicated on 4-point scales ranging from *never* (1) to *often* (4) the extent to which they perceived nine different forms of discrimination in the past 12 months. Example items include, "People act as if you are less intelligent than you are," and "You receive poorer service than others in restaurants or stores." Mean scores were calculated across the nine items. Internal consistency on the scale in our sample was high, $\alpha=.88$.

Female role models. On a 5-point scale from none to a great deal, participants indicated how much contact they had with female role models. Also, on a 5-point scale from *very negative* (1) to *very positive* (5), participants indicated whether this contact was negative or positive.

Social support. To assess family support, we asked participants "how encouraging was your family about your chosen field of study?" Responses were given on a 5-point scale anchored by *very discouraging* (1) and *very encouraging* (5).

An adapted version of the Interpersonal Support Evaluation List (Cohen & Hoberman, 1983) was used to measure social support on the dimensions of belonging (perceived availability of someone to do things with), appraisal help (perceived availability to talk with someone about problems), tangible support (perceived availability of material help), and self-esteem support (perceived availability of someone to positively compare oneself with). Participants rated 16 statements from *definitely false* (1) to *definitely true* (4). Overall social support was computed by taking the average of these items. Internal consistency on the scale in our sample was high, $\alpha = .89$.

Reactions to conference. On six items, participants were asked to indicate their sense of belongingness and interest regarding the conference. Three items measured belongingness (e.g., "I feel like I would belong at this conference;" alpha = .88), and three items measured interest in attending the conference (e.g., "I would be interested in attending the conference;" alpha = .96). Each item was presented on a 5-point scale ranging from *definitely disagree* (1) to *definitely agree* (5).

Results

Background Differences between Engineers and Nonengineers

As shown in Table 1, women faculty in engineering, compared with nonengineering women faculty, reported slightly more experiences of unfair treatment in the past 12 months ($p = .06$). Women engineers also reported great social support

Table 1. Descriptive Statistics, Scale Reliability and Group Differences of Individual Difference and Psychosocial Variables

Measure	Engineers M (SD)	Nonengineers M (SD)
Past discrimination	2.13(0.50)	1.90(0.50)
Contact with female role models	2.58(1.15)$_a$	3.48(1.50)$_b$
Positivity of female role models	3.60(1.25)	3.81(1.25)
Social support	1.82(0.51)$_a$	1.55(0.37)$_b$
Family support	4.12(1.11)	4.03(1.21)
Years since PhD	7.10(3.61)$_a$	11.50(6.50)$_b$

Note. Means with differing subscripts are significantly different ($p < .05$).

Table 2. Reported Belonging at, and Interest in Attending the Conference by Field and Conference Description

	Engineers		Nonengineers	
	Gender equal	Predominantly male	Gender equal	Predominantly male
	M (*SD*)	*M* (*SD*)	*M* (*SD*)	*M* (*SD*)
Belonging	3.96(0.85)	3.96(0.84)	4.18(1.11)	3.17(1.17)
Interest	3.88(1.22)	3.56(1.04)	4.15(0.96)	2.69(1.34)

outside of work and less contact with female role models in their graduate training ($ps < .05$). On average, female nonengineers held their doctorate degrees for longer than the female engineers ($p < .05$). Women engineers were comparable to the nonengineers in the positivity of their experiences with female role models and in family support for their careers.

Reactions to the Conference

To test our hypothesis about reactions to social identity threat, we analyzed received belongingness ratings with Conference Type (equal vs. predominately male) × Disciplinary Field (engineering vs. nonengineering) analysis of variance. In all the models, we analyzed the outcomes of belonging and interest separately because, even though they have comparable effects across all the analyses, they each provide unique insight into the factors that moderate social identity threat.

The predicted interaction approached significance, $F(1,54) = 3.72, p = .06$. As can be seen in Table 2, engineering women faculty did not respond differently to the gender-balanced versus male-dominated conference ($F < 1$). However, women faculty from nonengineering fields reported significantly less belongingness when the conference was male-dominated than when it was balanced, $F(1, 54) = 5.28$, $p < .05$. Similarly, in the analysis on how interested participants were in attending the conference, the interaction between field and video condition approached significance, $F(1, 54) = 3.55, p = .06$. Again, engineers' interest in attending the conference was not influenced by whether it was portrayed as balanced or imbalanced ($F < 1$), but nonengineers were significantly less likely to be interested in attending a gender-imbalanced than a gender-balanced conference, $F(1, 54) = 10.44, p < .01$.

Moderators of Identity Threat

To examine whether positive experiences with female role models and lack of discrimination buffered social identity threat, we constructed regression models in

Table 3. Correlations between Perceived Discrimination (PD), Social Support,
and Female Role Models

	Perceived discrimination	Social support	Positivity of female role models
Social support	0.23*		
Positivity of female role models	−0.29**	−0.15	
Family support	−0.37***	−0.07	0.37***

Note. *$p < .10$, **$p < .05$, ***$p < .01$.

which predictors that were continuous variables were standardized and interaction terms were computed between predictors. Table 3 shows the correlations between these variables. Following the suggestions of Cohen, Cohen, Aiken and West (2003), we interpreted the interactions by estimating simple slopes at one standard deviation below and one standard deviation above the mean of each moderator. Because of a priori predictions and our small sample size, we examined all simple slopes regardless of whether the overall interactions were significant.

Perceived discrimination. In support of our hypotheses, women engineers who perceived fair treatment in the past were less susceptible to social identity threat and reported a greater sense of belonging to the predominantly male conference than did those with higher levels of perceived discrimination, $t(53) = -2.46$, $p < .05$ (see Figure 1). Perceived discrimination did not influence reactions to the gender-equal conference by engineers or reactions to either conference by nonengineers (all $ts < 1$).

Positive experiences with female role models. In partial support of our predictions, having positive experiences with female role models did not buffer women from social identity threat, but not having positive experience was a vulnerability and increased negative responding to the threat. After controlling for overall contact with female role models, women engineers with less positive experiences with female role models expressed marginally less interest in attending a conference when it was represented as male dominated as compared to when it was gender balanced, $t(44) = -1.54$, $p < .10$ (see Figure 2). Engineers with more positive experiences with female role models did not respond differently to the balanced and imbalanced videos and nonengineers were more interested in attending the balanced conference, regardless of role model influence.

Social support. We anticipated that social support would be a generally ameliorative factor that promoted well-being and thereby buffered challenges for both engineers and nonengineers. As Figure 3 shows, this prediction held for the amount

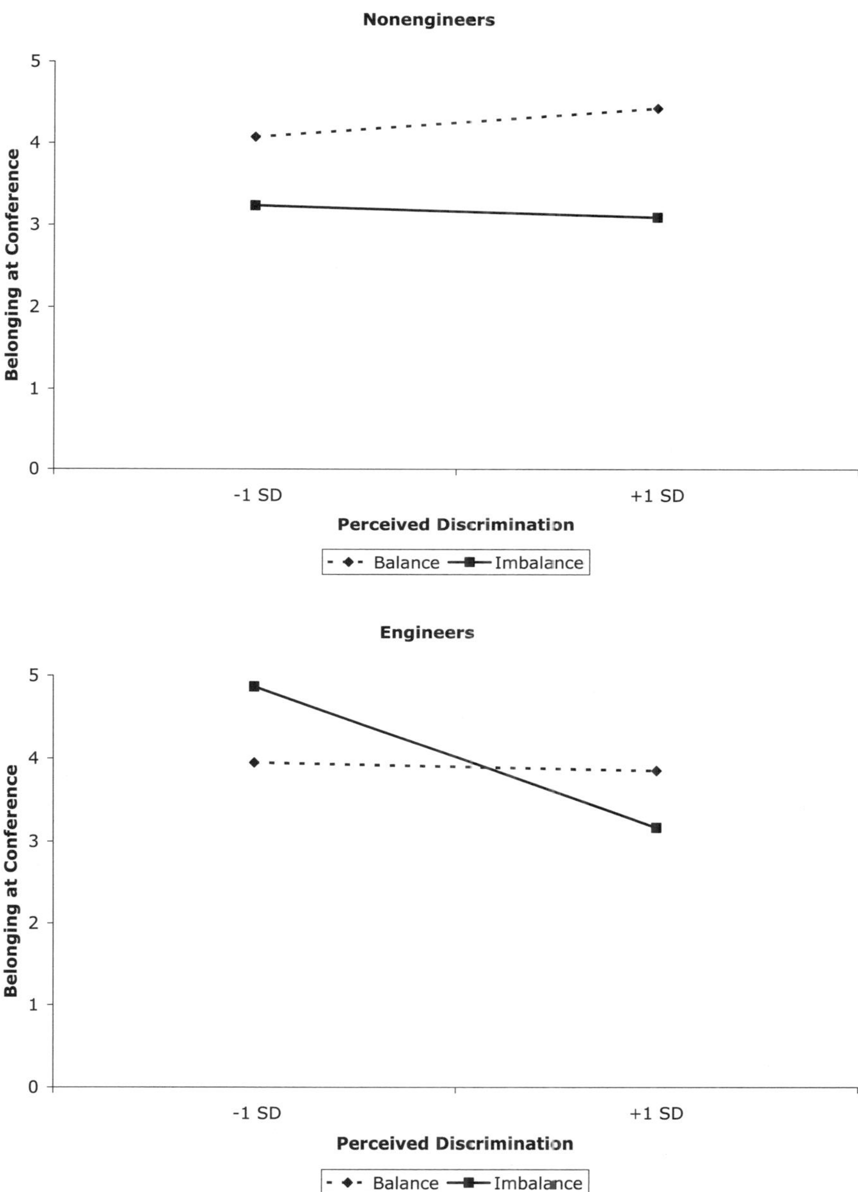

Fig. 1. Perceived belongingness at the conference as a function of field, gender balance of conference, and experiences with discrimination.

 Richman, vanDellen, and Wood

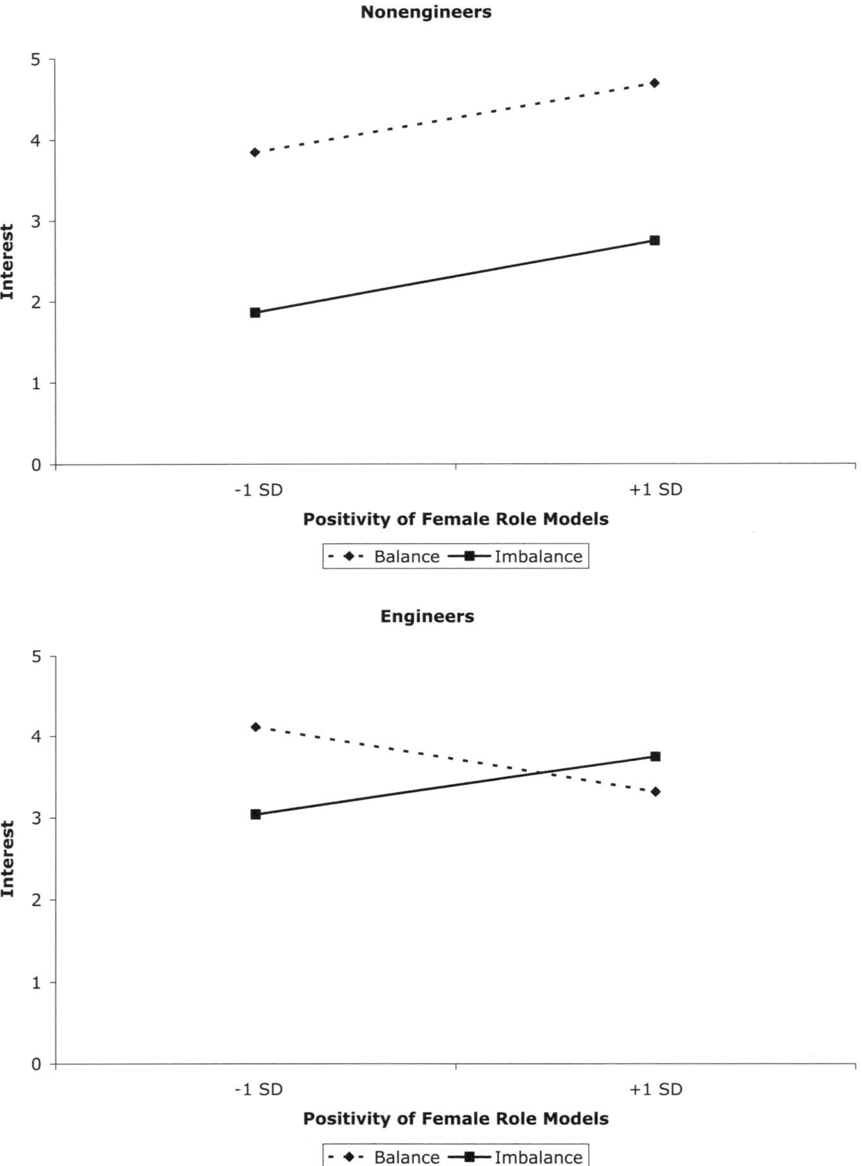

Fig. 2. Interest in attending the conference as a function of field, gender balance of conference, and positivity of interactions with female role models.

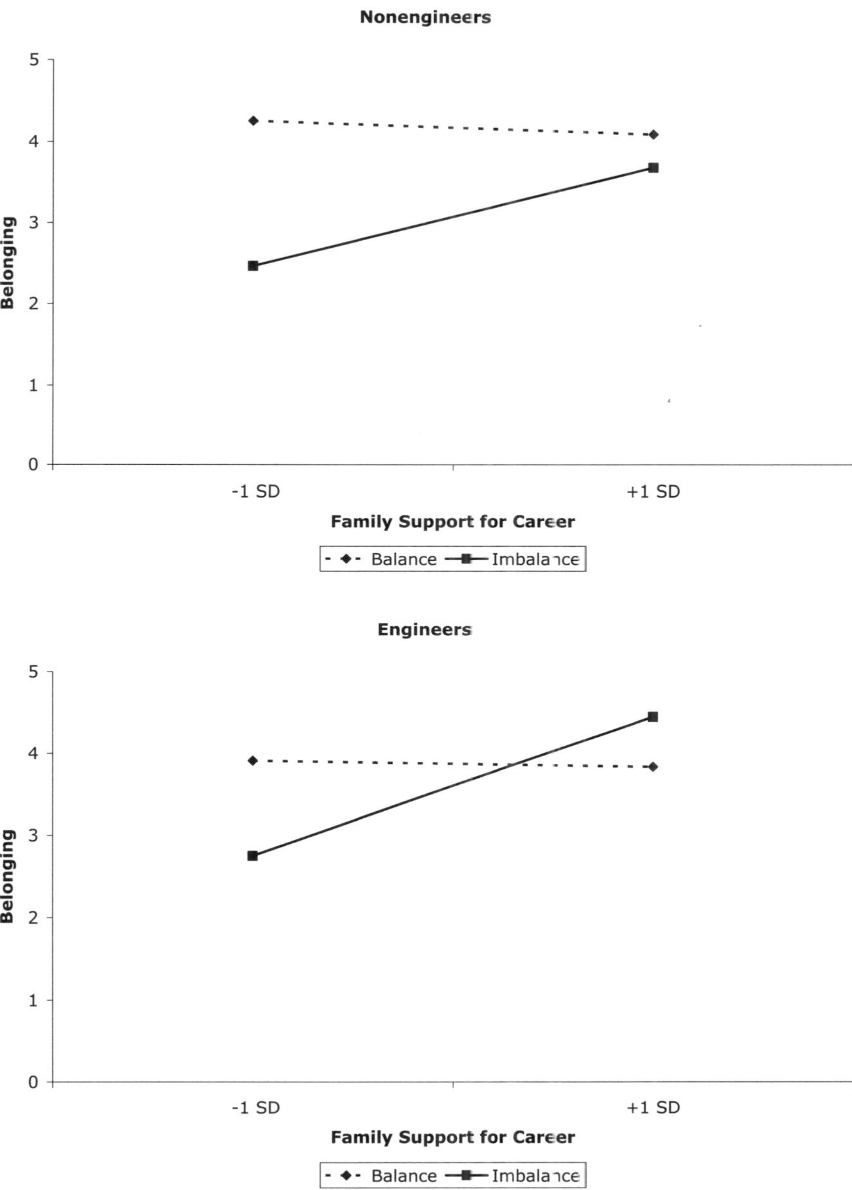

Fig. 3. Perceived belongingness at the conference as a function of field, gender balance of conference, and family support for field of study.

of family support for one's chosen career. Participants with higher levels of family support reported a greater expectation of belonging at the predominantly male conference than did those with lesser family support, and this effect held for engineers, $t(53) = 2.16$, $p < .05$, and nonengineers, $t(53) = 2.09$, $p<.05$. Family support did not influence responses to the gender equal conference for either group (all $Fs < 1$). Our prediction also held for general social support (see Figure 4). Participants with low levels of social support were less interested in attending the conference if it was portrayed as male dominated rather than gender equal. This was consistent for both engineers (marginally), $t(53) = 1.61$, $p < .08$ and nonengineers, $t(53) = 3.10$, $p < .01$. At high levels of social support, interest in attending the conference did not differ according to gender ratio portrayed in the video ($Fs < 1$).

Discussion

The central finding from this research is that academic women in the field of engineering were less reactive to the experience of social identity threat than were academic women from more gender-balanced fields. The women engineers' sense of belonging at, and interest in attending a professional conference were not influenced by the numbers of women portrayed at the conference, whereas the nonengineering women reported a reduced sense of belonging and less interest in attending a male-dominated rather than gender-balanced conference. The successful women engineers in our sample appear to have developed means of coping with the social identity threat that arises from their minority status in the field. In addition, certain academic and social experiences of these women were important moderators of whether their social identity was threatened.

For the women engineers, a history of fair treatment and minimal perceived exposure to discrimination was related to a decreased vulnerability to social identity threat. Engineering women who perceived less exposure to discrimination in the past year reported feeling more belonging at the male-dominated conference compared with those who perceived more exposure to discrimination. The nonengineers, in contrast, reported less belonging at the male-dominated conference, regardless of their perceived discrimination. This effect suggests an important qualification of the responses to the different videos. It is not simply that the engineering women had more experience with being in gender-imbalanced environments and were therefore relatively more comfortable in attending a predominantly male conference. Rather, the absence of perceived discrimination was related to the engineers' comfort at the male-dominated conference. Past research has found that experiences of observing the underrepresentation of women in a field and experiences with being a target of repeated, subtle discrimination can lead to a state of belonging uncertainty (Walton & Cohen, 2007) that impairs

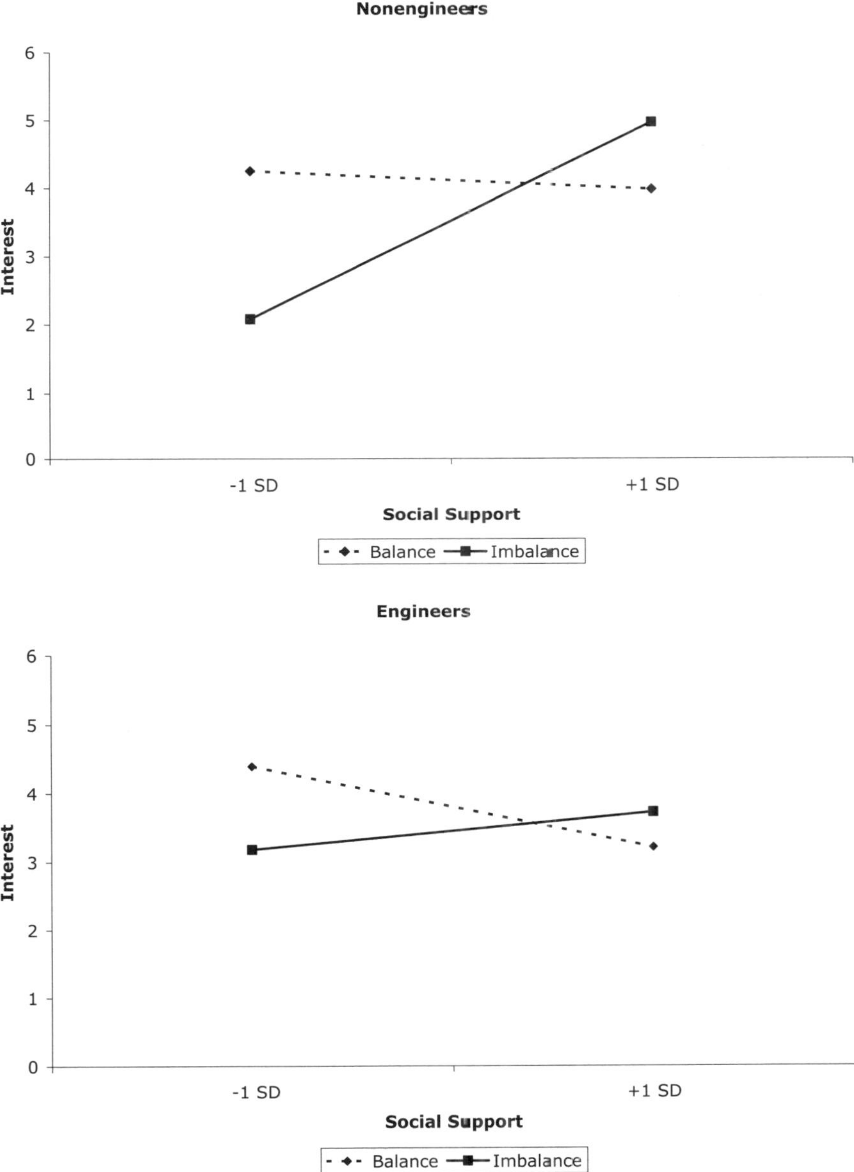

Fig. 4. Interest in attending the conference as a function of field, gender balance of conference, and social support.

achievement and motivation of underrepresented groups in academic settings. Our findings imply that working in environments where one perceives fair treatment can promote women's experience of belonging and engagement in similar environments in the future.

The absence of positive female role models also affected how women in engineering appraised the threat. Women engineers with less experience with positive female role models were marginally less interested in attending the predominately male, as compared to the gender-balanced conference. This effect suggests that the lack of supportive female role models heightens the threat in gender-imbalanced work environments.

For all of the women in our study, supportive social networks were important elements to success in an identity threatening environment. Having a strong support network encourages feelings of belonging and appraisals of intimacy and thereby contributes to an increased sense of interest and inclusiveness in the face of a potential social identity threat. We also found that for both groups of women, strong perceptions of the availability of social support provided a buffer to the experience of social identity threat. Typically, past research has focused on social support as an adaptive coping mechanism in response to social identity-based stressors. For example, people who have more social support after experiencing a social identity threat have better emotional and physical outcomes (e.g., Richman, Bennett, Pek, Siegler, & Williams, 2007). However, our findings suggest that perceived social support may also influence how people appraise a threatening environment. We found that both groups of women evaluated the threat as less severe when they considered themselves to have strong support networks. Future research would benefit from examining how these perceptions could in turn lead to a greater willingness to enter gender-imbalanced academic settings that hold the potential to be threatening environments.

Social support in the form of family encouragement for their chosen careers also was a positive buffer for both groups of women. This finding is consistent with the parent socialization model (Eccles, Adler, & Kaczala, 1982) in which the expectations that parents have of their children's future careers influence children's motivation to pursue these fields. For example, daughters of parents who hold egalitarian gender role attitudes maintain high levels of math and science achievement in adolescence. In a test of this model, Chhin, Bleeker, and Jacobs (2008) found that across three studies, parents' beliefs and expectations reported when their children were adolescents played an important role in shaping their children's gender-typed occupational choices during young adulthood. This research emphasizes that family support and encouragement in both traditional and nontraditional occupational domains enables women to be better able to cope with negative socialization pressures and social identity threat.

Conclusion

In summary, women in the field of engineering on average have developed the capacity to cope with their minority status in their predominantly male field and the stereotypic perceptions that are activated in such contexts. Thus, they were more likely to feel that they belonged in a male-dominated conference than women from more gender-balanced academic fields. The engineers were especially able to cope with social identity threat when they had experiences to suggest that they, personally, belonged in such settings. These included a history of minimal personal discrimination and a history of positive female role models. Women engineers without these buffering experiences reacted to the threat with reduced interest in attending the conference, and were in this way similar to the nonengineers.

Our findings indicate that efforts to reduce discrimination, provide positive female role models, and establish social support in traditionally male academic settings have meaningful implications for women's willingness to pursue and persist in these environments. This research also underscores the importance of fostering the careers of women in science, match, and technology fields to increase the likelihood that girls and women will stay in the pipeline. These efforts could then lead to an upward trend in which more women are available to serve as effective role models for future women during their training and careers, which could then encourage more women to seek out and flourish in these environments.

References

Adams, G., Garcia, D. M., Purdie-Vaughns, V., & Steele, C. M. (2006). The detrimental effects of a suggestion of sexism in an instruction situation. *Journal of Experimental Social Psychology, 42*, 602–615. doi:10.1016/j.jesp.2005.10.004.

Ben-Zeev, T., Fein, S., Inzlicht, M. (2005). Arousal and stereotype threat. *Journal of Experimental Social Psychology, 41*, 174–181. doi:10.1016/j.jesp.2003.11.007.

Ceci, S. J., & Williams, W. M. (Eds.). (2007). *Why aren't more women in science? Top researchers debate the evidence*. Washington, DC: American Psychological Association.

Chatman, J. A., Boisnier, A. D., Spataro, S. E., Anderson, C., & Berdahl, J. L. (2008). Being distinctive versus being conspicuous: The effects of numeric status and sex-stereotyped tasks on individual performance in groups. *Organizational Behavior and Human Decision Processes, 107*, 141–160. doi:10.1016/j.obhdp.2008.02.006.

Chhin, C. S., Bleeker, M. M., & Jacobs, J. E. (2008). Gender-typed occupational choices: The long-term impact of parents' beliefs and expectations. In H.M G. Watt and J. S. Eccles (Eds.), *Gender and occupational outcomes*. Washington, DC: APA.

Cohen, S., & Hoberman, H. M. (1983). Positive events and social support as buffers of life change stress. *Journal of Applied Social Psychology, 13*, 99–125. doi:10.1111/j.1559–1816.1983.tb02325.x.

Cohen, L. L., & Swim, J. K. (1995). The differential impact of gender rations on women and men: Tokenism, self-confidence, and expectations. *Personality and Social Psychology Bulletin, 21*, 876–884. doi:10.1177/0146167295219001.

Cohen, J., Cohen, P., West, S. G., & Aiken, L. S. (2003) *Applied multiple regression/correlation analysis for the behavioral sciences* (3rd ed.). Mahwah, NJ: Erlbaum.

Eagly, A. H., & Carli, L. L. (2008). *Through the labyrinth: The truth about how women become leaders.* Boston, MA: Harvard University Press.

Eccles, J. (1994). Understanding women's educational and occupational choices: Applying the Eccles et al. model of achievement-related choices. *Psychology of Women Quarterly, 18*, 585–609. doi:10.1111/j.1471–6402.1994.tb01049.x.

Eccles, J., Adler, T. F., & Kaczala, C. M. (1982). Socialization of achievement attitudes and beliefs: Parental influences. *Child Development, 53*, 322–339. doi:10.2307/1128973.

Gardiner, M., Tiggemann, M., Kearns, J., & Marshall, K. (2007). Show me the money! An empirical analysis of mentoring outcomes from women in academia. *Higher Education Research & Development, 26*, 425–442. doi:10.1080/07294360701658633.

Halpern, D. F., Benbow, C. P. Geary, D. C., Gur, R. C., Hyde, J. S., & Gernsbacher, M. A. (2007). The science of sex differences in science and mathematics. *Psychological Science in the Public Interest, 8*, 1–51. doi:10.1111/j.1529–1006.2007.00032.x.

Hedges, L. V., & Nowell, A. (1995). Sex differences in mental test scores, variability, and numbers of high-scoring individuals. *Science, 269*, 41–45. doi:10.1126/science.7604277.

Hyde, J., Lindberg, S. M., Linn, M. C., Ellis, A. B., & Williams, C. C. (2008). Gender similarities characterize math performance. *Science, 321*, 494–495. doi:10.1126/science.1160364.

Inzlicht, M., & Ben-Zeev, T. (2000). A threatening intellectual environment: Why females are susceptible to experiencing problem-solving deficits in the presence of males. *Psychological Science, 11*, 365–371. doi:10.1111/1467–9280.00272.

Kanter, R. (1977). *Men and women of the corporation.* New York: Basic Books.

Lippa, R. A. (2005). *Gender, nature, and nurture.* Mahwah, NJ: Erlbaum.

Lord, C. G., & Saenz, D. S. (1985). Memory deficits and memory surfeits: Differential cognitive consequences of tokenism for tokens and observers. *Journal of Personality and Social Psychology, 49*, 918–926. doi:10 1037/0022–3514.49.4.918.

Marx, D. M., & Roman, J. S. (2002). Female role models: Protecting women's math test performance. *Personality and Social Psychology Bulletin, 28*, 1183–1193. doi:10.1177/01461672022812004.

Murphy, M. C., Steele, C. M., & Gross, J. J. (2007). Signaling threat: How situational cues affect women in math, science, and engineering settings. *Psychological Science, 18*, 879–885. doi:10.1111/j.1467–9280.2007.01995.x.

National Science Foundation. (June, 2008). Thirty-three years of women in S&E faculty positions. Arlington, VA: National Science Foundation, Division of Science Resources Statistics. http://www.nsf.gov/statistics/infbrief/nsf08308/, accessed on line June 23, 2009.

Nauta, M. M., Epperson, D. L., & Kahn, J. H. (1998). A multiple-groups analysis of predictors of higher level career aspirations among women in mathematics, science, and engineering majors. *Journal of Counseling Psychology, 45*, 483–496. doi:10.1037/0022–0167.45.4.483.

Pascoe, E., & Richman, L. S. (2011). Effects of discrimination on food decisions. *Self and Identity, 10*, 396–406. doi:10.1080/15298868.2010.526384.

Richman, L. S., Bennett, G., Pek, J., Siegler, I. C.. & Williams, R. B. (2007). Discrimination, dispositions, and cardiovascular responses to stress. *Health Psychology, 26*, 675–683. doi:10.1037/0278–6133.26.6.675.

Schmader, T., Johns, M., & Forbes, C. (2008). An integrated process model of stereotype threat effects on performance. *Psychological Review, 115*, 336–356. doi:10.1037/0033–295X.115.2.336.

Steele, C. M. (1997). A threat in the air: How stereotypes shape the intellectual identities and performance of women and African-Americans. *American Psychologist, 52*, 613–629. doi:10.1037/0003–066X.52.6.613.

Syed, M., Azmitia, M., & Cooper, C. R. (2011). Identity and academic success among underrepresented ethnic minorities: An interdisciplinary review and integration. *Journal of Social Issues, 67*(3), 442–468.

Taylor, S. E., & Fiske, S. T. (1978). Salience, attention and attribution: Top of the head phenomena. In L. Berkowitz (Ed.), *Advances in experimental social psychology* (Vol. 11. pp. 249–288). New York: Academic Press.

Walton, G. M., & Cohen, G. L. (2007). A question of belonging: Race, social fit, and achievement. *Journal of Personality and Social Psychology, 92*, 82–96. doi:10.1037/0022–3514.92.1.82.

Williams, D. R., Yu, Y., Jackson, J. S., & Anderson, N. B. (1997). Racial differences in physical and mental health: Socioeconomic status, stress and discrimination. *Journal of Health Psychology, 2*, 335–351. doi:10.1177/135910539700200305.
Wong, C. A., Eccles, J. S., & Sameroff, A. (2003). The influence of ethnic discrimination and ethnic identification on African American adolescent's school and socioemotional adjustment. *Journal of Personality, 71*, 1197–1232. doi:10.1111/1467–6494.7106012.
Wood, W., & Eagly, A. H. (in press). Gender. In S. T. Fiske, D. T. Gilbert, & G. Lindzey (Eds.), *Handbook of social psychology* (5th ed.).

LAURA SMART RICHMAN is an Assistant Professor of social and health psychology in the Department of Psychology & Neuroscience at Duke University. Her research focuses on stress and coping processes associated with experiences of social inequality, with an emphasis on how perceived discrimination affects health-related behavior and outcomes.

MICHELLE VANDELLEN is a Franklin Postdoctoral Fellow at the University of Georgia. She received her PhD in Social Psychology from Duke University in 2008. Her research interests include how individuals manage threats to the self and how social and environmental factors influence self-control.

WENDY WOOD is Provost Professor of Psychology and Business at the University of Southern California. Her research interests are in gender, especially evolutionary origins of gender differences, and in habits and attitudes as determinants of behavior. She is a fellow of the American Psychological Association, the Association for Psychological Science, the *Society for Experimental Social Psychology*, and founding member of the *Society for Research Synthesis Methodology*.

Journal of Social Issues, Vol. 67, No. 3, 2011, pp. 510–530

Assessing the Role of Gender Rejection Sensitivity, Identity, and Support on the Academic Engagement of Women in Nontraditional Fields using Experience Sampling Methods

Bonita London,* Lisa Rosenthal, and Angel Gonzalez
Stony Brook University

Efforts to understand and alleviate the pervasive underrepresentation of women in science, technology, engineering, and mathematics (STEM) fields may benefit from the utilization of research methodologies that can model STEM engagement from multiple levels of analysis. We discuss the utility of experience sampling methodology (ESM) in capturing this broad range of factors that contribute to women's success and engagement in STEM fields—as well as other fields in which women have historically been underrepresented—with special focus on the importance of identity, social support, and gender-based rejection. We propose that the use of ESM may provide fine-grained details of women's STEM experiences, and thus model the challenges they face in STEM fields. The advantages of using ESM for capturing repeated measures of affect and behavior, the use of electronic methods of data collection, and the use of ESM to administer interventions are discussed.

Following the removal of many overt, structural barriers to women pursuing careers in nontraditional fields, there has been notable progress in women's advancement in such fields over the past several decades in many places, including the United States. For example, women have made substantial gains in the fields of medicine and law, where they now constitute nearly 50% of the entering classes of doctors and lawyers (Leadley, 2009; National Association for Law

*Correspondence concerning this article should be addressed to Bonita London, Department of Psychology, Stony Brook University, Stony Brook, NY 11794-2500 [e-mail: bonita.london@stonybrook.edu].

Portions of the work reported in this article were supported by a grant from the National Science Foundation (Award #0733918) awarded to the first author. Support in the preparation of this article was received while the first author was a Visiting Scholar at the Russell Sage Foundation.*

Placement, 2009), and earn more than 50% of the bachelor's degrees in science and engineering disciplines (NSF, 2009). Despite these substantive gains, gender inequalities remain pervasive and persistent at multiple levels across domains in which women have been historically negatively stereotyped, marginalized, and excluded. For example, women represent only 19.2% of private law firm partners, 21% of law school Deans, and 25% of District Court judges (National Association for Law Placement, 2009). In the field of medicine, starting salaries of female physicians in select markets are approximately $16,000 less than equivalently educated male physicians within the same specialties (Lo Sasso, Richards, Chou, & Gerber, 2011). Within science and engineering fields in the United States, women receive less than 25% of postdoctoral fellowships in computer sciences, mathematics, and physical sciences, hold only 39% of faculty positions in science and engineering departments at 4-year colleges, and have only 28% of tenure track faculty positions in science and engineering departments (NSF, 2009). Finally, in science, technology, and engineering, women are reportedly twice as likely as men to leave positions in these fields (Ceci, Williams, & Barnett, 2009).

Efforts to identify the causes of these disparities have focused on the influence of a wide range of potential contributing factors at multiple levels of analysis, including structural forms of discrimination and marginalization, and psychological processes that interfere with confidence and success. For example, research has demonstrated the impact of societal level factors such as negative stereotypes of women's math ability on stereotype threat activation and subsequent performance decrements for women enrolled in science, technology, engineering, and mathematics (STEM) disciplines (e.g., Pittinsky, Shih, & Ambady, 1999; Spencer, Steele, & Quinn, 1999; Steele & Ambady, 2006). Other work demonstrates the impact of institutional level factors, such as the absence versus presence of female role models on women's pursuit of professional development opportunities (Smart Richman, vanDellen, & Wood, 2011), and the influence of university single-sex STEM education programs on women's investment in STEM domains (e.g., Rosenthal, London, Levy, & Lobel, 2011). Still other work provides evidence of the impact of individual level beliefs in the compatibility between women's gender and STEM identities on their sense of belonging, motivation, and commitment to STEM careers (London, Rosenthal, Levy, & Lobel, in press; Rosenthal et al., 2011; Settles, 2004).

Importantly, the great diversity of research findings aimed at uncovering the processes through which women engage or disengage from STEM domains reflects the diversity in research methods used to capture that process—from large-scale cross-sectional surveys, to controlled experimental studies, to detailed qualitative interviews. In this article, we propose that a relatively underused methodology in the study of academic processes—experience sampling methodology (ESM)—has the potential to provide important and novel contributions to the aforementioned literature. We first summarize conceptualizations of "engagement" as a key construct. Second, we provide a brief review of the traditional methods used to study academic engagement. Third, we define and review the key features of ESM designs that can be used to address both the ways in which engagement has been operationalized in the literature and the challenges faced by traditional research methods for studying engagement. Fourth, we review research that has utilized ESM designs to explore three themes related to the experiences of women pursuing interests in STEM and other nontraditional domains: (1) perceptions of gender marginalization and sexism, (2) gender and STEM (or other career) identity compatibility, and (3) social support. Fifth, we discuss the benefits of ESM studies beyond empirical research—namely, its ability to capitalize on self-disclosure benefits for participants, and its potential use in intervention studies. Finally, we discuss the limitations of ESM designs.

Defining and Measuring Engagement in STEM Fields

Engagement and success in STEM fields is often defined and conceptualized broadly to reflect both conceptual ideologies and behavioral correlates. For example, conceptual definitions of STEM engagement include sense of belonging in a STEM field (e.g., London et al., in press; Rosenthal et al., 2011), centrality of a STEM identity (e.g., Settles, 2004; Syed, Azmitia, & Cooper, 2011), implicit and/or explicit attitudes toward STEM fields (e.g., Blickenstaff, 2005; Nosek et al., 2002), expectations for success (e.g., Eccles, 2007), as well as persistence, confidence, pride, and investment in the STEM domains (e.g., Blickenstaff, 2005; Brainard & Carlin, 1998; Ceci et al., 2009; Chemers, Zurbriggen, Syed, Goza, & Bearman, 2011; Eccles, 2007; Smart Richman et al., 2011).

Engagement has also been defined behaviorally. For example, engagement has been measured in terms of rates of participation in STEM related activities and groups (e.g., Brainard & Carlin, 1998; Chemers et al., 2011; Smart Richman et al., 2011), seeking and receipt of STEM support (e.g., Erwin & Maurutto, 1998), STEM performance and grades received (e.g., Erwin & Maurutto, 1998; Settles, 2004), class participation and perceptions of threat in the academic environment (e.g., London, Anderson, & Downey, 2007a), and selection of (e.g., Syed et al., 2011) or thoughts about changing one's STEM major (e.g., London et al., in press; Rosenthal, London, Levy, Lobel, & Herrera-Alcazar, in press; Steele et al., 2002). These broad and specific concepts highlight that researchers define engagement and success not simply in terms of one's academic performance within STEM fields, but also in the social, academic, and personal factors that contribute to the overall well-being of an individual pursuing a career in a nontraditional field.

Traditional Methods used to Study Academic Engagement

Much of the literature on the academic engagement of women in STEM has utilized cross-sectional survey methods, experimental lab studies, interview or

  513

focus group study designs, and longitudinal methods. Each methodology provides an important perspective on STEM engagement. For example, cross-sectional survey research has provided evidence of sex differences in STEM experiences, engagement and performance, differences in the experiences of women in STEM versus non-STEM fields, and the impact of constructs like identity interference and centrality on STEM performance, among many other insights (e.g., Ferreira, 2003; Nosek et al., 2002; Settles, 2004). Qualitative and focus group research involving either structured or free-form interview protocols have provided detailed accounts of personal experiences of men and women pursuing STEM careers (e.g., Erwin & Maurutto, 1998). For example, based on interviews with female science major undergraduates, Erwin and Maurutto (1998) reported that subtle slights and experiences of marginalization can create a "chilly climate" for women in STEM fields.

Experimental research designs provide controlled analyses of identified phenomena theorized to impact STEM engagement. For example, through experimental manipulations of situational cues of gender relevance (e.g., the number of gender in-group vs. out-group members present as one completes a math test), the stereotype threat literature has compellingly demonstrated that the presence of situational cues of threat can undermine women's performance on challenging math tasks—particularly those women who are invested in success in math and science fields (e.g., Inzlicht & Ben-Zeev, 2003; Logel et al., 2009; Shih et al., 1999; Spencer et al., 1999; Steele & Ambady, 2006).

Finally, longitudinal studies of women in STEM fields have provided valuable insight into the time course of academic engagement. For example, in a longitudinal study, Brainard and Carlin (1993) demonstrate that after the first year in college, women's academic self-confidence decreases substantially, rebounds over time, but never returns to baseline levels, and that women who changed majors did so in their first or second year.

Although each of these research methodologies offers unique and critically important information on the processes involved in STEM engagement for women, there remains room for research techniques that can incorporate some of the benefits of each method while addressing some of the challenges or limitations. A research approach that allows for the integrative and simultaneous exploration of: (1) between-group differences (e.g., comparisons of men and women pursuing STEM careers, or comparisons of individuals exposed to varying targeted interventions); (2) within-group differences (e.g., factors that impede STEM success for some women but not others); and (3) the process of change over time within individuals (e.g., shifts in STEM engagement throughout critical educational transition periods) at short-term (e.g., across days) and longer-term (e.g., across weeks or semesters) intervals, all within the naturalistic context of real world STEM environments can also provide a process-oriented investigation of the underlying mechanisms associated with successful academic engagement. ESM offers a research technique that can examine these three levels of data simultaneously, and thus can potentially integrate some of the advantages of cross-sectional, qualitative, longitudinal, and field research designs.

What is Experience Sampling Methodology?

ESM, also referred to as diary research, event sampling research, or everyday experience methods, is a methodology of collecting data in which researchers utilize repeated measures to sample behaviors, emotions, and experiences over a given period of time or around particular events generated by participants' self-reports (Bolger, Davis, & Rafaeli, 2003; Reis & Gable, 2000; Stone & Shiffman, 2002). Though ESM has been used in social, personality, and clinical psychology studies (e.g., Bolger & Zuckerman, 1995; Rafaeli, Rogers, & Revelle, 2007; Swim, Hyers, Cohen, & Ferguson, 2001), it has been relatively underused in studying academic engagement processes.

By capturing repeated points of data from participants over a period of time, ESM may address the challenges of maintaining experimental realism, reducing memory recall distortions, and compensating for few data points that often affect survey, experimental, and qualitative research designs (Bolger et al., 2003; London, Downey, Bolger, & Velilla, 2005; London, Downey, Rattan, & Tyson, unpublished data; Reis & Gable, 2000). The structure of ESM makes the methodology well suited to address research questions in which the phenomenon being studied is hypothesized to: (1) occur or be measured best within the natural context of the real world (rather than in laboratory simulations), (2) be compromised by recall or memory distortions, and (3) have a time course effect, i.e., to change or shift over some period of time such as in mood or behaviors, or have a repeated process (e.g., tallying of social behaviors). Based on the questions to be addressed, researchers can vary the type of questions (e.g., open-ended, Likert-type scale, etc.), the frequency (e.g., number of surveys completed, the rate of repetition of questions, the duration of the study), the form (e.g., paper-pencil or web-based), and the signal type (i.e., whether participants complete surveys at a predetermined time period, or an event-determined period, etc.) administration. According to Reis and Gable (2000), "the payoff [of ESM data] is a detailed, accurate, and multifaceted portrait of social behavior embedded in its natural context."

Example of an ESM Study Design

Three ESM studies used to address questions of the academic engagement of women in nontraditional fields are described with greater detail below. However, we describe a general example of an ESM design here to provide a context for discussions of the methodological advantages of ESM in the subsequent section.

A researcher interested in exploring the factors that contribute to STEM engagement might first identify the groups of interest: STEM women and comparison groups of STEM men and non-STEM men and women. Second, identify a critical period in which STEM engagement might be vulnerable: for example, during the first year of college when women are more likely to withdraw from a STEM discipline (Brainard & Carlin, 1998). Third, identify a particular environment in which STEM engagement processes might occur: an introductory STEM "gateway" course in which STEM students must perform well to be accepted into the STEM major. Fourth, identify the time course in which engagement processes might shift: given that students attend courses once or twice per week, a diary questionnaire completed at the end of each week over the course of the semester might capture shifts in engagement that occur in response to weekly classroom experiences. Fifth, determine the method for the diary administration: college students with access to computers might complete electronic/web-based diaries. Finally, determine the types of questions likely to capture the constructs of interest: a checklist of the tasks completed that week (e.g., had an exam, worked in research lab); reports of objective course performance (e.g., test grades, whether the student answered questions and participated in the course) and subjective ratings of engagement (e.g., feelings of competence, efficacy); an open-ended narrative of a positive or negative experience that increased or decreased feelings of engagement, competence, etc.; and ratings of coping strategies used to deal with negative STEM experiences.

Together, the ESM paradigm described would allow an investigator to obtain repeated measures of a wide variety of academic engagement outcomes, and of key factors that might contribute to levels of academic engagement from the same individual over a critical period of time. Further, the design would allow the investigator to explore whether between-person differences and within-person changes in engagement are associated with concurrent environmental or individual factors, are short lived or long lasting, are affected by particular forms of coping, are unique to STEM women or STEM students, among other questions.

Conceptual and Practical Benefits of ESM Techniques

In addition to the flexibility in addressing conceptual questions, ESM paradigms also offer an important practical benefit—the repeated measures approach helps to facilitate recall of events, experiences, and moods by reducing the time delay between the lived experience and the reporting of that experience. Research has shown that individuals may have poor recall for specific details of past events (Shiffman et al., 1997). For example, Shiffman et al. (1997) found that individuals generally have poor memory for their mood and general activities, especially for emotionally charged events, such as a smoking relapse for ex-smokers.

Further, comparisons of ESM data to retrospective reports underscore the potential discrepancy between these two forms of data collection methods.

Researchers have found that retrospective reports of events completed by an individual tend not to be good predictors of that same individual's daily report of the same events (Shiffman et al., 1997; Smith, Leffingwell, & Ptacek, 1999; Terry, Stevens, & Lane, 2005). For example, a subject's estimate of how often s/he participated in class discussions throughout the semester may be inflated when asked at the end of the semester, but may be more accurate when asked at the end of each day. Research has also found that one's current mood and affect can influence the recall of long past events, e.g., current mood can lead to an exaggerated appraisal of past mood states (e.g., Shiffman et al., 1997; Terry et al., 2005). This effect may be reduced as the need for retrospective recall of mood is eliminated in ESM studies in which mood is measured in the moment, such as with questions that assess how an individual is feeling "right now" rather than last week.

Applied to research on STEM engagement, there is a benefit to accurately measuring the relationship between day-to-day or week-to-week experiences in STEM courses where women may report experiences of threat and marginalization, and their waning sense of comfort and interest in pursuing STEM fields. The sexism literature has convincingly demonstrated that overt sexism may be declining given sanctions on discriminatory behavior, but subtle sexism (like the form the "chilly" STEM environment may take) continues to be pervasive (e.g., Swim et al., 2001). Given the subtlety and ambiguity of modern sexism cues, the perception and experience of threat may be strong and damaging to a woman in the moment that it occurs, but the emotion and certainty of that perception may wane once the subtle cues of that experience are further from one's immediate memory. Therefore, both the immediate experiences of threat and the accumulation of those experiences over time are important for modeling STEM engagement.

Modeling change. A second key benefit of ESM is in its ability to model the process of change over time. Of interest to many researchers studying gender disparities in STEM engagement is the issue of whether interest/investment in STEM disciplines is relatively stable over time (e.g., formed from early socialization experiences and relatively unchanging) or is reliably malleable and undergoes frequent changes and shifts as a result of life experiences (e.g., exposure to STEM role models at critical life transition periods enhancing engagement; Smart Richman et al., 2011; see Ceci et al., 2009, for a review). Studying the process of change requires methodological approaches that acknowledge time as a key contributing factor to the theoretical models. For example, if STEM engagement is conceptualized as a phenomenon that is rooted in stable environmental factors, such as the number of female STEM professors present, then measurements of STEM engagement should be relatively stable over time within that institution, and infrequent measures of engagement (e.g., cross-sectional correlational designs, in-depth qualitative interviews) are sufficient to test whether an individual perceives the environment as hostile or unsupportive. Alternatively, if engagement is conceptualized as being rooted in the social or academic cues of marginalization in an environment that may change from situation to situation (e.g., receiving one poor grade on an assignment or being excluded from STEM activities/meetings), then the stability of measures of engagement may be more transient and require repeated or multiple measures to capture the process of change.

Electronic diaries (ED). In recent years, researchers have also begun to utilize different media for ESM administration. Typically, ESM questionnaires were administered using paper and pencil surveys, with participants completing sequential questionnaires either in a controlled setting or in a natural setting (e.g., at home) and submitting completed questionnaires in bulk (e.g., in a group or individually over time). With the advent of technological advances, ED can be administered through a variety of mediums (e.g., Internet connection on a computer, palm pilots). The debate regarding the advantages of electronic data collection over paper-and-pencil data collection have highlighted both some important advantages of ED over paper-and-pencil diaries, and some critical challenges (e.g., Bolger, Shrout, Green, Rafaeli, & Reis, 2006; Broderick & Stone, 2006; Green, Rafaeli, Bolger, Reis, & Shrout, 2006; Takarangi, Garry, & Loftus, 2006; Tennen, Affleck, Coyne, Larsen, & DeLongis, 2006).

First, through the use of electronic signaling (e.g., email reminders or palm pilot alarms), researchers can ensure that participants have a consistent reminder to complete their diary entries (Bolger et al., 2003; Jamison et al., 2001). This removes participants' burden of remembering to complete entries, and may increase compliance, and reduce back-filing entries (i.e., participants completing multiple diary entries at a time and falsely dating those entries; Takarangi et al., 2006). Second, the use of ED may increase the accuracy of diary entries by presenting question items sequentially rather than simultaneously so that the presence of related questions on a page will not influence the response pattern (Green et al., 2006). Additionally, the use of ED allows researchers to tailor questionnaires to participants' specific experiences, e.g., presenting a predetermined set of followup questions only if a particular event is experienced. Finally, the ED method may allow researchers to expand their sample of target participants beyond those only readily available within the researchers' immediate environment more easily than typically done with paper-and-pencil research designs. For example, the use of the Internet can increase opportunities for wide-scale recruitment of participants through Internet invitations, groups, websites, and online forums (Bolger et al., 2003; Piasecki, Hufford, Solhan, & Trull, 2007), and help facilitate collaborative multi-institution studies via the web.

Although ED methods provide some important benefits to ESM studies, there are some noted challenges to this methodology. First, the use of handheld ED devices may restrict the length and depth of questions that can be probed given the space and memory limitations that may exist with handheld devices.

Second, the use of the Internet may pose certain challenges for participants. Internet ED methods require participants to have access to computers and an Internet connection for the study to be successful (Piasecki et al., 2007), which may restrict the participant pool to those with the economic means to afford computers and Internet access. For researchers primarily interested in college student populations, these issues may be less problematic.

Using ESM to Study the Academic Engagement of Women in Nontraditional Fields

Having outlined the basic premises of ESM research designs, in the following section we review a select sample of studies that utilize ESM to study processes related to academic engagement of women. The factors that can influence whether women remain engaged in nontraditional fields are numerous. Recent converging lines of research have focused on three distinct, yet related, constructs thought to impact the success and engagement of women in nontraditional domains: (1) perceptions of subtle and overt sexism or negative stereotypes within domains where women have been historically marginalized and excluded, (2) belief in the compatibility between being a woman and being successful in a nontraditional career, and (3) support from others as one pursues a career in a nontraditional field.

Perceptions of Sexism and Academic Engagement

Swim et al. (2001) conducted a series of ESM studies that sought to provide evidence of the exposure frequency, type, and consequence of incidences of sexism directed toward women. Across three studies, women and men were instructed to complete a diary questionnaire immediately following an observed incident of sexism (i.e., event related diary). The diary included open-ended questions in which participants described the observed incident of sexism—incidents ranged from traditional gender role prejudices to sexual objectification to subtle demeaning comments—and close-ended questions that assessed the impact of the event on participants' well-being. Swim et al. (2001) report that participants were exposed to one to two incidents of significant sexist events per week and that such exposure negatively impacted their self-esteem, emotional well-being, and sense of belonging. The diary approach allowed Swim et al. (2001) to capture the "lived experience" of participants as they encountered day-to-day forms of sexism, and determine the relative impact of that exposure on their sense of belonging and psychological well-being.

Similar to the plight of women in STEM fields, gender issues continue to pervade the experiences of women pursuing advanced degrees in a number of other fields, including law. The gender disparities in the representation of women in positions of power, and status within the field of law parallel those seen in STEM fields—women are increasingly absent at higher levels of achievement compared to men (ABA Commission on Women, 2005; Guinier, Fine, & Balin, 1997; US Bureau of Labor Statistics, 2001; Valian, 2005). Much research has focused on the factors that contribute to the disengagement of women in the field of law, typically utilizing the same methodologies used to study women in STEM—cross-sectional surveys, qualitative interviews, and few longitudinal panel studies (e.g., Guinier et al., 1997). Similar to work on women in STEM, research on women in law has demonstrated a similarly alienating and chilly environment for women in law (e.g., Guinier et al., 1997), where women report perceiving subtle cues of marginalization and sexism, and feeling silenced and alienated within the law school environment (e.g., Mertz, 2007).

Given the subtlety of some forms of sexism (e.g., Logel et al., 2009), appraising and coping with subtle or ambiguous cues may vary greatly from individual to individual. Experiencing the negative consequences of social marginalization or bias first requires the individual to detect the subtle or ambiguous cues of rejection in a given situation. London et al. (unpublished data) proposed the sensitivity to gender-based rejection (Gender RS) model to help explore the mechanism(s) through which perceptions of threat vary across individuals, and subsequently lead to differences in vulnerability to the negative achievement and well-being outcomes associated with exposure to sexism. The Gender RS model (London et al., 2010; London, Downey, & Mace, 2007b) hypothesizes that women with past experiences of or exposure to gender bias, marginalization, discrimination, or rejection would be more likely to develop greater attunement to cues that signal the potential for threat in gender-relevant situations. In an ESM study of women entering a highly competitive law school environment, London et al. (unpublished data) demonstrated that individual differences in Gender RS within women predicted different trajectories of engagement and disengagement over time.

London et al. (unpublished data) recruited men and women at a competitive law school prior to the start of classes in their first year. Students completed a background questionnaire before the first day of their law school classes and then completed a 3-week daily diary longitudinal study. The transition into law school was chosen as an appropriate time period to study given the research on social transitions (e.g., Eccles et al., 1993; Ruble & Seidman, 1996), which suggests that upon entry into new life roles and environments (e.g., new educational contexts), one's identities, competence, and confidence may become challenged. Thus, for women pursuing a nontraditional educational program (law or a STEM discipline), their confidence, competence, and sense of belonging may be most vulnerable as they attempt to meet the challenges of the new environment both academically and socially.

The background questionnaire provided assessments of basic sociodemographic information, achievement test scores and grades, self-reports of prior academic and social engagement in undergraduate institutions (e.g., office hours attendance, study group participation, etc.), expectations of law school, among other relevant personality and individual differences questionnaires. Students logged into an ED at the end of each day, and completed a series of open- and close-ended questions that assessed a variety of constructs that were hypothesized to impact their social and academic engagement. Measures included assessments of: (1) major academic and social stressors that occurred over the course of the day (e.g., academic work overload, conflicts with partners or family members, illness, financial difficulties), (2) self reports of mood, sense of belonging, and comfort with peers and professors, (3) academic engagement (e.g., volunteering in class, workload completion, participation in study groups, and frequency of visiting professor office hours), (4) academic goal orientation, confidence, and satisfaction with work, and (5) positive or negative events, coping strategies used to deal with the event and affect following the event, among other factors. In addition to responding to the directed questions used for quantitative analyses, the ESM technique also allowed for the inclusion of open-ended, qualitative questions that could be summarized and analyzed qualitatively. Finally, end of semester follow-up questionnaires were distributed to assess the long-term impact of those initial transition experiences on academic engagement.

Importantly, ESM data help to model the complexity of the process of engagement. For example, when simply exploring group-based differences in engagement, London et al. (unpublished data) found no significant gender differences in previous undergraduate achievements (e.g., undergraduate grade point average) or engagement (e.g., frequency of attending office hours, participating in class discussions and study groups) prior to the start of law school; however, group-based differences as well as within-group differences emerged during the first 3 weeks of law school. Using the Gender RS framework to identify women who are more highly attuned to subtle cues of sexism (high Gender RS women) than other women, London et al. (unpublished data) found that women high in Gender RS reported higher levels of self-doubt (e.g., feelings of insecurity, anxiety, intimidation) than men and than women lower in Gender RS on average across the 3 weeks. High Gender RS women were more likely to perceive negative gender related threats than men and low Gender RS women, and high Gender RS women were significantly more likely to cope with negative gender-related threats using self-silencing strategies (e.g., keeping it to themselves) rather than confrontational strategies. Further, when women self-silenced, they reported significantly greater feelings of alienation and threat immediately following the negative incident. Finally, utilizing the day-to-day structure of the diary data, London et al. (unpublished data) demonstrated that while men and low Gender RS women showed increasing confidence in the quality of their work and performance when called on to speak in class, high

Gender RS women showed no improvement over time in their level of academic confidence.

The open-ended questions utilized in the ESM study of law school engagement also provide some context for capturing the specific qualitative experiences that contribute to the disengagement and feelings of threat and alienation that women may experience in a traditionally male-oriented academic environment. For example, demonstrating the gendered effect of the classroom context on sense of belonging, one participant reported:

> I had my hand raised for a long time to answer a question, but I never got called on. Some guy in the back corner got called on twice (I am female). Some other female students were called on, but it seemed like males were more aggressive.

Yet another participant highlighted the sense of "entitlement" expressed by some students, which may contribute to the context of alienation and subsequently the need to prove one's worthiness for nontraditional students:

> His comments got me angry: I think he thinks that he is more deserving of being here than I am. I feel like I am going to have to work twice as hard as he will to prove that I belong here...

These findings suggest that variability in Gender RS within women can predict a variety of engagement outcomes, including feelings of self-doubt, perceptions of sexism, self-silencing, and alienation within the context of a competitive, male-dominated law school culture. The ESM design further allowed for an analysis of event-specific coping strategies and subsequent engagement outcomes following negative gender-relevant events.

Identity, Social Support, and Academic Engagement

Building on the ESM paradigm for studying engagement of women in nontraditional fields outlined in London et al. (2007a, 2010, in press), and Rosenthal et al. (2011) conducted a longitudinal project of women in STEM fields, using mixed experience sampling methods (e.g., background surveys, daily diaries during the transition to college, follow-up cross-sectional surveys). The goal of the study was to analyze the social and academic factors that enhance or hinder STEM engagement of women across several key college and career transition points, such as the transition from high school to college. Two key theoretically guided predictors of undergraduate women's engagement in STEM fields are being tested in this project: perceived identity compatibility between being a woman and being in a STEM field, and perceived social support.

In one study across the first year of college, Rosenthal et al. (2011) examined the roles of perceived identity compatibility and perceived social support for one's choice of major from both close others (e.g., friends and family) and a single-sex program for women in STEM fields. Multiple regression analyses revealed that at the beginning of women's second year in college, perceived identity compatibility, perceived support from close others, and perceived support from the single-sex program for STEM women were each independently associated with greater sense of belonging in their major, even when controlling for past high school academic achievement and expected sense of belonging at the beginning of their first year of college. As well, perceived identity compatibility and perceived support from the single-sex program were associated with greater sense of belonging at the university more generally. This study allowed for the longitudinal examination of these two key variables for women in STEM specifically who were enrolled in a single-sex program for women in STEM at a coeducational university, and revealed the importance of identity compatibility and social support across the first year of college in women's sustained engagement in STEM fields. These findings support other work that suggests that academic engagement can be influenced by an individual's perceptions of how compatible their identity is with an academic domain (e.g., Chemers et al., 2011; Syed et al., 2011) and the social support resources available to them (e.g., Smart Richman et al., 2011; Witkow & Fuligni, 2011).

Further, London et al. (in press) examined the importance of perceived identity compatibility and social support using a daily diary across the first 3 weeks of women's first year of college, among women STEM majors at a coeducational university. Using ESM in this study allowed for the uncovering of daily processes involved in women's engagement in their STEM majors during their initial transition to college. For example, London et al. (in press) found that greater perceived identity compatibility and perceived social support on a particular day during women's first 3 weeks of college predicted greater sense of belonging, motivation, and less insecurity in STEM disciplines on that same day, even when controlling for general mood on that day.

London et al. (in press) also conducted lagged analyses on the daily diary data, which is a great advantage of ESM, allowing for the test of whether these key variables have a lasting, or cumulative effect on important engagement outcomes, not just for the same day, but on subsequent days. These analyses revealed that greater identity compatibility and support on a given day corresponded to greater motivation and sense of belonging on subsequent days. Lagged analyses also allow for a greater understanding of the causal direction of effects between variables over time. Additionally, during a follow-up survey at the beginning of participants' Spring semester of their first year of college, they found that greater perceived identity compatibility and social support from close others predicted lower expectations of dropping out of one's STEM major, even when controlling for past high school academic achievement and expectations of dropping out of their major at the beginning of their first year of college. Taken together, the comprehensive, longitudinal ESM methodology used in this work has already begun to provide substantive evidence of the long-term process of STEM engagement of women.

Crocker, Karpinski, Quinn, and Chase (2003) also conducted a diary study examining the impact of grades on identity and self-worth of both male and female engineering and psychology students. Participants completed pretest questionnaires, then for 3 weeks, they completed web-based questionnaires three times a week and on any days that they received a grade back or took an exam in any of their classes. Finally, they completed posttest questionnaires at the end of the semester. Crocker et al. (2003) found that self-esteem, affect, and identification with their major increased on the days that students received better grades and decreased on the days that they received worse grades. Additionally, they found that the relationship between bad grades and self-worth was moderated by how much the individual based her or his self-esteem on academic competence. Bad grades were also found to cause a greater drop in self-esteem for women than men, and engineering majors than psychology majors, and thus the greatest drop was found for women engineering majors. Because of their use of ESM, this study was able to examine how events that occur on a particular day can affect academic engagement, identification with the major, and feelings of self-worth over time.

Applications of ESM beyond empirical research

Benefits of Disclosure

In addition to the wealth of empirical information that ESM paradigms can provide for the study of STEM engagement of women, the methodology has additional applications and benefits that are worth noting. The methodology involves the repeated self-report of personal information within one's natural context. Research has convincingly demonstrated that self-disclosure, (e.g., in the form of open-ended diaries) can have positive outcomes related to physical health, psychological well-being, and academic achievement in college student populations, particularly when disclosing stressful or negative events (Pennebaker & Beall, 1986; Pennebaker, Kiecolt-Glaser, and Glaser, 1988; Pennebaker, Colder, & Sharp, 1990; Sheese, Brown, & Graziano, 2004; Sloan & Marx, 2004). Self-disclosure has also been shown to lead to improved academic performance, such as increases in grade point average (Pennebaker et al., 1990), which may suggest a particular utility of the disclosure paradigm specific to college populations. Given that ESM is a form of disclosure, whether through the close- or open-ended questions often included in diary research, study participants may enjoy an additional benefit of participating that results in adaptive outcomes associated with self-disclosure separate from the specific goals of the diary study.

The benefits of associated with disclosure may stem from the self-reflection and perspective change that occurs with the processing of negative experiences. However, while the long-term benefits of disclosure may be positive, some research suggests that a more immediate effect may be an increase in negative affect following disclosure of negative events (Pennebaker & Beall, 1986; Pennebaker et al., 1990). Pennebaker and Beall (1986) found that participants reported increased negative affect and blood-pressure reactivity after writing about a traumatic life event. Thus, an unintended effect of ESM studies is in its ability to potentially change and shift the individuals' interpretation, experience, and motivations as they participate over time.

Tailored Interventions and Policy Implications

A second applied benefit of ESM is in the application of tailored interventions. Just as questions can be administered on a daily or weekly interval time course, researchers may utilize ESM (particularly ED) to administer daily or weekly "doses" of interventions to participants. Participants could be presented with intervention materials at the beginning of each diary period, and the repeated questions over the time course of the diary would assess not only long-term change in engagement, but also the effect of the intervention materials presented. For example, Rosenthal et al. (2009) presented women interested in pursuing a career related to their STEM major (i.e., careers in medicine) with biographies of female role models prior to the administration of a web-based questionnaire. Results indicated that being exposed to those biographies resulted in increased sense of belonging in their major field, and that an increased perceived compatibility between being a woman and being in their science field mediated the effect of the biographies on sense of belonging. Expanding on this methodology, researchers might present intervention materials (e.g., biographies of successful STEM women, information about STEM careers, manipulations, etc.) to participants followed by repeated measures of questions on STEM engagement and investment over the course of a longitudinal diary study. This method may allow for a cost-effective administration of intervention materials to participants by utilizing the ease of access of the Internet without requiring direct person-to-person contact. Further, utilization of the Internet may increase the number of participants served by both the ESM data collection and the intervention administered given the ease of accessibility of computers and the web, particularly for college student populations.

The ED paradigms may offer the opportunity for tailored interventions and/or feedback to participants. As previously discussed, the immediate accessibility to data via electronic sources may allow researchers to tailor the experience of the diary to particular participants. For example, participants who report having a negative experience may be prompted to elaborate on those experiences with additional questions generated only if a negative experience is reported.

Alternatively, participants who report a negative experience could be directed to specific intervention materials relevant to their experience, for example, by indicating that they received a poor grade in a STEM course that day, participants may then be directed to study modules for STEM courses or information regarding coping resources for dealing with academic challenges. Again, the accessibility of the electronic data may allow for countless targeted modifications for interventions.

In addition to researchers being interested in this approach to implementing an intervention, the methodology could be used at the institutional level and become part of a university's policy or normal programming. A university could have a policy implemented that all incoming freshmen, as part of an introductory course or as an extension of orientation, log onto a website daily, weekly, or monthly to receive intervention materials that may be tailored to students in their major or their specific concerns, and students could receive course credit for doing so. For example, all students who are in nontraditional fields, such as women or African Americans in STEM fields, could be provided by their university or department with web-based materials over the course of their first year (or all years) of college that are designed to buffer them and provide support and coping strategies for their unique challenges in those fields, while simultaneously allowing them to earn course credit. Findings from ESM studies point to ongoing changes that occur for students, which have important implications for academic engagement, suggesting that the resources and programming provided to students in nontraditional fields should be ongoing and address those day-to-day or week-to-week changes. ED provide an efficient and cost-effective way for universities or departments to provide those ongoing resources to many students.

Finally, findings from ESM studies suggest that ESM itself should be used to evaluate existing policies or intervention programs aimed at maintaining or boosting academic engagement for women in STEM fields. Taking into account the financial constraints under which most universities operate, it is vital to have a strong and continuous assessment of what types of policies or intervention programs work best. Analyzing, for example, the percentages of women who stay in a major based on their membership in an intervention group versus those women who are not members of an intervention group can provide us with very important information for making this type of evaluation, but there are also ongoing, day-to-day events and changes students experience that could be quite useful to examine when evaluating the success of a program or institutional policy. For example, an evaluation of a particular university program that collects daily or weekly diaries could provide insight into what processes are affected by the program, what the particular times or moments in a student's career when an intervention is the most helpful, or what moments an intervention is not successful and thus should be modified. Thus, ESM might prove quite useful in evaluating, developing, and modifying intervention programs and policies to increase academic engagement for women in nontraditional fields such as STEM.

Limitations and Challenges with ESM

Although the benefits of utilizing ESM to study academic and social engagement are broad, there are important limitations to the methodology. First, the time commitment required of participants to complete longitudinal studies often increases attrition rates compared to cross-sectional, qualitative, or experimental research designs. This limitation can be partially addressed by creating shorter measures, but this comes at the cost of limiting the amount and type of information that can be collected (Bolger et al., 2003). Second, the use of ESM methods can alter an individual's insight of a specific domain, e.g., by allowing them to recall details of a negative event, and release the emotional strain by writing about the experience. This may also prove to be a scientific challenge (Bolger et al., 2003). For most scientific research, an important challenge is in having the methodology operate as an invisible mechanism in the process being studied. However, with ESM research, the methodology itself may become a part of the phenomenon being measured and studied. Similarly, given that the benefit of ESM is in studying change in responses over time, the methodology typically involves the repeated administration of the same question over the diary period. The repeated administration of the same question may become a cue to participants of the phenomenon being studied by the researcher (Bolger et al., 2003).

Conclusion

Despite some limitations, ESM research designs have many strengths and allow for fine-grained analyses of the processes involved in academic engagement for women in STEM, or other groups in nontraditional fields. ESM may help the field progress in understanding the time course of engagement versus disengagement, the day-to-day and week-to-week challenges that may create an accumulation of rejection or bias, and some of the buffering factors or influences that are key for understanding how we may increase representation of women in STEM fields. The methodology is particularly applicable to student populations that may have easy access to computers and electronic devices, making electronic tracking of diaries a viable option that reduces a number of data management issues. Further, the ESM design provides a mechanism for testing short- and long-term longitudinal questions about STEM engagement in a natural context rather than an experimentally sterile context, and avoids many of the recall biases that plague survey and qualitative interview designs. ESM may also have indirect benefits for participants and may be useful for creating cost-effective, targeted interventions. Taken together, this methodology is a promising novel technique for studying STEM engagement.

References

American Bar Association (2005): Commission on Women in the Profession. Retrieved on December 19, 2009, from http://www.abanet.org/women/pastevents/WashDCflyer05.pdf.

Blickenstaff, J. C. (2005). Women and science careers: Leaky pipeline or gender filter? *Gender and Education, 17*(4), 369–386. doi:10.1080/09540250500145072.

Bolger, N., Davis, A., & Rafaeli, E. (2003). Diary methods: Capturing life as it is lived. *Annual Review of Psychology, 54,* 579–616. doi:10.1146/annurev.psych.54.101601.145030.

Bolger, N., & Zuckerman, A. (1995). A framework for studying personality in the stress process. *Journal of Personality and Social Psychology, 69*(5), 890–902. doi:10.1037/0022–3514.69.5.890.

Bolger, N., Shrout, P. E., Green, A. S., Reis, H. T., & Rafaeli, E. (2006). Paper or plastic revisited: Let's keep them both – Reply to Broderick and Stone (2006); Tennen, Affleck, Coyne, Larsen, and DeLongis (2006); and Takarangi, Garry, and Loftus (2006). *Psychological Methods, 11*(1), 123–125. doi:10.1037/1082–989X.11.1.123.

Brainard, S. G., & Carlin, L. (1998). A six-year longitudinal study of undergraduate women in engineering and science. *Journal of Engineering Education, 87*(4), 369–375.

Broderick, J. E., & Stone, A. A. (2006). Paper and electronic diaries: Too early for conclusions on compliance rates and their effects – Comment on Green, Rafaeli, Bolger, Shrout, and Reis (2006). *Psychological Methods, 11*(1), 106–111. doi:10.1037/1082–989X.11.1.123.

Ceci, S., Williams, W., & Barnett, S. (2009). Women's underrepresentation in science: Sociocultural and biological considerations. *Psychological Bulletin, 135*(2), 218–261. doi:10.1037/a0014412 (Supplemental).

Chemers, M. M., Zurbriggen, E. L., Syed, M., Goza, B. K., & Bearman, S. (2011). Assessing the role of efficacy and identity in science career commitment among underrepresented minority students. *Journal of Social Issues, 67*(3), 510-530.

Crocker, J., Karpinski, A., Quinn, D. M., & Chase, S. K. (2003). When grades determine self-worth: Consequences of contingent self-worth for male and female engineering and psychology students. *Journal of Personality and Social Psychology, 85*(3), 507–516. doi:10.1037/0022–3514.85.3.507.

Eccles, J. S. (2007). Where are all the women? Gender differences in participation in physical science and engineering. In S. J. Ceci & W. M. Williams (Eds.), *Why aren't more women in science?* (pp. 199–210). Washington, DC: American Psychological Association.

Eccles, J., Midgley, C., Wigfield, A., Buchanan, C., Reuman, D., Flanagan, C., et al. (1993). Development during adolescence: The impact of stage-environment fit on young adolescents' experiences in schools and in families. *American Psychologist 48*(2), 90–101. doi:10.1037/0003–066X.48.2.90.

Erwin, L., & Maurutto, P. (1998). Beyond access: Considering gender deficits in science education. *Gender and Education, 10*(1), 51–69. doi:10.1080/0954025982109.

Ferreira, M. M. (2003). Gender issues related to graduate student attrition in two science departments. *International Journal of Science Education, 25*(8), 969–989. doi:10.1080/09500690220000038259.

Green, A. S., Rafaeli, E., Bolger, N., Reis, H. T., & Shrout, P. E. (2006). Paper or plastic? Data equivalence in paper and electronic diaries. *Psychological Methods, 11*(1), 87–105. doi:10.1037/1082–989X.11.1.87.

Guinier, L., Fine, M. & Balin, J. (1997) *Becoming gentleman: Women, law school, and institutional change.* Boston, MA: Beacon Press.

Inzlicht, M., & Ben-Zeev, T. (2003). Do high-achieving female students underperform in private? The implications of threatening environments on intellectual processing. *Journal of Educational Psychology, 95*(4), 796–805. doi:10.1037/0022–0663.95.4.796.

Jamison, R. N., Raymond, S. A., Levine, J. G., Slawsby, E. A., Nedeljkovic, S. S., & Katz, N. P. (2001). Electronic diaries for monitoring chronic pain: 1-year validation study. *Pain, 91*(3), 277–285. doi:10.1016/S0304–3959(00)00450–4.

Leadley, J. (2009) Women in U.S. academic medicine: Statistics and benchmarking report 2008–2009. Washington, DC: Association of American Medical Colleges.

Logel, C., Iserman, E. C., Davies, P. G., Quinn, D. M., & Spencer, S. J. (2009). The perils of double consciousness: The role of thought suppression in stereotype threat. *Journal of Experimental Social Psychology, 45*, 299–312.

Lo Sasso, A. T., Richards, M. R., Chou, C.-F., & Gerber, S. E. (2011). The \$16,819 pay gap for newly trained physicians: The unexplained trend of men earning more than women. *Health Affairs, 30*, 193–201. doi:10.1377/hlthaff.2010.0597.

London, B., Downey, G., Bolger, N., & Velilla, E. (2005). A framework for studying social identity and coping with daily stress during the transition to college. In G. Downey, J. S. Eccles, & C. Chatman (Eds.), *Navigating the future* (pp. 45–63). New York: Russell Sage Foundation.

London, B., Anderson, V., & Downey, G. (2007a). Studying institutional engagement: Utilizing social psychology research methodologies to study law student engagement. *Harvard Journal of Law and Gender, 30*, 389–407.

London, B., Downey, G., & Mace, S. (2007b). Psychological theories of educational engagement: A multi-dimensional approach to studying individual engagement and institutional change. *Vanderbilt Law Review, 60*, 455–481.

London, B., Downey, G., Rattan, A., & Tyson, D. (2010) Gender rejection sensitivity: Implications for women's well-being and achievement in gender stereotyped contexts. Manuscript submitted for publication.

London, B., Rosenthal, L., Levy, S., & Lobel, M. (in press). The influences of perceived identity compatibility and social support on women in non-traditional fields during the college transition. *Basic and Applied Social Psychology*.

Mertz, E. (2007). Semiotic anthropology. *Annual Review of Anthropology*, 36337–36353. doi:10.1146/annurev.anthro.36.081406.094417.

National Association for Law Placement. (2009). *Law firm diversity demographics show little change, despite economic downturn representation in some markets declines while others show small gains*. [Press release] Retrieved March 18, 2011, from http://www.nalp.org/uploads/PressReleases/09NALPWomenMinoritiesRel.pdf.

National Science Foundation. (2009). Division of science resources statistics, *Women, Minorities, and Persons with Disabilities in Science and Engineering: 2009*, NSF 09-305 (Arlington, VA; January 2009). Available from http://www.nsf.gov/statistics/wmpd/.

Nosek, B. A., Banaji, M. R., & Greenwald, A. G. (2002). Math = male, me = female, therefore math ≠ me. *Journal of Personality and Social Psychology, 83*(1), 44–59. doi:10.1037/0022–3514.83.1.44.

Pennebaker, J. W., & Beall, S. K. (1986). Confronting a traumatic event: Toward an understanding of inhibition and disease. *Journal of Abnormal Psychology, 95*(3), 274–281. doi:10.1037/0021–843X.95.3.274.

Pennebaker, J. W., Kiecolt-Glaser, J. K., & Glaser, R. (1988). Disclosure of traumas and immune function: Health implications for psychotherapy. *Journal of Consulting and Clinical Psychology, 56*(2), 239–245.

Pennebaker, J. W., Colder, M., & Sharp, L. K. (1990). Accelerating the coping process. *Journal of Personality and Social Psychology, 58*(3), 528–537. doi:10.1037/0022–3514.58.3.528.

Piasecki, T. M., Hufford, M. R., Solhan, M., & Trull, T. J. (2007). Assessing clients in their natural environments with electronic diaries: Rationale, benefits, limitations, and barriers. *Psychological Assessment, 19*(1), 25–43. doi:10.1037/1040–3590.19.1.25.

Pittinsky, T., Shih, M., & Ambady, N. (1999). Identity adaptiveness: Affect across multiple identities. *Journal of Social Issues, 55*(3), 503–518.

Rafaeli, E., Rogers, G. M., & Revelle, W. (2007). Affective synchrony: Individual differences in mixed emotions. *Personality and Social Psychology Bulletin, 33*(7), 915–932. doi:10.1177/0146167207301009.

Reis, H. T., & Gable, S. L. (2000). Event-sampling and other methods for studying everyday experience. In H. T. Reis & C. M. Judd (Eds.), *Handbook of research methods in social and personality psychology* (pp. 190–222). Cambridge, UK: Cambridge University Press.

Rosenthal, L., London, B., Levy, S. R., Lobel, M., Guarino, M., Bermeo, J., et al. (2009). *Role models increase women's engagement in science.* Poster presentation, American Psychological Association Annual Convention. Toronto, Canada.

Rosenthal, L., London, B., Levy. S. R., & Lobel, M. (2011). The roles of perceived identity compatibility and social support for women in a single-sex STEM program at a co-educational university. *Sex Roles.* doi:10.1007/s11199-011-9945-0.

Rosenthal, L., London, B., Levy, S. R., Lobel, M., & Herrera-Alcazar. A. (in press). The relation between the Protestant work ethic and undergraduate women's perceived identity compatibility in STEM majors.

Ruble, D., & Seidman, E. (1996). *Social transitions: Windows into social psychological processes. Social psychology: Handbook of basic principles* (pp. 830–856). New York: Guilford Press.

Settles, I. H. (2004). When multiple identities interfere: The role of identity centrality. *Personality and Social Psychology Bulletin, 30*(4), 487–500. doi:10.1177/0146167203261885.

Sheese, B. E., Brown, E. L., & Graziano, W. G. (2004). Emotional expression in cyberspace: Searching for moderators of the pennebaker disclosure effect via e-mail. *Health Psychology, 23*(5), 457–464. doi:10.1037/0278–6133.23.5.457.

Shih, M., Pittinsky, T. L., & Ambady, N. (1999). Stereotype susceptibility: Identity salience and shifts in quantitative performance. *Psychological Science, 10*, 81–84.

Shiffman, S., Hufford, M., Hickcox, M., Paty, J. A., Gnys, M., & Kassel, J. D. (1997). Remember that? A comparison of real-time versus retrospective recall of smoking lapses. *Journal of Consulting and Clinical Psychology, 65*(2), 292–300.

Sloan, D. M., & Marx, B. P. (2004). Taking pen to hand: Evaluating theories underlying the written disclosure paradigm. *Clinical Psychology: Science and Practice, 11*(2), 121–137. doi:10.1093/clipsy/bph062.

Smart Richman, L., vanDellen, M., & Wood, W. (2011). How women cope: Being a numerical minority in a male-dominated profession. *Journal of Social Issues, 67*(3), 492–509.

Smith, R. E., Leffingwell, T. R., & Ptacek, J. T. (1999). Can people remember how they coped? Factors associated with discordance between same-day and retrospective reports. *Journal of Personality and Social Psychology, 76*(6), 1050–1061.

Spencer, S. J., Steele, C. M., & Quinn, D. M. (1999). Stereotype threat and women's math performance. *Journal of Experimental Social Psychology, 35*(1), 4–28. doi:10.1006/jesp.1998.1373.

Steele, J., & Ambady, N. (2006). 'Math is Hard!' The effect of gender priming on women's attitudes. *Journal of Experimental Social Psychology, 42*(4), 428–436. doi:10.1016/j.jesp.2005.06.003.

Steele, J., James, J. B., & Barnett, R. C. (2002). Learning in a man's world: Examining the perceptions of undergraduate women in male-dominated academic areas. *Psychology of Women Quarterly, 26*, 46–50.

Stone, A. A., & Shiffman, S. (2002). Capturing momentary, self-report data: A proposal for reporting guidelines. *Annals of Behavioral Medicine, 24*(3), 236–243.

Swim, J. K., Hyers, L. L., Cohen, L. L., & Ferguson, M. J. (2001). Everyday sexism: Evidence for its incidence, nature, and psychological impact from three daily diary studies. *Journal of Social Issues, 57*(1), 31–53.

Syed, M., Azmitia, & Cooper (2011). Identity and academic success among under-represented ethnic minorities: An interdisciplinary review and integration. *Journal of Social Issues, 67*(3), 442–468.

Takarangi, M. K. T., Garry, M., & Loftus, E. F. (2006). Dear diary, is plastic better than paper? I can't remember: Comment on Green, Rafaeli, Bolger, Shrout, and Reis (2006). *Psychological Methods, 11*(1), 119–122. doi:10.1037/1082–989X.11.1.119.

Tennen, H., Affleck, G., Coyne, J. C., Larsen, R. J., & DeLongis, A. (2006). Paper and plastic in daily diary research: Comment on Green, Rafaeli, Bolger, Shrout, and Reis (2006). *Psychological Methods, 11*(1), 112–118. doi:10.1037/1082–989X.11.1.112.

Terry, P. C., Stevens, M. J., & Lane, A. M. (2005). Influence of response time frame on mood assessment. *Anxiety, Stress & Coping: An International Journal, 18*(3), 279–285. doi:10.1080/10615800500134688.

Thompson, A., & Bolger, N. (1999). Emotional transmission in couples under stress. *Journal of Marriage & the Family, 61*(1), 38–48.

U.S. Bureau of Labor Statistics. (2001). *Annual average tables from the January 2001 issue of Employment and Earnings (Table 11: Employed persons by detailed occupation, sex, race, and Hispanic origin)*. Retrieved on August 18, 2003 from http://www.bls.gov/cparticipantsaatab.htm.

Valian, V. (2005). *Sex disparities in advancement and income*. Retrieved on September 10, 2006, from http://www.hunter.cuny.edu/genderequity/equitymaterials.html.

Witkow, M. R., & Fuligni, A. J. (2011). Ethnic and generational differences in the relations between social support and academic achievement across the high school years. *Journal of Social Issues, 67*(3), 531–552.

BONITA LONDON is an Assistant Professor of Psychology in the Social and Health Psychology program at Stony Brook University, and an affiliate of the Women Studies Department. Dr. London's research focuses on the impact of social identity threat and coping on the social, health, and academic outcomes of women and students of color in the United States.

LISA ROSENTHAL completed her PhD in Social and Health Psychology at Stony Brook University and is currently a post-doctoral associate in Public Health at Yale University. Her research focuses on prejudice, discrimination, and intergroup relations. Her interests include intergroup ideologies and their relationships with intergroup attitudes; the consequences of being a member of a stigmatized group, including social, health, and academic outcomes; and the intersections of social identities, such as gender and race.

ANGEL GONZALEZ is a fifth-year doctoral student in the Social and Health Psychology program at Stony Brook University. His research focuses on the experience of discrimination from the targets perspective. His research interests include the impact of discrimination on affective and cognitive processes; ways in which negative intergroup interactions can be processed to diminish negative outcomes; and intragroup rejection concerns of members of traditionally stigmatized groups.

Journal of Social Issues, Vol. 67, No. 3, 2011, pp. 531–552

Ethnic and Generational Differences in the Relations between Social Support and Academic Achievement across the High School Years

Melissa R. Witkow*
Willamette University

Andrew J. Fuligni
University of California

Changes in adolescents' reports of social support from parents and friends were examined across the 4 years of high school to examine associations between support and academic achievement. Results from 541 adolescents from diverse backgrounds suggest that changes in encouragement from parents and friends within individual adolescents are associated with concurrent changes in grade point average (GPA). Between-person analyses indicate that adolescents who report higher levels of encouragement in ninth grade are more likely to enroll in courses and receive grades that make them eligible to enroll in California's public university system. Both GPA and eligibility, in turn, were associated with higher rates of enrollment in college after high school. Many of these findings varied according to ethnicity and generation, reinforcing the importance of understanding the extent to which adolescents from diverse backgrounds have access to the information and support that is necessary to take advantage of the postsecondary educational system.

With the growing immigrant population in the United States (e.g., Zhou, 1997), an important question is the extent to which this group is able to take advantage of the postsecondary educational system that is critical for a successful transition to adulthood (Halperin, 1998). Most research examining ethnic and

*Correspondence concerning this article should be addressed to Melissa R. Witkow, Psychology Department, Willamette University, 900 State St. Salem, OR 97301 [e-mail: mwitkow@ willamette.edu].

Support for this study was provided by the Russell Sage Foundation and the John Randolph and Dora Haynes Foundation.*

immigrant generational differences in educational experiences during adolescence has tended to focus on grades and test scores during high school (e.g., Fuligni, 1997; Kao & Tienda, 1995). These studies have demonstrated that youth from immigrant families often receive grades at least as good as those from nonimmigrant families (Fuligni, 1997; Fuligni and Witkow, 2004; Hagelskamp, Suarez-Orozco, & Hughes, 2010; Kao & Tienda, 1995), and youth from Asian backgrounds perform better than youth from Latino families (Fuligni & Witkow, 2004; Hagelskamp et al., 2010). These ethnic differences are at least partially attributable to higher education levels of parents with Asian backgrounds prior to immigration.

Receiving high grades in high school, however, is not enough to ensure that an adolescent will qualify for college admissions, particularly a 4-year college or university. The extent to which students successfully complete college preparatory courses is critical because even the highest of grades does not guarantee college admissions if high school course requirements are not met. To be eligible for many 4-year colleges, adolescents have to have successfully completed a specific set of courses. For example, the two public university systems in the state of California, the University of California and the California State University, have a set of high school course requirements that go beyond the graduation requirements of many high schools in California, including the three schools reported on in this study. These requirements, termed the "a-g" requirements, include 3 years of math, including algebra I, geometry, and algebra II, 2 years of a foreign language, and a grade of at least a "C" in each academic course (California State University Admissions, 2009; University of California Admissions, 2009). In contrast, high school graduation often requires only 2 years of math, without specifying what courses these should be, does not require a foreign language, and allows grades as low as "D" as passing. Other requirements, including those of English, history/social science, and laboratory science, tend to be similar to high school graduation requirements.

Many youth from immigrant families report working hard in school and getting good grades out of a sense of obligation to their parents (Fuligni & Pedersen, 2002). Unlike working hard to get good grades, however, enrolling in a college preparatory curriculum and meeting postsecondary admissions requirements often involves external support and information (see also Aurora, Schneider, Thal, & Meltzer, 2011). That is, the default curriculum may not be one that would allow a student to be University of California/California State University (UC/CSU) eligible upon graduation. The purpose of this study is therefore to examine ethnic and generational differences in both the extent to which parents and friends are sources of support for academics, and whether this support is associated with high school academic achievement and UC/CSU eligibility. Additionally, we will examine the extent to which grades, UC/CSU eligibility, and high school math course enrollment are associated with enrollment in a 4-year college or university 2 years after graduating from high school.

One important feature of the current study is our ability to examine within-person change in social support over the 4 years of high school. We are therefore able to model normative change within individual adolescents across the high school years as a function of their UC/CSU eligibility upon graduation. Yet individual adolescents may change quite a bit from year to year in their perceptions of support, without necessarily heading in a single linear direction (see also Green, Rhodes, Hirsch, Suarez-Orozco, & Camic, 2008). Analysis of normative change by itself does not allow for examination of how that change is associated with concurrent changes within individual adolescents in other aspects of their lives. By longitudinally correlating within-person fluctuations in social support with fluctuations in grades, we can obtain important information on how these two experiences unfold simultaneously.

In all of the analyses, we will examine the extent to which patterns vary according to ethnicity, between Latino (primarily Mexican), Asian (primarily Chinese), and European-American adolescents. Further, for the Latino and Asian participants, we will examine differences according to immigrant generation. For both groups, the majority of the participants are of the second generation. Finally, we will examine the extent to which parent education, as a measure of socioeconomic status, accounts for any ethnic differences that are observed.

It is our hope that these analyses will allow us to suggest specific ways in which schools can take advantage of parental and peer support to promote success beyond the high school classroom. In particular, given current economic realities, high schools should aim for preparing their students of all ethnic, immigrant, and socioeconomic backgrounds for college, and particularly for degrees and careers in math, science, and engineering. These are the fields that will allow the United States to continue to be competitive in the international field, and in which ethnic minority youth continue to be underrepresented (Gándara & Maxwell-Jolly, 1999).

Parents and Friends as Sources of Social Support

Parents and friends can both be important sources of support and encouragement for education during adolescence (Brown, Mounts, Lamborn, & Steinberg, 1993). However, the extent to which they can help an adolescent prepare for postsecondary admissions depends upon the extent to which they have access to information about admissions requirements. Whether one's parents and friends have this information likely varies according to individual background characteristics, including the ethnicity and immigrant status of the adolescent (see Syed, Azmitia, & Cooper, 2011). On the one hand, ethnic minority youth and youth from immigrant families have parents who value education strongly and the youth themselves are likely to work hard in school out of a sense of obligation to their parents (Fuligni & Pedersen, 2002; Kao & Tienda, 1995). However, one challenge facing many youth from immigrant families, particularly those with Latino backgrounds, is that their parents may not have the social capital (e.g., Crosnoe, Cavanagh, & Elder, 2003) to enable them to make informed decisions about their educational careers, even if they value and encourage education strongly (see also Coleman, 1988). For example, parents may not have experience in navigating the college admissions process (Cooper, Chavira, & Mena, 2005), and are often unfamiliar with the U.S. educational system in general and the role that they are expected to play in their children's education (Kao & Tienda, 1995; Seidman et al., 1999). Parents may also feel uncomfortable interacting with school personnel if they are not comfortable speaking English or do not speak it well (Kao & Tienda, 1995). Further, while parents of Asian adolescents are more likely than parents of European-American adolescents to attempt to provide resources to help their children excel in school (Coleman, 1988), they tend to be somewhat less involved in the day to day experiences of their children's schooling, in terms of activities such as attending school programs and helping with homework (Crosnoe, 2001). Because of these differences in social capital and cultural practices, the sense of obligation that ethnic minority and immigrant youth feel is more likely to be related to grades than to enrollment in a college preparatory curriculum.

Regardless of the extent to which parents can and do provide support, friends can be an important source of information, social capital, and support, provided that they themselves have access to information. Peers whose parents do not face the barriers described above are able to share the information they are in possession of with their friends. However, because adolescents tend to be friends with others who share their ethnic background (Kandel, 1978; Way & Chen, 2000), adolescents from ethnic minority backgrounds are more likely to be friends with adolescents who have similarly low levels of social capital, and therefore do not "come across" useful information about college. Whether or not they have information, there are also ethnic differences in the extent to which peer groups tend to be supportive of academics more generally, with Asian adolescents experiencing the most support from same-ethnic friends (e.g., Crosnoe et al., 2003; Steinberg et al., 1992). These ethnic differences are likely to be exacerbated because of ethnic differences in patterns of enrollment in college preparatory courses. Enrollment in college preparatory courses therefore has multiple benefits: preparation for college admissions and a higher likelihood of access to friends with social capital. It is therefore expected that differences between adolescents in the extent to which support from friends is associated with achievement will be consistent with overall ethnic differences in achievement.

Forms of Social Support

Social support can take multiple forms. From both parents and friends, we examine two forms of support in this study: talking about school, including future educational plans, and encouragement for taking high-level courses and continuing one's education beyond high school. These may vary in terms of both the reasons for the support and the role that social capital plays in the existence of the support. While one parent and adolescent may talk about school as a form of parental monitoring because the adolescent has not done well in the past (Crosnoe, 2001), another parent and adolescent may talk about school because the adolescent is engaged and wants to share that with his/her parent. A low level of talking about school, however, is likely to be associated with poor achievement because it reflects negatively on the parent–child relationship (Melby, Conger, Fang, Wickrama, & Conger, 2008), particularly because both the parent and adolescent have to be willing partners in the conversation. Some adolescents may choose not to share information about school with their parents, particularly in cases in which they feel as though they may not be living up to their standards (Qin, Way, & Mukherjee, 2008).

In terms of friends, talking about school is likely to be associated with higher levels of achievement because students who are engaged and achievement oriented are likely to share that with their friends (e.g., Ryan, 2001). Further, adolescents with friends at school to talk with about school are likely to be more engaged, which is also associated with achievement (Goodenow, 1993). More so than for talking, encouragement is likely to reflect an assessment of the adolescents' actual prospects (Crosnoe, 2001). Encouragement, from both parents and friends, is therefore more likely when the adolescent is doing well in school and future prospects seem good, and is expected to be more strongly predictive of achievement than talking.

Because talking is less specific than encouragement, it is expected to be less strongly tied to social capital, and thus less variable according to ethnicity and generation. That is, a parent who does not understand the U.S. educational system can still talk with his/her child about school. Indeed, transmission of parents' values of the importance of school is likely one of the reasons that immigrant children work so hard in school (Fuligni, Tseng, & Lam, 1999). However, encouragement carries with it an expectation that the adolescent, if he/she works hard, will be able to attend college. Parents may be less likely to encourage their adolescent if they are unsure of his/her prospects and/or their ability to pay for postsecondary education. Immigrant and/or ethnic minority parents may therefore be less likely to encourage their adolescents to take high-level courses and continue their education beyond high school than European-American parents.

The Current Study

The goal of this study is to examine both within- and between-person achievement-related correlates of social support from friends and parents. Within adolescents, we will examine year-to-year changes in social support as they relate to concurrent changes in grade point average (GPA). Between adolescents, we will examine trajectories of social support according to UC/CSU eligibility. Finally, we will examine the extent to which these variables are associated with postsecondary enrollment.

Within adolescents, it is hypothesized that support from both parents and friends in the forms of talking and encouragement will be positively associated with GPA. That is, in years in which an adolescent reports receiving support, he/she will also receive higher grades. However, it is hypothesized that the relations between support from parents and grades will be weaker for Asian and Latino students than for European-American students, particularly those from immigrant families, as their parents are likely to have less social capital and be less comfortable in their relationships with teachers and administrators at school.

Between adolescents, it is hypothesized that those who are UC/CSU eligible will report higher levels of support throughout high school, and that this difference will already exist by ninth grade. Even at the very beginning of high school, students are segregated from other peers through the courses in which they are enrolled. Those who are enrolled in college preparatory courses and doing well in those courses, and therefore more likely to be UC/CSU eligible upon graduation, are likely to have a high-achieving friendship group (Ryan, 2001) that provides them with support. Ethnic differences in support from parents are expected, mirroring ethnic differences in parental involvement in their children's academic careers (see Crosnoe, 2001).

Across ethnic groups, the extent to which these differences will manifest themselves in different trajectories over time is unclear. On the one hand, for high-achieving adolescents, friends may continue with their same high levels of support and parents may actually reduce their levels of support as they stop needing to actively monitor their adolescent and can give him/her more independence (Crosnoe, 2001; Muller, 1998). On the other hand, both parents and friends may increase their levels of support as college planning becomes more immediate and students begin to have realistic assessments of their postsecondary prospects.

Finally, it is hypothesized that enrollment in a 4-year college or university 2 years after high school graduation will be associated with both GPA and UC/CSU eligibility. In particular, we hypothesize that adolescents who are UC/CSU eligible upon graduation will be more likely to be enrolled in a 4-year college or university. Additionally, consistent with our conceptualization of UC/CSU eligibility being associated with differences in social support as early as ninth grade, we hypothesize that differences will exist in high school grades according to enrollment in college. That is, differences in grades will be apparent in the high school data prior to college enrollment. Given that there are likely to be some students enrolled in a 4-year college or university who were not UC/CSU eligible, we will further examine the extent to which high school math course enrollment in particular is associated with 4-year college enrollment. Math enrollment may be particularly important given that most 4-year colleges require 3 years of math coursework, while not necessarily following the other UC/CSU requirements.

Method

Sample

Beginning in ninth grade and continuing yearly through twelfth grade, students from three public high schools in the Los Angeles area were recruited for participation in a longitudinal study. The sample used in the present analyses was the 541 participants from European, Asian, and Latin American families who had participated in the study for at least two of the four years during high school ($M = 3.50$ years, $SD = 0.70$). The sample was evenly split by gender (263 male, 278 female). The majority of the 244 participants from Asian families were from Chinese backgrounds (77.0%), and the majority of the 196 participants from Latin American families had Mexican backgrounds (87.8%). Of the Asian participants, 79 were of the first generation (i.e., the students were foreign-born themselves), 151 were of the second generation (i.e., the students were born in the United States), and 14 were of the third generation or greater (i.e., both the students and their parents were born in the United States). Asian first-generation participants were on average 7.43 years old ($SD = 3.92$) when they came to the United States. Of the participants from Latin American families, 35 were of the first generation, 122 were of the second generation, and 39 were of the third generation or greater. Latino first-generation participants were on average 4.09 years old ($SD = 3.50$) when they came to the United States. Of the 101 participants from European-American families, 8 were of the first generation, 6 were of the second generation, and 87 were of the third generation or greater. See Kiang, Witkow, Baldelomar & Fuligni (2010), for a more complete description of the high school sample.

Of the 541 participants included in the main sample, 341 participants also completed the follow-up study 2 years after high school and are included in the postsecondary analyses. The subsample was ethnically diverse: 30% Latino, 53% Asian, and 17% European-American, although compared to the full sample, Asian participants were over-represented while Latino participants were under-represented, χ^2 (2, $N=541$) $= 23.16$, $p<.001$. Much of this difference is due to the fact that adolescents who were UC/CSU eligible were more likely to participate, χ^2 (1, $N=519$) $= 37.56$, $p < .001$.

Procedure

During high school, students completed a questionnaire during class time each spring. Consent forms and study materials were available in English, Chinese, and Spanish. Fewer than eight participants chose to complete the questionnaires in a language other than English during any single year. Students' courses and grades for each academic year were obtained from their official school records after the completion of the school year.

Two years after high school, those who had participated in twelfth grade were contacted by phone, email, and mail. Those who agreed to complete a follow-up survey were given access to an online survey; a paper survey was completed by 10 participants without internet access.

Measures: Within-Person Variables

GPA. Course grades were collected from school records and GPAs were computed for each year of high school based on participants' grades in their academic courses (i.e., those meeting UC/CSU a-g requirements; California State University Admissions, 2009; University of California Admissions, 2009). GPAs were computed on a 5-point scale ($0 =$ "Fail" to $4 =$ "A").

Social support from friends. Each year, participants reported the extent to which they talked to their friends about academics and received encouragement from friends to take advanced courses and pursue postsecondary education. The talk variable consisted of three items, based on Fuligni and colleagues (1999). Participants reported how often, with their friends, they talk about "future job plans," "future educational plans," and "the classes you are taking in school." Participants responded to each item on a 5-point scale ($1 = almost never$, $5 = almost always$). Internal consistencies were similarly high for members of all three ethnic groups across the 4 years of the study, $\alpha s = .66$ to $.87$. The encouragement variable consisted of two items. Participants reported how often their friends "encouraged you to take college placement or honors courses" and "encouraged you to continue your education after high school." Participants responded to each item on a 5-point scale ($1 = almost never$, $5 = almost always$). The two items were highly correlated for all three ethnic groups across the 4 years of the study, $rs = .38$ to $.75$, $ps < .001$. Both variables were recoded to a $0-4$ scale for ease of interpretation.

Social support from parents. The talk with parents and encouragement from parents variables mirrored the social support from friends items described above. For the talk with parents variable, internal consistencies were similarly high for members of all three ethnic groups across the 4 years of the study, $\alpha s = .60$ to $.87$. For the encouragement from parents variable, the two items were highly correlated for members of all three ethnic groups across the 4 years of the study, $rs = .30$ to $.48$, $ps < .01$, with the exception of European-American adolescents in twelfth grade, for whom the correlation was somewhat weaker, $r = .22$, $p < .05$.

Measures: Between-Person Variables

UC/CSU eligibility. Students were classified as being UC/CSU eligible if it could be determined that their courses and grades exceeded their high school graduation requirements to meet those required for admission to the University of California and the California State University (0 = did not meet UC/CSU eligibility requirements, 1 = did meet UC/CSU eligibility requirements). In particular, students were determined to be eligible if they had successfully completed algebra I, geometry, and algebra II, and 2 years of the same foreign language, and had received at least a "C" in all of their academic courses. Eligibility could be determined for some adolescents who were missing course record information in at least 1 year of the study. For example, a student who had record information from just 1 year and in that year received many grades of D could not be eligible. Eligibility could not be determined for 22 participants because they were missing at least 1 year of course records and the information from that missing year(s) was needed to determine whether or not they were eligible.

Postsecondary enrollment. Two years after completing high school, participants were asked whether they were currently taking courses at a 2- or 4-year college. If so, they were asked whether they were enrolled in a "community college," "4-year college or university," "vocational school," "technical school," or "trade school." Participants were classified as to whether or not they were enrolled in a 4-year college of university (0 = not enrolled in a 4-year college or university, 1 = enrolled in a 4-year college or university).

Results

Within-Person Associations between Social Support and GPA

Our first goal was to examine the concurrent relations between social support and GPA, within individual adolescents, across the high school years. Hierarchical linear models (Bryk & Raudenbusch, 1992) were used, given our longitudinally nested, within-person data. This method allows for the partitioning of variance into within- and between-person components to examine the extent to which within-person associations between social support and GPA vary according to features of the individual, such as gender and ethnicity. Because there was a maximum of four time points per person, and some participants had only two or three time points, we did not have enough degrees of freedom to estimate all of the support variables simultaneously. Separate models were therefore estimated for each of the four support variables (i.e., talk with friends, encouragement from friends, talk with parents, and encouragement from parents). The general form of the model used for these analyses was as follows:

$$\text{GPA}_{ij} = b_{0j} + b_{1j}(\text{Support}) + b_{2j}(\text{Year}) + e_{ij} \tag{1}$$

$$b_{0j} = c_{00} + c_{01}(\text{Gender}) + c_{02}(\text{Ethnicity}) + u_{0j} \tag{2}$$

$$b_{1j} = c_{10} + c_{11}(\text{Gender}) + c_{12}(\text{Ethnicity}) + u_{1j}. \tag{3}$$

Equation 1 shows how adolescents' GPA in a particular year (i) for a particular individual (j) was modeled as a function of the individuals' average GPA (b_{0j}) and social support. Equations 2 and 3 show how the average GPA and the effect of social support were modeled as a function of gender and ethnicity. Gender was effects coded such that males $=-1$ and females $=1$. Ethnicity was indicated with two dummy codes representing Latino and Asian, leaving European-American as the baseline condition. Year of study was included in Equation 1 as a control variable, given normative declines in GPA over the four years of high school, and was coded such that year $1 = 0$, year $2 = 1$, year $3 = 2$, and year $4 = 3$. Social support was uncentered, given that a score of zero on this scale is conceptually meaningful, allowing for straightforward interpretation of the results (see Schwartz & Stone, 1998).

As shown in Table 1, in contrast to our hypothesis, talking with friends was not associated with GPA, nor were there ethnic differences in this association. Consistent with our hypothesis, however, there was a positive association between encouragement from friends and GPA, a relation that held across ethnic groups. In contrast, the patterns for the relations between social support from parents and GPA did vary according to ethnic group. For Latino adolescents only ($b = .12, p < .001$), talking with parents was positively associated with GPA. Encouragement from parents was positively associated with GPA for European-American adolescents and Asian adolescents, although the relation was weaker for Asian adolescents ($b = .06, p < .05$), but not for Latino adolescents ($b = .02$, n.s.).

For the two analyses in which ethnic differences were found (i.e., talking with parents and encouragement from parents), follow-up analyses were conducted to determine whether these differences could be explained by socioeconomic status. For these analyses, parent education was added to Equations 2 and 3. In both of these tests, the ethnic differences were unchanged and parent education was not a significant predictor.

Finally, additional tests were performed to examine differences according to immigrant generation. Because generation and ethnicity were confounded, these tests were conducted within ethnic group. For Latino adolescents, Equations 2 and 3 were modified such that ethnicity was replaced with dummy codes representing second generation and third generation, with first generation serving as the baseline

Table 1. Hierarchical Linear Models Predicting GPA According to Social Support

	Talk with friends b (SE)	Encouragement from friends b (SE)	Talk with parents b (SE)	Encouragement from parents b (SE)
Intercept	2.89 (.13)	2.87 (.10)***	3.05 (.16)***	2.42 (.18)***
Gender	.08 (.05)	.14 (.05)**	.24 (.06)***	.22 (.07)**
Asian	.15 (.14)	.09 (.12)	−.01 (.18)	.47 (.21)*
Latino	−.65 (.16)***	−.54 (.13)***	−1.07 (.19)***	−.15 (.22)
Support	.06 (.05)	.08 (.03)*	−.01 (.05)	.19 (.05)***
Gender	.01 (.02)	−.02 (.01)	−.05 (.02)**	−.03 (.02)
Asian	−.05 (.06)	−.03 (.04)	02 (.05)	−.13 (.05)*
Latino	−.02 (.06)	−.08 (.04)	12 (.06)*	−.17 (.06)**
Year	−.11 (.02)***	−.10 (.02)***	−.09 (.02)***	−.09 (.02)***
Gender	.01 (.01)	.01 (.01)	.00 (.01)	.00 (.01)
Asian	.01 (.03)	.00 (.03)	.00 (.03)	.00 (.03)
Latino	−.01 (.03)	.00 (.03)	−.01 (.03)	−.03 (.03)

Notes. Gender was coded boys $= -1$, girls $= 1$.
Gender, ethnicity, year, and support were uncentered.
*$p<.05$, **$p<.01$, ***$p<.001$.

group. For Asian adolescents, because there were so few third-generation participants, comparisons were only conducted between first- and second-generation adolescents. Generation analyses were not conducted for European-American adolescents because so few were from immigrant families. For these analyses, there was no effect of generation for Latino adolescents, and just one for Asian adolescents. While there was no relation between parent encouragement and GPA for first-generation Asian adolescents, there was a positive relation for second-generation Asian adolescents ($b = .13, p < .05$).

This first set of analyses suggests that, in general, support from parents and friends is associated with GPA. Some of these relations vary by ethnicity, with a weaker relation between encouragement from parents and GPA for Latino and Asian (particularly first generation) adolescents, compared to European-American adolescents.

Change Over Time in Social Support According to UC/CSU Eligibility

The goal of the next set of analyses was to examine the association between UC/CSU eligibility and social support trajectories across the high school years. Of the 519 participants for whom UC/CSU eligibility could be determined, 142 (27.4%) were eligible. This varied according to ethnic group, χ^2 (2, $N=519$) $= 62.51$, $p<.001$, such that Latino participants (7.3%) were less likely to be eligible than Asian (39.1%) and European-American (39.6%) participants.

Hierarchical linear models were used to examine the extent to which adolescents reported changing levels of social support across the high school years, and whether these trajectories varied according to UC/CSU eligibility. An interaction term was included to test whether the effect of eligibility was moderated by ethnicity. The general form of the model used for these analyses was as follows:

$$\text{Support}_{ij} = b_{0j} + b_{1j}(\text{Year}) + e_{ij} \tag{4}$$

$$b_{0j} = c_{00} + c_{01}(\text{Gender}) + c_{02}(\text{Ethnicity}) + c_{03}(\text{UC/CSU eligibility}) \\ + c_{04}(\text{UC/CSU eligibility} \times \text{Ethnicity}) + u_{0j} \tag{5}$$

$$b_{1j} = c_{10} + c_{11}(\text{Gender}) + c_{12}(\text{Ethnicity}) + c_{13}(\text{UC/CSU eligibility}) \\ + c_{14}(\text{UC/CSU eligibility} \times \text{Ethnicity}) + u_{1j} \tag{6}$$

As shown in Equation 4, adolescents' reports of social support (i.e., talk with friends, encouragement from friends, talk with parents, encouragement from parents) in a particular year (i) for a particular individual (j) was modeled as a function of the average level of social support by the individual (b_{0j}) and the year of the study (b_{1j}). Equations 5 and 6 show how both the average social support and the effect of the year of the study were modeled as a function of adolescents' gender, ethnicity, whether or not they were UC/CSU eligible, and an interaction between ethnicity and UC/CSU eligibility.

As shown in Table 2, there were increases over time in adolescents' reports of talking with their friends and encouragement from friends. While Asian and Latino adolescents reported higher levels of encouragement from their friends in ninth grade, compared to European-American adolescents, the increase over time did not vary according to ethnic group. In contrast, while there was no change over time for European-American adolescents in social support from parents, Latino adolescents reported comparative decreases over time in encouragement from parents. Compared to European-American adolescents, Asian adolescents reported lower levels of talking with their parents in ninth grade, but higher levels of encouragement from their parents, differences that held steady across the high school years.

UC/CSU eligibility was not associated with changes over time in social support for members of any ethnic group. As hypothesized, however, it was associated with differences in adolescents' reports of encouragement from both friends and parents such that adolescents who were eligible reported higher levels of encouragement throughout high school. The effect of UC/CSU eligibility on encouragement from friends was weaker for Asian ($b = .29$,

Table 2. Hierarchical Linear Models Predicting Change over Time in Social Support as a Function of UC/CSU Eligibility

	Talk with friends $b\,(SE)$	Encouragement from friends $b\,(SE)$	Talk with parents $b\,(SE)$	Encouragement from parents $b\,(SE)$
Intercept	2.09 (.12)***	1.61 (.16)***	2.88 (.10)***	3.04 (.12)***
Gender	.15 (.04)***	.21 (.05)***	.00 (.04)	−.01 (.04)
Asian	.11 (.14)	.58 (.18)**	−.30 (.13)*	.28 (.13)*
Latino	.10 (.14)	.43 (.18)*	−.11 (.12)	.21 (.13)
UC/CSU eligibility	.28 (.16)	.99 (.23)***	.10 (.15)	.52 (.15)***
Asian×eligibility	−.17 (.20)	−.70 (.27)**	−.08 (.19)	−.40 (.18)*
Latino×eligibility	−.10 (.27)	−.80 (.37)*	.36 (.25)	−.28 (.21)
Year	.18 (.05)***	.17 (.06)**	.05 (.04)	−.03 (.04)
Gender	−.01 (.02)	−.03 (.02)*	.04 (.02)*	.02 (.01)
Asian	−.01 (.06)	−.01 (.07)	−.03 (.05)	−.08 (.05)
Latino	−.04 (.06)	−.07 (.07)	−.06 (.05)	−.11 (.05)*
UC/CSU eligibility	−.01 (.07)	−.01 (.08)	−.02 (.05)	−.01 (.05)
Asian×eligibility	.02 (.08)	.03 (.10)	.01 (.07)	.06 (.07)
Latino×eligibility	−.01 (.10)	.02 (.13)	−.05 (.10)	−.05 (.11)

Notes. Gender was coded boys $= -1$, girls $= 1$.
Gender, ethnicity, and year were uncentered.
*$p<.05$, **$p<.01$, ***$p<.001$.

$p < .05$) and Latino ($b = .19$, n.s.) adolescents than for European-American adolescents. Similarly, the effect of UC/CSU eligibility on encouragement from parents was weaker for Asian ($b = .12$, n.s.) adolescents compared to European-American adolescents.

Follow-up analyses were again conducted to determine whether parent education could explain any of the ethnic differences. In no case was parent education a significant predictor. With parent education in the model, only one ethnic difference was changed. Controlling for parent education, the difference between Asian and European-American adolescents in talking with parents in ninth grade was no longer significant ($b = -.23$, n.s.).

Finally, there were no generation differences for Asian adolescents and just one difference for Latino adolescents. In ninth grade, second- ($b = -.50$, $p < .01$) and third- generation ($b = -.58$, $p < .01$) Latino adolescents reported talking with their friends less about school than first generation Latino adolescents. However, they also reported increases in talking with their friends over time (second generation: $b = .20$, $p < .05$; third generation: $b = .26$, $p<.01$).

This set of analyses suggests that, even though support trajectories vary across the high school years, UC/CSU eligibility is more strongly related to support in ninth grade than to change in support across the high school years. The relation between eligibility and support in the form of encouragement varied by ethnicity, with a weaker relation for Latino (in the parent domain) and Asian adolescents (in both the parent and peer domains) than for European-American adolescents.

Postsecondary Enrollment

The final goal of this study was to examine the extent to which high school grades and UC/CSU eligibility were associated with postsecondary enrollment. Because almost 90% of participants reported being currently enrolled in some type of postsecondary education and because both the University of California and California State University are 4-year institutions, participants were classified as to whether or not they were enrolled in a 4-year college or university 2 years after completing high school. A total of 203 participants (59.5%) reported being currently enrolled in a 4-year college or university. This varied by ethnicity, χ^2 (2, $N=341$) $= 62.90$, $p < .001$, such that Latino participants (27%) were less likely to be enrolled in a 4-year college or university than Asian (72%) and European-American (78%) participants. While 99 (72%) of the students who were not enrolled in a 4-year college or university were enrolled in a 2-year college, we included these students in the group not currently enrolled in a 4-year college or university because the transfer rate in California from 2- to 4-year colleges is very low, with only 40% of students attempting to transfer successfully doing so within 6 years (California Community College Chancellor's Office, 2009).

To examine whether postsecondary enrollment was associated with trajectory of high school grades, Equations 4, 5, and 6 were modified such that GPA was the outcome variable in Equation 4 and enrollment and enrollment by ethnicity interactions replaced eligibility in Equations 5 and 6. As shown in Table 3, as hypothesized, participants who were enrolled in a 4-year college or university had higher grades in ninth grade. This effect was stronger for Latino than European-American participants, although significant for members of all three ethnic groups. For European-American adolescents, while grades declined over time for participants who were not enrolled, this effect was reduced for those who were enrolled. For Latino and Asian adolescents, grades declined over time regardless of enrollment status.

Parent education was also a significant predictor in this set of analyses. Adolescents whose parents had more education had higher grades in ninth grade ($b=.05, p<.05$), but a sharper decrease in their grades over time ($b=-.02, p<.01$). Inclusion of parent education reduced to nonsignificance the main effects of ethnicity on change in GPA over time. However, the interactions between enrollment and ethnicity remained unchanged. There were no differences according to generation for Latino or Asian adolescents.

As hypothesized, as with grades there was a significant association between UC/CSU eligibility and enrollment in a 4-year college or university, χ^2 (1, $N=329$) $= 87.79$, $p<.001$. While 92.5% of UC/CSU eligible high school students were

Table 3. Hierarchical Linear Model Predicting Change over Time in GPA as a Function of Whether or not a Participant is Enrolled in a 4-Year Degree Program 2 years after High School

	GPA $b\,(SE)$
Intercept	$2.89\,(.14)^{***}$
Gender	$.06\,(.03)$
Asian	$-.28\,(.17)$
Latino	$-.60\,(.16)^{***}$
Enrollment	$.45\,(.15)^{**}$
Asian×enrollment	$.32\,(.17)$
Latino×enrollment	$.45\,(.21)^{*}$
Year	$-.22\,(.04)^{***}$
Gender	$-.01\,(.01)$
Asian	$.11\,(.05)^{*}$
Latino	$.10\,(.05)^{*}$
Enrollment	$.17\,(.04)^{***}$
Asian×enrollment	$-.13\,(.06)^{*}$
Latino×enrollment	$-.23\,(.07)^{***}$

Notes. Gender was coded boys $= -1$, girls $= 1$.
Gender, ethnicity, and year were uncentered.
$^{*}p<.05$, $^{**}p<.01$, $^{***}p<.001$.

enrolled in a 4-year college or university 2 years after high school (although not necessarily a UC or CSU), only 39.7% of non-UC/CSU eligible high school students were enrolled. This relation was similar across ethnic groups, χ^2 (1, $Ns = 56-173) = 16.40-27.81, ps < .001$ and did not vary according to generation.

Given that many students in our sample were enrolled in a 4-year college or university without having met UC/CSU requirements, a final analysis was conducted to determine the extent to which math course enrollment during high school was associated with 4-year college enrollment. While 75.0% of participants who had completed algebra I, geometry, and algebra II during high school were enrolled in a 4-year college or university, only 18.6% of those who did not complete these courses were enrolled, χ^2 (1, $N=330) = 84.48, p<.001$.

This final set of analyses confirms that UC/CSU eligibility during high school is associated with enrollment in a 4-year college or university after graduation. Adolescents who were enrolled in college also had higher grades throughout high school, although the association between enrollment and trajectory of grades varied according to ethnic group.

Discussion

To identify the extent to which adolescents from immigrant families are able to realize their parents' wishes for them in terms of financial and occupational success

(Fuligni, 1997), it is critical that they are able to access the postsecondary education system (Halperin, 1998). The current study extends previous research examining adolescents' grades during high school (e.g., Fuligni, 1997) to understand ethnic and immigrant generational differences in adolescents' access to social supports that can enable them to navigate college eligibility requirements during high school, and enroll in a 4-year college or university after graduation. In line with other work on social capital (e.g., Coleman, 1988; Crosnoe, 2001), we found that patterns of support for education, particularly for pursuing high-level course work in high school and college admissions, is related to the likelihood one is able to access educational information.

Consistent with work examining ethnic differences in achievement during high school, we found many ethnic differences in the roles of support from parents and friends on academic achievement. As hypothesized, within adolescents, the relation between encouragement from parents and GPA was stronger for European-American adolescents than for Asian or Latino adolescents, with the relation being significant only for European-American adolescents and second-generation Asian adolescents. This suggests that immigrant parents may not feel confident in their abilities to specifically encourage their sons and daughters to take high-level courses and pursue postsecondary education, potentially because of a lack of understanding of the U.S. educational system (Cooper et al., 2005).

In contrast, the relation between encouragement from friends and GPA was consistent across groups, suggesting that even though members of some ethnic groups are less likely to have engaged and supportive friends (e.g., Steinberg et al., 1992), when encouragement is received it operates similarly across groups. This finding may also reflect differences in one's friendship group as a function of one's academic track. Regardless of ethnicity, adolescents in college preparatory classes are more likely to have high achieving and academically supportive friends than those enrolled in lower level classes. Further, college planning is likely to be more relevant for those in college preparatory courses.

In contrast to the relation between encouragement and GPA, with the exception of the association between talking with parents and GPA for Latino adolescents, neither talking about school with parents nor friends was associated with GPA for members of any group. This may reflect the different reasons for talking about school. For instance, some adolescents may talk with their friends about school to complain, while others to seek out support or study together. Similarly, some low-achieving adolescents may talk with their parents about school because their parents are actively monitoring their progress. High-achieving adolescents, in contrast, may talk with their parents about school to obtain help or to discuss future opportunities (Crosnoe, 2001; Muller, 1998). The significant relation for Latino adolescents between talking with parents about school and GPA potentially reflects the importance of education that Latino parents, particularly those from immigrant families, convey to their children (Fuligni et al., 1999).

While the relations between support and GPA were examined within adolescents, to determine the extent to which change in support in a given year was associated with concurrent changes in GPA, the relations between support and UC/CSU eligibility were examined somewhat differently. Because UC/CSU eligibility was not a time-varying predictor, we instead examined the extent to which eligibility was associated with changes in perceptions of support over time. It is important to note that eligibility is not something that could be determined prior to the completion of high school. However, our results suggest that by the time they are in ninth grade, at least for European-American adolescents, the experiences of those who are going to be eligible are different than those who are not going to be eligible, with those who are going to be eligible reporting much higher levels of encouragement from both their parents and friends. This higher level of encouragement held constant across the high school years.

Like the results described for GPA, the relations between eligibility and support varied according to ethnicity. In particular, eligibility had a weaker effect on encouragement from friends for Asian than European-American adolescents, and was not significant for Latino adolescents. For Asian adolescents, this difference may reflect high levels of support for academics within the peer group (Steinberg et al., 1992). Indeed, non-UC/CSU eligible Asian adolescents reported higher levels of encouragement from friends than European-American adolescents. For Latino adolescents, this difference may reflect both higher levels of encouragement overall, as well as the very small percentage of Latino adolescents who were actually eligible. Similar to the finding regarding support from friends, the effect of eligibility on encouragement from parents was not significant for Asian adolescents, potentially reflecting generally higher levels of encouragement and support from parents (Coleman, 1988).

Finally, we demonstrated that patterns of adolescents' grades in high school and whether or not they were UC/CSU eligible were related to their postsecondary enrollment 2 years after graduation. Students who are able to enroll in college do not necessarily do so, as needs to contribute financially to the family and/or a lack of ability to finance one's education could prevent enrollment. Other work has demonstrated that youth from immigrant and Latino families are more likely to support their families financially in the years immediately after high school, and that Asian youth are less likely than other youth to work at a job while enrolled in college (Fuligni & Witkow, 2004). It is therefore important that there were not ethnic or generational differences in the relation between eligibility and enrollment in that potential obligations such as these did not seem to interfere with eligible students' ability to enroll in a 4-year college or university. Instead, virtually everybody who was eligible to enroll in a UC or CSU campus was enrolled in a 4-year college 2 years after graduating from high school.

Some non-UC/CSU eligible students also managed to be enrolled in a 4-year college or university 2 years after graduation. While this number was substantially smaller than that of those who were eligible, it is still important to understand how these students were able to do so. One explanation is that these students may have been enrolled in private or out-of-state schools with different requirements than UC/CSU. Even though requirements can vary, most schools require 3 years of math coursework, as supported by our follow-up analyses examining patterns of college enrollment according to high school math courses. Another explanation is that students who had not met UC/CSU requirements were able to remedy missing courses after high school graduation and prior to college enrollment.

It is important to note that for most analyses, parent education was not a significant predictor and did not account for ethnic differences (see also Azmitia, Cooper, & Brown, 2009). This suggests that differences in parental support, and its correlates, are not just due to education levels but are instead likely due to a constellation of factors which prevent ethnic minority parents from having access to the same kinds of information as European-American parents.

Limitations

While this study helps advance our understanding of the relations between social support and academic success among a diverse sample of adolescents, it is important to consider a number of limitations. First, we argued that adolescents may vary in their social capital, in the form of access to information about the U.S. educational system and college entrance requirements. However, we did not directly ask adolescents the extent to which they, their parents, or their friends were in possession of this information. While no amount of information can be conveyed without talking and encouragement, it is possible that some adolescents talk with their parents and friends about school without getting useful information and this possibility should be explored in future research.

We were also not able to directly test whether support from friends or parents was more important, or to test their interactive effects. In fact, it is likely that they are related to each other, as adolescents with good relationships with their parents are likely to have good relationships with their friends (Brown et al., 1993). These adolescents are likely to share information obtained from their parents with their friends, as well as the reverse. In future work it will be important to consider support from other sources as well, such as older siblings, teachers, mentors, and school counselors (Azmitia et al., 2009; Blake-Beard, Bayne, Crosby, & Muller, 2011; Chemers, Zurbriggen, Syed, Goza, & Bearman, 2011; Green et al., 2008; Hurtado et al., 2011; Phinney, Torres Campos, Padilla Kallemeyn, & Kim, 2011). However, while teachers are important in adolescents' achievement, the teachers one encounters are largely determined by one's course enrollment. Further, as demonstrated by Woolley, Kol, and Bown (2009), it is likely that support from teachers and other adults at school mediate the relations between support from parents and friends and achievement outcomes. That is, support from parents and/or friends enables adolescents to obtain support and information from teachers and counselors at school.

Additionally, our encouragement variable consisted of only two items, which were potentially tapping somewhat different constructs, depending on a students' track in school. In particular, the items asking about the extent to which participants' friends and parents have encouraged them to take college placement or honors courses likely has very different meanings for students already in AP or honors classes, compared to those who are not. Future studies should attempt to develop items that measure encouragement for academics more globally.

Finally, the participants in the follow-up sample were not entirely representative of the full high school sample, but instead were more likely to have been UC/CSU eligible during high school. Because of this, the majority of participants were enrolled in college 2 years after graduation. A more representative sample would have allowed us to better examine the extent to which high school experiences (both academically and in terms of support) predicted attending a 2-year college versus not attending college, instead of collapsing these two categories as we did in this study. Examining this sample as they continue on in their educational experiences will allow us to further distinguish between those who go on to graduate with a 4-year degree and those who do not. If patterns of support in high school are predictive of the extent to which adolescents go on to graduate from college, the findings reported here would have even larger implications in terms of policy and intervention.

Implications and Conclusions

Overall, these results demonstrate the importance of intervention early in the high school years in making sure that adolescents know and understand college eligibility requirements. The strong associations between reports of support and UC/CSU eligibility in the ninth grade suggest that at the very beginning of high school many adolescents are already on a path that will either lead them toward or away from college. Part of the explanation for the importance of course enrollment in ninth grade has to do with the sequential nature of many courses. A student who does not start on a college preparatory trajectory early enough in math, for example, will not be able to catch up by taking multiple courses in a single year. Math course enrollment in high school is critical not only for college admissions, but also in preparing adolescents for careers in science and engineering. These are fields in which ethnic minority youth continue to be underrepresented (Gándara & Maxwell-Jolly, 1999). Equality in our society across ethnic and immigrant groups is dependent on equal access to careers in these domains.

Math also offers opportunities for intervention in that unlike subjects such as English, adolescents are not required to enroll in advanced math courses during high school. Changing high school graduation requirements, or having school personnel actively encourage more adolescents to enroll in advanced math courses early in high school may help offset a lack of parental knowledge and encouragement that may exist for some adolescents. This may be particularly important Latino adolescents, who are striking in the tremendous difference in their rate of UC/CSU eligibility, compared to European-American and Asian adolescents.

Given that parents who have gone to college are more easily able to guide their children through the college admissions process, interventions aimed at increasing college eligibility, enrollment, and graduation will have benefits for future generations as well. There is no time like the present to begin this process of increasing college access through high school course enrollment.

References

Aurora, V., Schneider, B., Thal, R., & Meltzer, D. (2011). Design of an intervention to promote entry of minority youth into clinical research careers by aligning ambition: The TEACH (training early achievers for careers in health) research program. *Journal of Social Issues, 67*(3), 580–598.

Azmitia, M., Cooper, C. R., & Brown, J. R. (2009). Support and guidance from families, friends, and teachers in Latino early adolescents' math pathways. *The Journal of Early Adolescence, 29*(1), 142–169. doi:10.1177/0272431608324476.

Blake-Beard, S., Bayne, M., Crosby, F., & Muller, C. (2011). Matching by race and gender in mentoring relationships: Keeping our eyes on the prize. *Journal of Social Issues, 67*(3), 622–643.

Brown, B. B., Mounts, N., Lamborn, S. D., & Steinberg, L. (1993). Parenting practices and peer group affiliation in adolescence. *Child Development, 64*(2), 467–482. doi:10.2307/1131263.

Bryk, A. S., & Raudenbush, S. W. (1992). *Hierarchical linear models: Applications and data analysis methods*. Thousand Oaks, CA: Sage.

California Community College Chancellor's Office. (2009). *Focus on Results: Accountability reporting for the California Community Colleges*. Retrieved on October 21, 2009, from http://www.cccco.edu/Portals/4/TRIS/research/ARCC/arcc_2009_final.pdf.

California State University Admissions (2009). *Undergraduate admissions requirements*. Retrieved on May 19, 2009, from http://www.calstate.edu/admission/.

Chemers, M. M., Zurbriggen, E. L., Syed, M., Goza, B. K., & Bearman, S. (2011). The role of efficacy and identity in science career commitment among underrepresented minority students. *Journal of Social Issues, 67*(3), 469–491.

Coleman, J. S. (1988). Social capital in the creation of human capital. *American Journal of Sociology, 94*, S95–S120.

Cooper, C. R., Chavira, G., & Mena, D. D. (2005). From pipelines to partnerships: A synthesis of research on how diverse families, schools, and communities support children's pathways through school. *Journal of Education for Students Placed at Risk, 10*(4), 407–430. doi:10.1207/s15327671espr1004_4.

Crosnoe, R. (2001). Academic orientation and parental involvement in education during high school. *Sociology of Education, 74*(3), 210–320.

Crosnoe, R., Cavanagh, S., & Elder, G. H. (2003). Adolescent friendships as academic resources: The intersection of friendship, race, and school disadvantage. *Sociological Perspectives, 46*(3), 331–352. doi:10.1525/sop.2003.46.3.331.

Fuligni, A. J. (1997). The academic achievement of adolescents from immigrant families: The roles of family background, attitudes, and behavior. *Child Development, 68*(2), 351–363.

Fuligni, A. J., & Pedersen, S. (2002). Family obligation and the transition to young adulthood. *Developmental Psychology, 38*(5), 856–868. doi:10.1037/0012–1649.38.5.856.

Fuligni, A. J., & Witkow, M. (2004). The postsecondary educational progress of youth from immigrant families. *Journal of Research on Adolescence, 14*(2), 159–183. doi:10.1111/j.1532–7795.2004.01402002.x.

Fuligni, A. J., Tseng, V., & Lam, M. (1999). Attitudes toward family obligations among American adolescents with Asian, Latin American, and European backgrounds. *Child Development, 70*(4), 1030–1044. doi:10.1111/1467–8624.00075.

Gándara, P., & Maxwell-Jolly, J. (1999). *Priming the pump: Strategies for increasing the achievement of underrepresented minority undergraduates*. New York, NY: The College Board.

Goodenow, C. (1993). Classroom belonging among early adolescent students: Relationships to motivation and achievement. *Journal of Early Adolescence, 13*(1), 21–43. doi:10.1177/0272431693013001002.

Green, G., Rhodes, J., Hirsch, A. H., Suarez-Orozco, C., & Camic, P. M. (2008). Supportive adult relationships and the academic engagement of Latin American immigrant youth. *Journal of School Psychology, 46*, 393–412. doi:10.1016/j.jsp.2007.07.001.

Hagelskamp, C., Suarez-Orozco, C., & Hughes, D. (2010). Migrating to opportunities: How family migration motivations shape academic trajectories among newcomer immigrant youth. *Journal of Social Issues, 66*(4), 717–739. doi:10.1111/j.1540–4560.2010.01672.x.

Halperin, S. (Ed.). (1998). *The forgotten half revisited: American youth and young families, 1988–2008*. Washington, DC: American Youth Policy Forum.

Hurtado, S., Eagan, M. K., Tran, M. C., Newman, C. E., Chang, M. J., & Velasco, P. (2011) "We do science here": Underrepresented students interactions with faculty in different college contexts. *Journal of Social Issues, 67*(3), 553–579.

Kandel, D. B. (1978). Homophily, selection, and socialization in adolescent friendships. *American Journal of Sociology, 84*(2), 427–436. doi:10.1086/226792.

Kao, G. & Tienda, M. (1995). Optimism and achievement: The educational performance of immigrant youth. *Social Science Quarterly, 76*(1), 1–19.

Kiang, L., Witkow, M. R., Baldelomar, O. A. & Fuligni, A. J. (2010). Change in ethnic identity across the high school years among adolescents with Latin American, Asian, and European backgrounds. *Journal of Youth and Adolescence, 39*(6), 683–693. doi:10.1007/s10964–009–9429–5.

Melby, J. N., Conger, R. D., Fang, S., Wickrama, K. A. S., & Conger, K. J. (2008). Adolescent family experiences and educational attainment during early adulthood. *Developmental Psychology, 44*(6), 1519–1536. doi:10.1037/a0013352.

Muller, C. (1998). Gender differences in parental involvement and adolescents' mathematics achievement. *Sociology of Education, 71*(4), 336–356. doi:10.2307/2673174.

Phinney, J. S., Torres Campos, C. M., Padilla Kallemeyn, D. M., & Kim, C. (2011). Processes and outcomes of a mentoring program for Latino college freshman. *Journal of Social Issues, 67*(3), 599–621.

Qin, D. B., Way, N., & Mukherjee, P. (2008). The other side of the model minority story: The familial and peer challenges faced by Chinese American adolescents. *Youth & Society, 39*(4), 480–506. doi:10.1177/0044118×08314233.

Ryan, A. M. (2001). The peer group as a context for the development of young adolescent motivation and achievement. *Child Development, 72*(4), 1135–1150. doi:10.1111/1467–8624.00338.

Schwartz, J. E. & Stone, A. A. (1998). Strategies for analyzing ecological momentary assessment data. *Health Psychology, 17*(1), 6–16. doi:10.1037/0278–6133.17.1.6.

Seidman, E., Chesir-Teran, D., Friedman, J. L., Yoshikawa, H., Allen, L., Roberts, A., et al. (1999). The risk and protective functions of perceived family and peer microsystems among urban adolescents in poverty. *American Journal of Community Psychology, 27*(2), 211–237. doi:10.1023/A:1022835717964.

Steinberg, L., Dornbusch, S. M., & Brown, B. B. (1992). Ethnic differences in adolescent achievement: An ecological perspective. *American Psychologist, 47*(6), 723–729. doi:10.1037/0003–066X.47.6.723.

Syed, M., Azmitia, M. & Cooper, C. R. (2011). Identity and academic success among under-represented ethnic minorities: An interdisciplinary review and integration. *Journal of Social Issues, 67*(3), 442–468.

University of California Admissions (2009). *Undergraduate admissions requirements*. Retrieved on May 19, 2009, from http://www.universityofcalifornia.edu/admissions/undergraduate.html.

Way, N., & Chen, L. (2000). Close and general friendships among African American, Latino, and Asian American adolescents from low-income families. *Journal of Adolescent Research, 15*(2), 274–301. doi:10.1177/0743558400152005.

Woolley, M. E., Kol, K. L., & Bowen, G. L. (2009). The social context of school success for Latino middle school students: Direct and indirect influences of teachers, family, and friends. *The Journal of Early Adolescence, 29*(1), 43–70. doi:10.1177/0272431608324478.

Zhou, M. (1997). Growing up American: The challenge confronting immigrant children and children of immigrants. *Annual Review of Sociology, 23*, 63–95. doi:10.1146/annurev.soc.23.1.63.

MELISSA R. WITKOW is Assistant Professor of Psychology at Willamette University. Dr. Witkow studies the intersection between peer relationships and academic motivation and achievement during adolescence, and how adolescents from diverse backgrounds negotiate the demands in their lives.

ANDREW J. FULIGNI is Professor of Psychology and Psychiatry at the University of California, Los Angeles. Dr. Fuligni's research has focused on family relationships and adolescent development among culturally and ethnically diverse populations.

Journal of Social Issues, Vol. 67, No. 3, 2011, pp. 553–579

"We Do Science Here": Underrepresented Students' Interactions with Faculty in Different College Contexts

Sylvia Hurtado,* M. Kevin Eagan, Minh C. Tran, Christopher B. Newman, Mitchell J. Chang, and Paolo Velasco

University of California

Faculty members play a key role in the identification and training of the next generation of scientific talent. In the face of the need to advance and diversify the scientific workforce, we examine whether and how specific institutional contexts shape student interactions with faculty. We conducted a mixed methods study to understand institutional contextual differences in the experiences of aspiring scientists. Data from a qualitative five-campus case study and a quantitative longitudinal study of students from over 117 higher education institutions were analyzed to determine how aspiring scientists interact with faculty and gain access to resources that will help them achieve their educational goals. Findings indicate that important structural differences exist between institutions in shaping students' interactions with faculty. For example, students at more selective institutions typically have less frequent, less personal interactions with faculty whereas Black students at historically Black colleges and universities report having more support and frequent interactions with faculty.

It is a critical national priority to develop, recruit, and retain talent in science and engineering to maintain U.S. economic competitiveness in the context of rapid globalization. In its report titled *Rising Above the Gathering Storm*, the National

---

*Correspondence concerning this article should be addressed to Sylvia Hurtado, 405 Hilgard Ave., 3005 Moore Hall, University of California, Los Angeles, CA 90095–1521 [e-mail: sylvia.hurtado@gmail.com].

All of the authors are affiliated with the Higher Education and Organizational Change program, Graduate School of Education and Information Studies, UCLA. This study was made possible by the support of the National Institute of General Medical Sciences, NIH Grant Numbers 1 R01 GMO71968–01 and R01 GMO71968–05 as well as the National Science Foundation, NSF Grant Number 0757076. This independent research and the views expressed here do not indicate endorsement by the sponsors.*

Academies' Committee on Science, Engineering and Public Policy (2007) issued a strong call to action that resulted in the passage of the 2007 America Competes Act to strengthen science-related education, programs, and research. However, the report did not address the substantial gaps between racial/ethnic groups or pose recommendations to address how the production of scientists may be affected by the culture of science within institutions with substantially different resources.

The underrepresentation of racial/ethnic minorities in scientific careers is not necessarily attributable to a lack of interest in science fields but rather poor science degree completion rates as underrepresented racial minority students have much lower science, technology, engineering, and mathematics (STEM) completion rates than their White and Asian-American counterparts (Higher Education Research Institute [HERI], 2010). Although student preparation and ability represent important predictors of students' navigation along their scientific pathways, progression through undergraduate science majors may be strongly influenced by the types of opportunities, experiences, and support students receive in college (Phinney, Campos, Kallemeyn, & Kim, 2011). Having regular contact with faculty has been linked with increased student success, particularly among underrepresented students, as students who interact more frequently with faculty tend to earn higher grades, increase their likelihood of degree completion, and increase their degree aspirations (Cole, 2010; Kim & Sax, 2009).

Diversifying the scientific workforce has remained an important goal for both the National Science Foundation and the National Institutes of Health (NIH). NIH initiatives, in particular, have provided funds to support undergraduate research training in institutions that graduate a large number of science baccalaureates from diverse racial/ethnic and socioeconomic groups. These funds are intended to assist with both individual training and to compensate for institutional resource differences in colleges that enroll high numbers of underrepresented racial minority (URM) students. Given the differences in institutional resources and structures of opportunity, this study examines whether and how specific institutional contexts shape student interactions with faculty.

To examine variations in students' experiences in interacting with faculty, we draw from quantitative data on students' first-year experiences and qualitative data from upper-division students to identify how the educational context affects the nature and frequency of science students' interactions with faculty. We chose to focus on this type of interaction because students' connections to faculty have been shown to be an important source of recognition and encouragement for navigating through the undergraduate science pipeline (Carlone & Johnson, 2007; Chemers, Zurbriggen, Syed, Goza, & Bearman, 2011). Faculty members also serve as an important resource for students' access to opportunities due to their role in recognizing talent for scientific work. Because students' first-year experiences affect their chances of advancing along scientific educational pathways (Phinney et al., 2011), it is important to investigate the nature of faculty-student interactions at an early stage in students' course of studies.

Individual and Contextual Factors Affecting Student-Faculty Interactions

Prior research has established the importance of support from family (Witkow & Fuligini, 2011) and from faculty (Cole, 2007) in predicting future success of students. Syed, Azmitia, and Cooper (2011) suggest that family, friends, and faculty can act as identity agents for students by offering social support and facilitating individuals' identity development and academic success. These identity agents become critical forces for URM students, who often face isolation and stereotyping in the academic environment (Syed et al., 2011).

A number of individual characteristics and contextual factors influence the quality and frequency of student-faculty interactions in college (Cole, 2007; Cotten & Wilson, 2006). For instance, Cole (2007) found racial differences in students' propensity to report having interacted with faculty. Specifically, Asian-American and Black students were less likely than their White peers to enter into a mentoring relationship with a professor. Moreover, White students were more likely to interact with faculty during class. Cole also found that being female, mother's level of education, and average high school grade point average (GPA) positively predicted course-related student-faculty contact.

Cole's (2007) study also makes clear the importance of accounting for accessibility cues. According to Wilson, Woods, and Gaff (1974), the actions of faculty members in the classroom provide students with cues concerning the accessibility of faculty outside of the classroom. In other words, they claim that "faculty who have little contact with students do little to invite such contact, indeed may do much to discourage it" (p. 85). Cotten and Wilson (2006) similarly found that students perceived negative attitudes from faculty or felt like faculty seemed rushed, and such views made students less likely to attempt to connect with faculty. Additionally, students who felt that their professor did not take their comments seriously had significantly reduced course-related contact with faculty and reported a lower likelihood of establishing mentoring relationships with faculty (Cole, 2007). These findings suggest that the signals students receive from faculty in classroom settings can significantly influence the quality and frequency of their future interaction with faculty both in and outside of the classroom.

Given research that suggests the quality and frequency of faculty interaction vary by race (Cole, 2007), the question arises as to whether URM students are better served in specific college environments or whether structured interaction in students' experiences within college environments can facilitate their development of relationships with faculty. Kraft (1991) found that Black students at predominantly White institutions (PWIs) may be especially susceptible to feeling intimidated by their faculty. Prior research also has indicated that URM students' experiences with faculty contribute to their perceptions of the campus racial climate (Hurtado, 1994). However, in a study of a predominantly White public university in California, Loo and Rolison (1986) found that, despite the fact that minority students experienced greater levels of sociocultural alienation than White students, White and racial minority students had little difference in their perceptions of faculty support.

By contrast, multi-institutional studies have indicated that the experiences of students at minority-serving institutions can differ significantly from the experiences of their counterparts at PWIs. For instance, Allen (1992) and Nelson Laird, Bridges, Morelon-Quainoo, Williams, and Holmes (2007) found that African-American students at historically Black colleges and universities (HBCUs) reported greater levels of engagement, higher academic performance, and more favorable relations with professors than their African-American peers at PWIs. Nelson Laird et al. (2007), however, did not find a similar pattern of results when comparing experiences of Latino students at Hispanic-serving institutions (HSIs) to Hispanic students at PWIs. More specifically, the results of their study did not show any statistically significant differences between the two groups in the frequency with which grades, readings, and career plans were discussed with faculty; the likelihood of receiving prompt feedback from faculty; or the chances of working with faculty outside of class. Studies have been unable to capture whether Latinos have more contact with Latino faculty, as Black students do with Black faculty at HBCUs. However, at least one study (Dayton, Gonzalez-Vasquez, Martinez, & Plum, 2004) has suggested that, for some Latino students, the race of a faculty member was not as important to them as the faculty member's ethic of caring. By contrast, Blake-Beard, Bayne, Crosby, and Muller (2011) found that matching students and faculty by race and gender in creating mentoring relationships significantly increased the amount of help students reported receiving.

The Impact of Faculty Interactions for Students in STEM Majors

Based on research highlighting the supportive nature of HBCUs, it is not surprising that these colleges and universities serve as a significant pipeline for the production of minority scientists and engineers. Perna et al. (2009) report that HBCUs produce approximately 22% of all bachelor's degrees earned by Black students but account for 30% of all STEM degrees earned by Black students. Black STEM students who attend an HBCU as an undergraduate tend to enroll in graduate STEM programs at higher rates than their counterparts at PWIs (Wenglinsky, 1997).

According to Johnson (2007), several departmental practices and values serve to discourage minority women in the sciences, which may be instructive for considering key differences in URM support across institutions. Johnson found that conducting classes in large lecture halls made the students feel like a "face in a crowd" (p. 811). In addition, Johnson argued that professors' practice of asking questions during their lecture disadvantaged students who were taught to avoid attracting attention in classes. Johnson also pointed out the problem associated with a "narrow focus on decontextualized science" (p. 814), whereby the lived experiences of students are not made a more integral part of the process of learning science, which makes it more difficult for students to identify with the course content. Last, Johnson discussed the problems associated with the false assumption that the science classroom is meritocratic and neutral in regard to race, ethnicity, and gender. When science faculty do not account for how the science learning environment may be more negative for women of Color, for example, it likely discourages women from further pursuing their science major.

The body of research concerning science education also stands to benefit from a broader conceptualization of how individual and institutional factors impact the lives of developing scientists. Carlone and Johnson (2007) recommend focusing on the development of science identity as a useful lens to interpret the experiences of URMs and women. According to this research, exploring science identity can provide a better understanding of the cognitive and social processes surrounding learning, which gives researchers the tools to reconceptualize "a more equitable science education" (p. 1189). Carlone and Johnson (2007) developed a conceptual model of science identity, which included three overlapping components of performance, recognition, and competence. Their model suggests that a disruption of a student's science identity may occur through feelings of being "overlooked, neglected, or discriminated against by meaningful others within science" (p. 1202). These "meaningful others" include individuals who have power over a student's academic career, and they are typically faculty members; however, recognition from peers and graduate students may also be important (Phinney et al., 2011). Chemers et al. (2011) also concludes that research and mentoring experiences with faculty significantly improves students' self-rated science efficacy. Thus, under Carlone and Johnson's (2007) framework, a student's identity as a developing scientist is informed by student-faculty interactions that represent the norms of the culture of science within institutions.

Norms surrounding science play an important role in defining the culture of science in specific institutions. Becher's (1989) work on cultures of academic disciplines explains how the culture of science may serve as a disrupting source for the development of science identities among URM students. Becher (1989) contends that "academic tribes" define "their own identities and defend their own patches of intellectual ground by employing a variety of devices geared toward the exclusion" of others that do not fit their ideal (p. 24). These devices include the creation of folklore, myths, and legends by academic disciplines. Becher (1989) maintains that "initiates," which include undergraduates, "are steeped in a folklore and a code of accepted or required practice which conditions the way they see the world," and disciplinary culture is "gradually shaped through the interaction of students with one another, with their instructors, and with their work" (p. 25).

Driver, Asoko, Leach, Mortimer, & Scott (1994) argue that the culture of science has two primary tenets: culture, which dictates acceptable practices within the discipline, and individualistic, which refers to how an individual practices science. Students thus gain exposure to scientific culture and are actively taught or shown the way in which "science is done," having to navigate both areas within their university-specific setting. Preliminary research reveals that not only is the culture of science experienced differently in coursework and in work on scientific projects with faculty, but also that these distinctions are informed by the overall institutional ethos (Hurtado, Cabrera, Lin, Arellano, & Espinosa, 2009). Thus, the culture of science may differ according to individual experiences within different institutional contexts.

Given the importance of faculty interaction in shaping students' experiences in their disciplines and the literature reviewed above, the current study assumes that faculty play a critical role in shaping the culture of science on a campus and that undergraduate contact with faculty is an important part of their socialization in becoming a scientist. We examine the effects of specific institutional contexts on this socialization process, as prior researchers have concluded that institutional culture, in addition to disciplinary culture, matters for preparing future scientists (Allen, 1992). Additionally, we examine how out-of-class interactions with faculty assist URM STEM students in overcoming some of the challenges they face associated with perceived negative aspects of their studies (Johnson, 2007). To address these issues, we test a statistical model predicting student-faculty interaction for aspiring scientists, including institutional and URM interactions that address distinctions identified in previous literature. We also draw from qualitative accounts of science students' interactions with faculty among students who have successfully navigated their way into and through a science major.

Method

To examine the institutional contexts and students' characteristics and experiences that increase the chances of interacting with faculty, we employed a sequential explanatory strategy, whereby quantitative data were collected during the first phase of research followed by the collection of qualitative data in the second phase. According to Creswell (2003), the qualitative data and analyses in a sequential explanatory strategy provide support for the quantitative findings and offer "broader perspectives as a result of using the different methods as opposed to using the predominant method alone" (p. 214). The following subsections first describe the quantitative techniques used in this study and conclude with a description of the qualitative methods.

Quantitative Methods

Sample. The quantitative sample comes from two surveys administered by the Cooperative Institutional Research Program: the 2004 Freshman Survey and the 2005 Your First College Year (YFCY) survey. Students in our sample completed the 2004 Freshman Survey as they entered college in the fall of 2004. During the spring term of 2005, we followed up with these same students as they completed their first year of college. We used a matched sample technique so that, within each institution, for every URM aspiring scientist we also identified a White or Asian-American aspiring scientist. Details of the sampling and weighting procedures may be found in Hurtado et al. (2007).

Because this study focuses on students' experiences and the institutional characteristics that affect the frequency with which biomedical and behavioral science students interact with faculty, we limited the quantitative sample to 3,003 aspiring scientists across 117 institutions who answered both the Freshman Survey and YFCY survey. Analyses of the demographic characteristics of the sample show that 78% of respondents were women. Approximately 30% of students identified as Black or African-American, 21% as Latina/o, 11% as Asian, 4% as American Indian, and 34% as White. Approximately 55% of the institutions in the study were privately controlled. HBCUs accounted for 13% of institutions in the sample, whereas HSIs accounted for 9% of the institutions.

Variables. The dependent variable in the quantitative analysis measured students' self-reported frequency of interacting with faculty during their first year of college. Using principal axis factoring with promax rotation, we identified a factor representing students' interaction with faculty, and this factor included four survey items: frequency of interaction with faculty during office hours; frequency of interaction with faculty outside of class or office hours; frequency with which students received advice from faculty about their educational program; and frequency with which students received emotional support from faculty. These items had a Cronbach's alpha coefficient of 0.68.

Table 1 shows all of the measures and scale ranges in the quantitative analysis. The independent variables in our analyses accounted for students' demographic traits, prior academic preparation, college entry characteristics, and first-year college experiences. The set of variables that targeted prior academic preparation included students' self-reported high school GPA, the frequency with which they interacted with teachers in high school, and whether they participated in a precollege summer research program. Additionally, we controlled for students' sense of connection with their intended science major through a factor labeled "science domain identification," a measure of science identity that tapped into students' life objectives, including the personal importance of their desire to make a theoretical contribution to science and to be recognized for contributions to their

Table 1. Description of Variables and Measures

Variable	Coding
Dependent variable	
Faculty-student interactions	Factor composed of four variables relating to the frequency of: interacting with faculty outside of class (0.62), interacting with faculty during office hours (0.60), receiving advice from faculty about the educational program (0.60), and receiving emotional support from faculty (0.59); (alpha = 0.68)
Individual characteristics (Level 1)	
Background characteristics	
Sex: Female	$0 = male$, $1 = female$
Race: Latino	$0 = no$, $1 = yes$ (referent White)
Race: Black	$0 = no$, $1 = yes$ (referent White)
Race: Asian	$0 = no$, $1 = yes$ (referent White)
Race: American Indian	$0 = no$, $1 = yes$ (referent White)
Father's education	$1 = grammar\ school\ or\ less$ to $8 = graduate\ degree$
Mother's education	$1 = grammar\ school\ or\ less$ to $8 = graduate\ degree$
Parental income	$1 = less\ than\ \$10,000$ to $14 = \$250,000\ or\ more$
Precollege Experiences	
High school GPA	$1 = D$ to $8 = A\ or\ A+$
Felt bored in class in high school	$1 = not\ at\ all$ to $3 = frequently$
Asked teacher for advice after class in high school	$1 = not\ at\ all$ to $3 = frequently$
Participated in precollege summer research program	$0 = no$, $1 = yes$
Science domain identification in 2004	Factor composed of four variables relating to the goals of: obtaining recognition from colleagues (0.71), making a theoretical contribution to science (0.62), becoming an authority in my own field (0.59), and working to find a cure for a health problem (0.55), (alpha = 0.71)
College experiences	
Studied with other students in college	$1 = not\ at\ all$ to $3 = frequently$
Felt overwhelmed in college	$1 = not\ at\ all$ to $3 = frequently$
Felt intimidated by faculty	$1 = not\ at\ all$ to $4 = frequently$
Family responsibilities interfered with academics	$1 = not\ at\ all$ to $4 = frequently$
Faculty here are interested in students' personal problems	$1 = strongly\ disagree$ to $4 = strongly\ agree$
Students here are treated like numbers in a book	$1 = strongly\ disagree$ to $4 = strongly\ agree$
Faculty here are interested in students' academic problems	$1 = strongly\ disagree$ to $4 = strongly\ agree$

(*Continued*)

Table 1. *(Continued)*

Variable	Coding
Participated in first-year seminar course	$0 = no$, $1 = yes$
Participated in preprofessional or departmental club	$0 = no$, $1 = yes$
Participated in an academic enrichment program for minority students	$0 = no$, $1 = yes$
Discussed course content with students outside class	$1 = not\ at\ all$ to $4 = frequently$
Worked on a professor's research project	$1 = not\ at\ all$ to $4 = frequently$
Received negative feedback about academic work	$1 = not\ at\ all$ to $4 = frequently$
Studied	$1 = none$ to $9 = over\ 30\ hours/week$
Cumulative GPA at the end of the first year of college	$1 = C-\ or\ less$ to $6 = A$
Success at managing the academic environment	Factor composed of five variables assessing students' success at: understanding professors' academic expectations. developing effective study skills, adjusting to academic demands of college, managing time effectively, and getting to know faculty. (alpha = 0.78)
Sense of belonging	Factor composed of three variables assessing students' agreement with the statements: I see myself as a part of the campus community, I feel I am a member of this college, and I have a sense of belonging to this college. (alpha = 0.84)
Positive cross-racial interactions	A factor with seven variables assessing how often students have experienced the following with students from a different racial/ethnic group from their own: socialized, dined/shared a meal, had meaningful and honest discussions about race/ethnicity, shared personal feelings and problems, had intellectual discussions outside of class, studied or prepared for class, socialized or partied. (alpha = 0.90)
Institutional contexts (level 2)	
Control: Private	$0 = no$, $1 = yes$
Offer research experiences to first-year students	$0 = no$, $1 = yes$
Institutional selectivity	Continuous; range 400–1600, rescaled to 4–16
Undergraduate FTE enrollment	Continuous; natural log of total undergraduate FTE enrollment

(Continued)

Table 1. *(Continued)*

Variable	Coding
Proportion of undergraduate students majoring in biomedical and behavioral sciences	Continuous
Average science domain identification of students entering college in 2004	Average of science domain identification (level-1 variable) for each institution
Average opinion: Students here are treated like numbers in a book	Average of this opinion variable (level 1) for each institution
HBCU	$0 = no$, $1 = yes$
Research expenditures	Continuous; natural log of research expenditures

Note. Authors will provide means, standard deviations, and correlations upon request. FTE is full-time equivalent (three part-time students are equivalent to one full-time student).

field (Chang, Eagan, Lin, & Hurtado, in press). The science domain identification factor has a Cronbach's alpha of 0.71.

Our analyses also statistically controlled for a number of student perceptions and activities. Specifically, we accounted for students' success at managing the academic environment, the extent to which students felt they belonged to the campus community, and the frequency with which they interacted with students of other races and ethnicities, among other experiences (see Hurtado et al.,2007, for more information about these factors). The final block of variables in the analyses controlled for the uniqueness of students' own campus characteristics and climate (measured by aggregating key student-level variables for each institution).

Analyses. To examine separately the individual and institutional effects on students' frequency of interaction with faculty members, we utilized hierarchical linear modeling (HLM). According to Raudenbush and Bryk (2002), HLM appropriately partitions variance to the individual (student) and group (institution) levels when data are clustered. By separating variance attributable to student effects and to institutional ones, HLM reduces the risk of making a Type I statistical error. To determine the proportion of variance attributable to institutional effects, we computed the intraclass correlation per Raudenbush and Bryk's (2002) recommendation and found that 15.4% of the variance in students' interactions with faculty was due to institutional effects. We chose to grand-mean center all of our continuous variables at level 1 except for those variables being modeled with level-2 predictors, which were group-mean centered. We left all dichotomous variables uncentered.

Qualitative Methods

Site selection. To better understand students' experiences with science in different contexts, we went to five different campuses located in different states across the United States. Taken together, we conducted 10 focus groups and 16 interviews with science faculty and key administrators of undergraduate science research programs. The campus case study sites, which included two PWIs, two HSIs, and one HBCU, were purposefully selected because they offered formal undergraduate science research programs and have high rates of science degree completion. This sampling strategy strengthened the study by offering insights into key similarities and differences across various institutional contexts. Participants in both the student focus groups and individual faculty/administrator interviews were purposefully recruited through science undergraduate research programs. We utilized purposeful sampling to capture the experiences of students who had successfully navigated the scientific pipeline.

Table 2 provides a description of each campus site. Southern State University is a master's comprehensive university ranked nationally among the highest number of baccalaureate degrees awarded to Latina/os in the biological sciences. Southwestern Flagship University (SWFU) is a research university that offers doctoral degrees in the sciences and in the schools of engineering, medicine, and pharmacy. Latina/o students comprise more than a third of the undergraduate enrollments. Southern Private University (SPU) is a relatively small HBCU, and its undergraduate enrollment is approximately 75% Black. While SPU offers a small number of graduate degrees, and it boasts a relatively large school of pharmacy, SPU's strong focus on undergraduate education has made it a national leader in African-American baccalaureate degrees in the biological and physical sciences.

Western University (WU) is a large, public, research university with a prominent medical school. WU is ranked nationally among the best institutions in engineering and research in the biological sciences. The student population is predominantly White and Asian-American, and a large proportion of WU's undergraduate students are biological science majors. North East University (NEU) is an elite research university consistently ranked among the top doctoral degree granting institutions in the country. The undergraduate population is also predominantly White and Asian-American, but it also maintains high ranking among the top producers of URM degrees in science.

Interviews. Focus group interviews were conducted by at least two researchers, with one or two facilitating the discussion while another took notes. The 71 student participants represented a racially diverse group: 56% Latina/o, 18% Black, 13% Asian-American, 8% multiracial, 2.5% American Indian, and 2.5% White. Women constituted 60% of the sample, and the majority of students (70%) were biology, biochemistry, or chemistry majors. We also conducted individual

Table 2. Site Visit Institutional Profiles

Pseudonym	Southern State University	Southwestern Flagship University (SWFU)	Southern Private University (SPU)	Western University (WU)	North East University (NEU)
Size	20,000	15,000	5,000	20,000	5,000
Control	Public	Public	Private	Public	Private
Type	HSI	HSI	HBCU	PWI	PWI
Selectivity (admittance rate)	90%	70%	60%	50%	20%
Ethnic enrollment	44% Latino 39% White 8% Black 6% Asian	47% White 34% Latino 4% Asian 3% Black 6% American Indian	75% Black 8% Asian 2% White 1% Latino	46% Asian 28% White 12% Latino 1% Black	37% White 26% Asian 12% Latino 7% Black 1% American Indian

interviews with a faculty member or administrator affiliated with an undergraduate research program on campus (e.g., Minorities Accessing Research Careers). The sample primarily consisted of coordinators, assistant directors, and directors of science research programs but also included science faculty and upper-level campus administrators. For both sets of interviews, we employed a semistructured protocol, which addressed the following broad thematic categories: types of support offered by the program, program evaluation, students' interest in science, educational and careers goals, undergraduate research experience, and obstacles facing URM students.

Analyses. Each site visit lasted between 1 and 2 days. At the end of each visit, we compiled notes from interviews, campus documents, and observations in a single notebook along with supplemental institutional documents. These documents provided the basis for triangulation across multiple sources of data (Creswell, 2003). We recorded and transcribed all interviews. Using a pattern matching technique, we coded transcriptions and organized the results using NVivo® software (QSR International, Australia) to identify emergent themes across the distinct interviews and campuses (Bazeley, 2007). The coding process is further described in Hurtado et al. (2009).

Cross-site comparisons were conducted across the five different institutions to examine how faculty, staff, and students involved in undergraduate research programs made sense of the process related to "becoming scientists" in different college contexts. According to Miles and Huberman (1994), cross-case analyses permit us to "deepen understanding and explanation" (p. 173) of a particular experience. The use of cross-case comparisons allowed us to examine the types of structural elements in place, such as faculty approachability and their ethic of care for students that facilitated student-faculty interactions and students' development as scientists.

Limitations

The mixed method design is intended to make up for some of the shortcomings in each of the quantitative and qualitative components. For example, the generalizability of the qualitative five campus sample is limited, but the quantitative data help by extending the sample to 117 institutions. The quantitative data alone, however, cannot provide enough information about how students experience science in these contexts and therefore is aided by specific examples and themes generated by the qualitative data. Other limitations include the fact that the sample for the quantitative portion of the study was overrepresented by women and the longitudinal response rate between the Freshman Survey and the YFCY survey was 22.5%. To attenuate nonresponse bias we developed normalized response weights to approximate the responses of the entering freshmen classes at participating institutions (for additional information on the weighting procedure used, see Hurtado et al., 2007). Additionally, it is important to note that we collected the quantitative data from first-year students whereas the qualitative data came from interviews of students in their third and fourth year of college. Students who successfully navigated their way into the major and an undergraduate research program may not have experienced some of the barriers that other freshmen have experienced; however, even these successful students did not hold uniformly positive assessments of their experiences in science on their campuses.

Results and Discussion

Table 3 presents the results from the HLM analyses. For the sake of simplicity, only the results of the final (i.e., intercept and slopes as outcomes) model are presented. Overall, the level-1 predictors accounted for approximately 28% of the variance in faculty interactions attributed to student characteristics. The level-2 model accounted for nearly 61% of the variance in the outcome attributed to institutional characteristics. Combined, the models accounted for slightly more than 33% of the total variance in students' interactions with faculty during their first year of college.

We examined three student-level predictors that significantly varied across institutions (cross-level interactions): the effect of being Black, participation in a preprofessional or departmental club, and working on a professor's research project. In Table 3, we found significant variation across institutions for the effect of being a Black student on student-faculty interactions. This significant variation indicated that Black students appeared to experience a unique impact on their propensity to interact with faculty based on where they attended college. To examine what accounted for this variation across institutions, we used institutional variables to assist in explaining what college contexts either encourage or discourage Black students' frequency of interaction with faculty. Black students, on average across institutions, had less frequent interactions than White students ($b=-.79$, $p<.05$); however, cross-level interaction terms revealed that Black students who attended an HBCU ($b=.62$, $p<.001$), a more selective institution ($b=.35$, $p<.01$), and a larger institution ($b=.33$, $p<.05$) interacted with faculty significantly more often than their Black peers at predominantly White, less selective, and smaller institutions, respectively. Thus, HBCU status, selectivity, and size appear to mitigate first-year Black students' propensity to interact less frequently with their professors. By contrast, after controls were introduced, Latina/o students did not exhibit any significant differences in interaction with faculty compared to White students nor was attending an HSI significant in the model, indicating no further investigation regarding differential contextual effects for Latina/o students was necessary.

Table 3. Results of Hierarchical Linear Modeling (HLM) Analyses Predicting Student-Faculty Interaction among Science Students

	Coef.	*SE* Sig.
Level 1		
Background characteristics		
Sex: Female	−0.09	0.10
Race: Latino	−0.19	0.13
Race: Black	−0.79	0.33*
Cross-level interaction: HBCU	0.62	0.17***
Cross-level interaction: Institutional selectivity	0.35	0.11**
Cross-level interaction: Undergraduate FTE enrollment	0.33	0.14
Race: Asian	−0.22	0.11*
Race: American Indian	0.51	0.28
Father's education	0.04	0.02
Mother's education	−0.01	0.03
Parental income	−0.02	0.02
Precollege experiences		
High school GPA	−0.01	0.04
Felt bored in class in high school	−0.18	0.07**
Asked teacher for advice after class in high school	0.31	0.06***
Participated in precollege after summer research program	0.23	0.15
Science domain identification in 2004	0.07	0.02***
College experiences		
Studied with other students in college	0.38	0.07***
Felt overwhelmed in college	0.10	0.07
Felt intimidated by faculty	0.04	0.05
Family responsibilities interfered with academics	0.17	0.05**
Faculty here are interested in students' personal problems	0.48	0.06***
Students here are treated like numbers in a book	−0.10	0.07
Faculty here are interested in students' academic problems	0.20	0.08*
Participated in first-year seminar course	0.13	0.08
Participated in preprofessional or departmental club	0.46	0.12***
Cross-level interaction: Research Expenditure	−0.02	0.01*
Cross-level interaction: Average science domain identification	0.38	0.20*
Cross-level interaction: Average opinion students are treated like numbers in a book	0.55	0.27*
Participated in academic enrichment program for minority students	0.30	0.09**

(Continued)

Table 3.   *(Continued)*

	Coef.	*SE* Sig.
Discuss course content with student outside class	0.29	0.07***
Worked on a professor's research project	0.22	0.05***
Cross level interaction: Research expenditures	0.02	0.01*
Received negative feedback about academic work	0.25	0.05***
Studied	0.10	0.03***
Cumulative GPA at the end of the first year of college	−0.14	0.04***
Success at managing the academic environment	0.79	0.11***
Sense of belonging	−0.18	0.09*
Positive cross-racial interaction	0.21	0.05
Level 2		
Intercept	5.50	0.70
Control private	0.13	0.14
Offers research experiences to first-year students.	0.14	0.11
Institutional selectivity	−0.47	0.13**
Undergraduate FTE enrollment	−0.74	0.18***
Proportion of undergraduate students in biomedical behavior	−0.01	0.00*
Average science domain identification of students entering college in 2004	−0.57	0.32
Average opinion: Students here are treated like numbers in a book	−0.89	0.35*

Note. $^*p < .05$, $^{**}p < .01$, $^{***}p < .001$.
Source. HLM analysis of 2004 Freshman Survey and 2005 Your First College Year data.

A second cross-level interaction shown in Table 3 relates to the variability of the effect of participating in a preprofessional or departmental club on students' frequency of interaction with faculty. Students who participated in these clubs appeared to interact with faculty significantly more often than their peers who did not join these organizations ($b=.46$, $p<.001$). Students who attended institutions where their peers had a stronger connection to science tended to reap even greater advantages from participation in departmental clubs ($b=.38$, $p<.05$). Likewise, students who joined these clubs and who attended institutions where more students reported that faculty treated them "like numbers in a book" tended to report even higher levels of interaction with faculty. It may be that, on campuses where a large proportion of students experience a strong sense of anonymity perhaps because of large institutional or class size, these academic clubs provide more opportunities to connect with peers and faculty in purposeful ways that enhance socialization in science. The final institutional moderator related to participation in academic clubs is an institution's level of research expenditure. Higher research expenditures tended to reduce the strength of academic club participation and the frequency with which undergraduates interact with faculty ($b=-.02, p<.05$).

The final cross-level interaction we examined in the analyses related to the effect of working on a professor's research project. On average, as students spent more time working on a professor's research project, their frequency of interacting with faculty increased significantly ($b=.22, p<.001$). Attending an institution that spends more money on research activities appeared to strengthen the effect of working on a professor's research project. Perhaps these better-resourced institutions provide financial incentives to students who participate on faculty research projects, as students at better-resourced institutions might receive stipends for their work on research projects. This finding may be directly related to federal grant supplements that provide additional stipends for undergraduate research training in specific research projects.

In addition to these cross-level effects, we identified a number of significant institution-level variables that affected the average frequency of students' interactions with faculty (as indicated by the intercept in the model). On average, students who attended more selective institutions tended to interact with faculty significantly less frequently than their peers did at less-selective colleges and universities. A 100-point increase in institutional selectivity resulted in almost a half-point reduction in the average student's interaction with faculty ($b=-.47, p<.001$). Likewise, students who enrolled at larger institutions tended to interact with faculty significantly less often than their peers at smaller institutions ($b=-.74, p<.001$). Finally, students who attended institutions where their peers, on average, perceived that faculty treated them "like numbers in a book" tended to interact with faculty significantly less often than their counterparts at colleges and universities where students, on average, perceived that faculty treated them as individuals ($b=-.89, p<.05$).

Curiously, students' individual perception (student-level) that faculty treated them "like numbers in a book" had no significant effect on their propensity to interact with faculty, but other student-level characteristics and experiences did have a significant effect. Students who reported more frequent contact with teachers in high school were prone to interact with college faculty more frequently ($b=.31, p<.001$). Similarly, students who reported feeling that their college faculty cared about their personal ($b=.48, p<.001$) and academic ($b=.20, p<.05$) problems also had higher frequencies of interacting with their professors during their first year of college. Being academically engaged, as measured by time spent studying ($b=.10, p<.01$), discussing course content with students outside of class ($b=.29, p<.001$), or participating in an academic enrichment program geared toward minority students ($b=.30, p<.01$), tended to also increase the frequency of interactions between students and their college faculty.

By contrast, students who struggled academically in their first year of college also interacted more often with faculty. Students with lower first-year cumulative

GPAs tended to report interacting with faculty more often than their peers with higher GPAs ($b=-.14, p<.01$). Likewise, students who reported that they received negative feedback from faculty about their academic work also tended to report more frequent interactions with their professors ($b=.25, p<.001$). It appears then that first-year students who need more academic assistance are also reporting to be interacting more with faculty, but the nature of this interaction is likely different from those students who are more engaged academically by, for example, participating in faculty research.

Supporting the findings from the quantitative analyses, several themes from analysis of the qualitative data connected to students' interactions with faculty. We provide information based on three themes: faculty approachability, students' views about an ethic of care (as opposed to being treated "like numbers in a book"), and how faculty seem to balance rigor and support for students. These themes originate from student, faculty, and program administrator interviews and include several contextual differences related to faculty accessibility and support both inside and outside of the classroom.

Faculty Approachability

Upon first entering college, students described feeling intimidated about approaching faculty. While this concern was common among nearly all students who had successfully navigated into the major, the intensity also varied to a certain degree across the five institutions, with students perceiving faculty to be most approachable at SPU and least approachable at NEU. A student at a NEU commented that, "Just recently, maybe last year, I started talking to a few of my professors when after class I did not understand something, but it took me 2 years to finally do it." Some students reported that they developed a reluctance to approach faculty over time after detecting certain accessibility cues. One of these cues was whether a faculty member encouraged students to ask questions in class. If not, students seemed more likely to view that faculty member as being unapproachable. As one NEU student explained, "Some professors are really inviting, like they motivate you to ask them questions and they are more available. Other professors, you go to ask them a question, and they are always like, 'Yeah, just go through the lecture'."

Generally, most of these cues regarding approachability are based largely on a faculty member's in-class behavior and demeanor. For example, another cue that focus group participants raised related to whether faculty members relied mainly on didactic versus interactive teaching methods, as those faculty who used interactive strategies tended to be perceived as more approachable. Students also pointed to a few out-of-class cues that signaled a professor's approachability. One indicator of accessibility related to posted office hours, as a student from WU explained, "There's faculty office hours, but it'll maybe be an hour a week. I did not really attend a lot of those. It's kind of hard to know if they did not encourage interaction or if it was just structured that way." Students see office hours as limiting interaction rather than evidence that faculty are willing to accommodate their needs for course assistance, academic and career advising.

Perhaps faculty accessibility to undergraduates is closely linked with the reward structure of an institution. A student at SWFU perceptively noticed this tension for her faculty mentor:

> She wasn't able to get any work done because she spent a lot of her time trying to help out her students, and that's why these professors might be a little bit reluctant to help with the students just because they're judged so much on how much progress they make, how many publications they get.

Both the institution and the reward system offer few if any incentives for faculty to engage in mentoring or include undergraduates in research. A faculty director of an undergraduate research program at WU described this challenge and discussed some alternative measures:

> It's a challenge to bring more new faculty on [to work with the program]. . .because there are no tenure perk points, and I've gone through that myself. It's "I've got to publish and I've got to do other things, I have to serve on this committee, I don't get any points if I [help you], so no." So one of the things we've talked about is trying to make service to the university and working with undergraduates in the program get some sort of points or somehow feel weighted so that I get more faculty [involved in the program].

Unfortunately, the lack of incentives for faculty to mentor and engage undergraduates was a recurrent theme among the staff and faculty we interviewed at the two HSIs and the two PWIs.

Faculty inaccessibility was also exacerbated by the scarcity of URM science faculty. A faculty program director at WU shared this sentiment and said, "There are very few professors who share [students'] background, so there might be something. . .off-putting or intimidating about a department where they never see anyone who looks like them who made it." Conversely, students attending SPU (the HBCU) reported that it was easier for them to identify science faculty members to serve as mentors and same-race role models.

Despite these obstacles, by the third year of college most students began to actively approach professors. One student at NEU described overcoming his initial sense of intimidation: "I did not start reaching out until last year, and, ever since I started reaching out to professors and other groups and stuff like that, it's been very fruitful." These students also found that once they made this effort, professors took an interest in their welfare and were generally willing to assist them. For instance, students frequently noticed that faculty became more attentive once they became aware of the students' intentions to pursue a research career and/or graduate school. One student at SPU said, "If [faculty] hear you say you want to go to grad school, that's when they really start pushing and really want you to do well and really give you all the resources that you need to do well." Students were able to establish relationships with faculty by discovering simple strategies, such as clearly communicating with faculty about their career goals and interest in science. After students began connecting with faculty, several seemed to find their efforts reciprocated, as students across all institutions reported gaining resources, encouragement, and valuable opportunities.

Ethic of Care

Students not only relied on cues to assess faculty approachability but also to determine whether a certain ethic of care existed within science departments. For instance, many students cited problems with large and impersonal class sizes and the overabundance of courses taught by unqualified teaching assistants, all of which was common for introductory science courses taken the first year of college. An SWFU student shared her experience: "You take biology, and you go into the class, and there are hundreds of students there. They are not all going to get their questions answered by the professor. If you are lucky, you might get the TA (teaching assistant) to answer it right, but you never know."

Subsequently, students enrolled in the PWIs tended to describe science environments as rather uncaring due to a perceived low emphasis on teaching and a lack of opportunities for meaningful interactions with science faculty and other undergraduates. As one student from NEU shared, "From the engineering department's viewpoint, I did not feel like they were supportive or they cared at all." Similarly, regarding the lack of opportunities to interact with faculty, one student at a NEU noted, "That seems to happen when you have really good professors that are doing other things besides teaching, like doing world-renowned research. They tend to not care about the other responsibilities that come along with that." Students' dissatisfaction related to teaching was not an issue that affected only students at PWIs. Several students at one of the HSI campuses in the sample also remarked about problems with large class sizes and the preponderance of courses taught by TAs.

Students from two institutions, SPU and SWFU, discussed having received personal attention from faculty. Students noted that faculty on their respective campuses tended to take a holistic approach to education by providing them with a great deal of individualized attention and by showing concern for both their academic and nonacademic lives. The following quote from a student at SWFU captures this notion of a holistic approach:

> They treat you as a whole person rather than just what you have to offer academically, and that made a big difference for me, just knowing that they're real people too, and you can go to them outside of academics, and then that in turn, the advice that they give you benefits you academically because, you know, they push in the right direction.

Comparatively, a student attending SPU shared her experience after spending a brief period at one PWI:

> I did go to [another university] for a semester and it's a big difference [at SPU] in how the teachers [interact with students]... they're more receptive of your feelings [at SPU] and what you're going through versus a big university. So that's a big difference.

Another SPU student echoed this sentiment:

> Generally HBCUs may not get as much funding, so they're not as equipped as other schools and you see that. When I went from the lab in [SPU's] classroom and then I go to [another university] and I go to the lab in their classroom, they have an incubator almost half the size of our class. At the same time, with what we have, [SPU] does give you a quality education and people tend to look over that.

Despite resource differences at some minority-serving institutions, such as SPU, students pointed to the ethic of care as the key feature that contributed most to the quality of their science education.

Rigor versus Support

Another theme that emerged from the case studies was the tenuous balance between rigor and support as they relate to science curriculum and instruction. This tension was most obvious at both of the PWIs, where a vast majority of students and faculty indicated that stressful and demanding science environments were the norm. Many interviewees suggested that a major contributing factor to this stress was the "gatekeeper" courses that students often took during their first year of college. Deeply ingrained in the culture of science at this institution was the process of gatekeeping, as one senior administrator who oversees undergraduate research at WU explained, "When they first come in, they really hit some barrier courses...If you are an educator, you see those as I do, as barrier courses that something needs to be done about it if possible." These "barrier" courses appear to be designed around a single objective: to differentiate students' capacity for absorbing large amounts of information. Consequently many students became excessively focused on grades rather than learning, as one NEU student explained: "I think there's just an issue with academics and the grading system in general because a lot of times you are just focused on getting a good grade." Further illustrating this problem, a student from NEU said:

> I think for a lot of the core classes, most people approach them as, "I just want to pass it." Most people don't approach them as, "This is going to be a building block that's going to help me out a lot later on when I'm going to be seeing it over and over again, so let me take this time to actually understand it."

Many students described grading on a curve as a common practice in introductory science courses, which discourages the "average" student from pursuing further coursework in the major. According to students at NEU and WU, such grading practices tend to promote rote memorization rather than deep understanding and application of knowledge.

Because the quality of precollege preparation varies widely, those who attended lower performing high schools, for example, are at a severe disadvantage in this grading system. A faculty program director at WU explained how rigorous yet naïve standards negatively affected persistence in the major and graduate school aspirations for first-generation and underrepresented students:

> Students who don't do well in the first year have a very hard time continuing in the major. . . I think it disproportionately affects first-generation students who aren't prepared for it, and I think a number of underrepresented students aren't prepared for those courses either, so we try to do some intervention with students taking those courses.

This high-stakes environment appears resistant to change as explained by the faculty program director at WU, "I think it's really tricky to talk to some professors about introducing certain kinds of supportive elements into a class," and he adds that attempts to intervene by calling attention to problems within the classroom were commonly met with stiff resistance among faculty. This point resonates with Becher's (1989) notion of academic cultures and their boundaries that inform not only teaching disciplinary knowledge but also ones' approach toward student support for learning.

Faculty can establish a healthy balance between rigor and support in science instruction and curriculum, as a faculty member at SPU describes:

> We're so teaching-oriented, you know. It's all about the students. You really care about the students. In every field, they put extra time into making it easy for a student and not in the sense of making the material easy. We expect them to learn, but we do help them achieve and especially in sciences.

That SPU offers an environment of faculty support was reinforced by a student at SPU: "I guess they are really more concerned about you here as far as how well you do, and they always ask me, 'Well, how are you doing in your class'? If you need any extra help, they are willing to help you if you come to their office hours." SPU offered a distinctive culture of support, where even rigorous elements can serve to motivate aspiring science students rather than to discourage them. As one student stated, "they are always trying to take you to the next level [here]."

Conclusions

At the conclusion of our site visit, one undergraduate science major aptly captured his own sense of science identity at SPU by proudly stating, "We do science here." Such student identification with both the institution and science does not happen by chance but is nurtured through some key student experiences, including having received substantive recognition and meaningful support from faculty. As suggested by Carlone and Johnson's (2007) discussion of science identity development and Becher's (1989) insights into how that identity is formed within disciplines, institutions and faculty members can play key roles in shaping the aspirations, opportunities, and experiences of URM science majors. Unfortunately, the culture that students often experience as part of their science education curtails rather than advances their studies. Becher (1989) acknowledges that it is very difficult to change the academic culture of a discipline or department, as "any systematic questioning of the accepted disciplinary ideology will be seen as heresy and may be punished by expulsion" (p. 37). However, we found that specific campuses and patterns of faculty engagement with students can make a significant difference in establishing a culture of support while still maintaining rigor in science training.

Our key findings from this mixed-method study point to the importance of institutional context in establishing meaningful student-faculty interaction that can facilitate students' development as scientists. Findings from the survey of first-year students suggest that both the structural characteristics of the institution and peer normative contexts matter in facilitating student-faculty interaction. Specifically, first-year aspiring scientists tended to report lower frequencies of interaction with faculty at institutions with larger undergraduate enrollments, more selective environments, or with faculty who treated students impersonally. Interview data confirmed that many students viewed the science classroom environment as impersonal and competitive. Program directors reported that faculty members are reluctant to introduce supportive mechanisms for learning in the classroom. Unfortunately, these problems are not unusual in science education but are instead commonly experienced by first-year students across the country. Becher (1989) argues that some of the key obstacles to improving undergraduate science education include the availability of faculty, grading practices in introductory courses, and the pressure on faculty to focus more on publishing rather than on teaching.

Overcoming these common practices, maintained by disciplinary traditions and socialization, will be an especially difficult challenge for large and selective institutions that often attract top scientific talent among faculty and students. Although findings from our cross-level analyses show that Black students at selective institutions may fare somewhat better in their level of contact with faculty, this effect is strongest for those Black students who attend HBCUs. This finding supports prior work that shows that HBCUs tend to promote stronger connections between Black students and faculty than their PWI counterparts (Allen, 1992; Nelson Laird et al., 2007), which increases the chances of retaining first-year science students (Chang et al., 2008). Only a few students at the HSIs mentioned similar connections, and no significant effects were evident in the quantitative findings. That there were no detectable cross-level effects for HSIs may be explained in large part by the fact that many HSIs began historically as PWIs and thus are still in the process of making institutional changes that would allow them to better serve the educational needs of their Latina/o students (Hurtado et al., 2007; Nelson Laird et al., 2007).

Even though the ways in which students are generally trained in the sciences appear to differ across institutional types, our findings also suggest that much can be done within institutions to facilitate students' progress in their science education. As noted in previous studies (Cole, 2007; Dayton et al., 2004), students often take their initial cues from faculty in the classroom when assessing faculty approachability. The qualitative findings confirm that students pay close attention to certain cues such as whether or not their instructor displays an ethic of caring to gauge if a faculty member is approachable.

We also identified several key opportunities that are associated with more frequent student-faculty interaction during an undergraduate student's first year of study, which may counteract the negative effects of other contextual factors such as large size and high selectivity. These experiences include participation in academic clubs, minority support programs, and taking advantage of opportunities to work on a professor's research project. Besides enhancing interaction with faculty, those structured research and student support programs may also help to socialize students into the culture of science at an early yet important stage in their studies. Through those experiences that occur within more supportive communities, students develop a better understanding of how to navigate their way through their major, what it means to become a scientist, and how to participate in the culture of science at their institution.

It is becoming increasingly clear that faculty involvement in the identification and training of developing scientists is essential to sustaining economic competitiveness and leadership in science. To meet the need to develop a talented and more diversified scientific workforce, policymakers and institutions can support undergraduate initiatives and faculty resources devoted to advancing the production of scientists. For example, it is important for National Science Foundation and NIH to continue to award research grants that require the training of undergraduates in ways that can produce more women and racial minority scientists. We found that first-year students who attended institutions that spent more money on research activities appear to benefit even more from working on faculty research projects. This finding suggests that research resources can play a key role in facilitating contact through the mutual goal of discovery, but, as students also indicated, faculty support also constitutes a significant resource. Allen (1992) indicated that the tradeoff between resources at a PWI and HBCU hinged on this very element of faculty support versus access to material resources, a theme that was repeated by students who were aware of these differences between institutions.

Likewise, those faculty and program administrators whom we interviewed emphasized the difficulty they had with balancing the demands of academia and the needs of their programs and students. Several program administrators who have faculty appointments also indicated a difficulty in recruiting new faculty mentors for their respective undergraduate research programs because of the lack of tangible institutional incentives and rewards. One way to reverse this trend is for institutions to reward faculty involvement with undergraduate research and academic support initiatives when considering tenure and promotion, which would also signal a stronger commitment to students and place a higher priority on faculty accessibility and support.

Another important implication from our research concerns institutional norms and how some practices tend to derail more than advance students' progress and interest in pursuing scientific inquiry. It appears most institutions can benefit from actively reshaping their culture of science on campus to balance rigor and support in ways that better acquaint students with the empowering and collaborative side of scientific discovery (Hurtado et al., 2007). Based on our findings, it is prudent for institutions to promote innovations for teaching and learning that engage students in science and minimize the widespread perception among first-year students that the science environment tends to be impersonal and competitive. Although this study further establishes the importance of intentionally shaping the unique context in which undergraduate science education takes place, especially with respect to facilitating higher levels of student-faculty interaction, the next phase of research should focus on how intervention strategies can be scaled-up from the program to the institutional level to increase the production of young scientists from diverse populations.

References

Allen, W. R. (1992). The color of success: African-American college student outcomes at predominantly White and historically Black public colleges and universities. *Harvard Educational Review, 62*(1), 26–44.

Bazeley, P. (2007). *Qualitative data analysis with NVivo*. Thousand Oaks, CA: Sage.

Becher, T. (1989). *Academic tribes and territories: Intellectual enquiry and the cultures of disciplines*. Milton Keynes, Buckingham, UK: The Society for Research into Higher Education and Open University Press.

Blake-Beard, S., Bayne, M., Crosby, F., & Muller, C. (2011). Matching by race and gender in mentoring relationships: Keeping our eyes on the prize. *Journal of Social Issues, 67*(3), 622–643.

Carlone, H. B., & Johnson, A. (2007). Understanding the science experiences of successful women of color: Science identity as an analytic lens. *Journal of Research in Science Teaching, 44*(8), 1187–1218. doi:10.1002/tea.20237.

Chang, M. J., Cerna, O., Han, J., & Saenz, V. (2008). The contradictory roles of institutional status in retaining underrepresented minorities in biomedical and behavioral science majors. *The Review of Higher Education, 31*(4), 433–464. doi:10.1353/rhe.0.0011.

Chang, M. J., Eagan, M. K., Lin, M. L, & Hurtado, S. (in press). Considering the impact of racial stigmas and science identity: Persistence among biomedical and behavioral science aspirants. *Journal of Higher Education*.

Chemers, M. M., Zurbriggen, E. L., Syed, M., Goza, B. K., & Bearman, S. (2011). The role of efficacy and identity in science career commitment among underrepresented minority students. *Journal of Social Issues, 67*(3), 469–491.

Cole, D. (2007). Do interracial interactions matter? An examination of student-faculty contact and intellectual self-concept. *Journal of Higher Education, 78*(3), 249–281. doi:10.1353/jhe.2007.0015.

Cole, D. (2010). The effects of student-faculty interactions on minority students' college grades: Differences between aggregated and disaggregated data. *Journal of the Professoriate, 3*(2), 137–160.

Committee on Science, Engineering, and Public Policy. (2007). *Rising above the gathering storm: Energizing and employing America for a brighter economic future.* Washington, DC: National Academies Press.

Cotten, S. R., & Wilson, B. (2006).Student-faculty interactions: Dynamics and determinants. *Higher Education, 51,* 487–519. doi:10.1007/s10734–004-1705–4.

Creswell, J. W. (2003). *Research design: Qualitative, quantitative, mixed methods, approaches* (2nd ed.). Thousand Oaks, CA: Sage.

Dayton, B., Gonzalez-Vasquez, N., Martinez, C. R., & Plum, C. (2004). Hispanic-serving institutions through the eyes of students and administrators. In A. M. Ortiz (Ed.). *Addressing the unique needs of Latino American students. New Directions for Student Services* (Vol. *105*, pp. 29–40). San Francisco, CA: Jossey Bass.

Driver, R., Asoko, H., Leach, J., Mortimer, E., & Scott, P. (1994). Constructing scientific knowledge in the classroom. *Educational Researcher, 23*(7), 5–12. doi:10.3102/0013189×023007005.

Higher Education Research Institute (2010). *Degrees of success: Bachelor's degree completion rates among initial STEM majors.* Retrieved July 24, 2011, from http://www.heri.ucla.edu/nih/HERI_ResearchBrief_OL_2010_STEM.pdf.

Hurtado, S. (1994). The institutional climate for talented Latino students. *Research in Higher Education, 35*(1), 21–41. doi:10.1007/BF02496660.

Hurtado, S., Han, J. C., Saenz, V. B., Espinosa, L. L., Cabrera, N. L., & Cerna, O. S. (2007). Predicting transition and adjustment to college: Minority biomedical and behavioral science students' first year of college. *Research in Higher Education, 48*(7), 841–887. doi:10.1007/s11162–007-9051-x.

Hurtado, S., Cabrera, N. L., Lin, M. H., Arellano, L., & Espinosa, L. L. (2009). Diversifying science: Underrepresented minority experiences in structured research programs. *Research in Higher Education, 50*(2), 189–214. doi:10.1007/s11162–008-9114–7.

Johnson, A. C. (2007). Unintended consequences: How science professors discourage women of color. *Science Education, 91*(5), 805–821. doi:10.1002/sce.20208.

Kim, Y. K., & Sax, L. J. (2009). Student-faculty interaction in research universities: Differences by student gender, race, social class, and first-generation status. *Research in Higher Education, 50,* 437–459. doi:10.1007/s11162–009-9127-x.

Kraft, C. L. (1991). What makes a successful Black student on a predominantly White campus? *American Educational Research Journal, 28*(2), 423–443. doi:10.3102/00028312028002423.

Loo, C. M., & Rolison, G. (1986). Alienation of ethnic minority students at a predominantly White university. *Journal of Higher Education, 57*(1), 58–77. Retrieved July 24, 2011, from http://www.jstor.org.

Miles, M., & Huberman, M. (1994). *Qualitative data analysis: An expanded sourcebook.* Thousand Oaks, CA: Sage.

Nelson Laird, T. F., Bridges, B. K., Morelon-Quainoo, C. L., Williams, J. M., & Holmes, M. S. (2007). African American and Hispanic student engagement at minority serving and predominantly White institutions. *Journal of College Student Development, 48*(1), 39–56. doi:10.1353/csd.2007.0005.

Perna, L. W., Lundy-Wagner, V., Drezner, N. D., Gasman, M., Yoon, S., Bose, E., et al. (2009). The contribution of HBCUs to the preparation of African American women for STEM careers: A case study. *Research in Higher Education, 50*(1), 1–23. doi:10.1007/s11162–008-9110-y.

Phinney, J. S., Campos, C. M. T., Kallameyn, D. M. P., & Kim, C. (2011). Processes and outcomes of a mentoring program for Latino college freshmen. *Journal of Social Issues, 67*(3), 599–621.

Raudenbush, S. W., & Bryk, A. S. (2002). *Hierarchical linear models: Applications and data analysis methods* (2nd ed.). Thousand Oaks, CA: Sage.

Syed, M., Azmitia, M., & Cooper, C. R. (2011). Identity and academic success among under-represented ethnic minorities: An interdisciplinary review and integration. *Journal of Social Issues, 67*(3), 442–468.

Wenglinsky, H. (1997). *Students at historically Black colleges and universities: Their aspirations & accomplishments.* Policy Information Report. Princeton, NJ: Educational Testing Service.

Wilson, R. C., Woods, L., & Gaff, J. G. (1974). Social-psychological accessibility and faculty-student interaction beyond the classroom. *Sociology of Education, 47*(1), 74–92.

Witkow, M. R., & Fuligini, A. J. (2011). Ethnic and generational differences in the relations between social support and academic achievement across the high school years. *Journal of Social Issues, 67*(3), 531–552.

SYLVIA HURTADO is Professor in Education and Director of the Higher Education Research Institute, UCLA. Her research interests include sociology of education, diversity in higher education, and student educational outcomes.

M. KEVIN EAGAN earned his PhD in Education at UCLA and serves as a postdoctoral research fellow at the Higher Education Research Institute. His research interests focus on equity, STEM, research methods, and institutional contexts.

MINH C. TRAN is a doctoral candidate in Education. His primary research interests are concerned with the intersectionality between science identity and multiple social identities.

CHRISTOPHER B. NEWMAN is a doctoral candidate in Education. His research focuses on African–Americans' pathways to and through the STEM pipeline.

MITCHELL J. CHANG is Professor in Education, with a joint appointment in Asian-American Studies. His research focuses on the educational efficacy of diversity-related initiatives on college campuses, including research concerning race-conscious admissions practices.

PAOLO VELASCO is a doctoral student in Education. His research interests include the impact of classroom pedagogy and diversity on students' learning and development.

Journal of Social Issues, Vol. 67, No. 3, 2011, pp. 580–598

Design of an Intervention to Promote Entry of Minority Youth into Clinical Research Careers by Aligning Ambition: The TEACH (Training Early Achievers for Careers in Health) Research Program

Vineet Arora[*]
University of Chicago

Barbara Schneider
Michigan State University

Rebecca Thal and David Meltzer
University of Chicago

The theory of aligned ambition posits that adolescents' career aspirations are shaped by both contextual and attitudinal factors. Minority students are less likely to exhibit career-specific knowledge, realistic attitudes, and successful behaviors, which could exacerbate racial disparities in the health care workforce. This article describes the theoretical grounding and preliminary implementation of an intervention designed to promote aligned ambition from an early stage of career development. The Training Early Achievers for Careers in Health Research Program provides exposure to realistic career experiences and multitiered mentorship, with the goal of cultivating aligned ambition toward clinical research careers among minority high school students. We discuss program operations in detail and consider whether this method can be used nationally to promote entry of minority youth into clinical research careers.

Many of the most pressing health problems facing the United States disproportionately affect minority groups (Centers for Disease Control and

---

*Correspondence concerning this article should be addressed to Vineet Arora, 5841 S. Maryland Ave., MC 2007, AMB W216, Chicago, IL 60637 [e-mail: varora@medicine.bsd.uchicago.edu].

This research was supported by 1 R01 GM075292 National Institute for General Medical Sciences/National Institute of Health; Effectiveness of TEACH Research (PI Meltzer).*

Prevention, 2011; LaVeist, 2005). Researchers with personal experience as members of less privileged racial or socioeconomic groups may be particularly well suited to understand and address the deep social determinants at work in minority health. However, relatively few individuals from such backgrounds enter careers in health research, which has motivated efforts by the National Institutes of Health and others to address this important national need. Designing an effective intervention to address this important national need requires an understanding of the barriers faced by minority youth in entering careers in health research.

Recent research suggests that minority youth have high aspirations for successful professional careers, such as those in health research, but often lack the knowledge, attitudes, and behaviors needed to pursue and achieve their occupational goals. This article describes the design of an intervention guided by the theory of aligned ambition to promote the entry of minority youth into careers in health research, Training Early Achievers for Careers in Health (TEACH) Research. The article will pay special attention to two concepts underpinning the design and evaluation of TEACH: the importance of engagement as mechanism to encourage and predict success of educational programs, and the importance of mentors in the course of career development.

Theoretical Underpinnings: The Importance of Promoting Clinical Research Careers to Minority Youth

A diverse health care work force is an important part of expanding health care access for the underserved, enriching the pool of leaders and policymakers to meet the needs of an increasingly diverse population, and fostering biomedical and clinical research to address diseases that affect minority groups (Cohen, Gabriel, & Terrell, 2002). Clinical research—such as patient-oriented research, which often directly involves patients and/or aims to understand the social factors that impact health—can be especially important for minority populations (Bierman, Lurie, Collins, & Eisenberg, 2002; NIH Director's Panel on Clinical Research, 2003). Because clinical research relies on human interaction, the ability to communicate and relate to patients is a critical component to success. Furthermore, clinical researchers often rely on personal experience and background to formulate their questions. As such, the lack of appropriate representation of underrepresented minority leaders in clinical research can be a barrier to adequate study of health conditions relevant to minority groups. In addition, the lack of minority-led clinical investigations can increase skepticism toward research that already exists among underrepresented groups. This skepticism is deeply rooted in historical events, such as the Tuskegee syphilis study, in which investigators deliberately withheld diagnosis and treatment of syphilis from a group of Black men (Freimuth et al., 2001).

For these reasons, it is critical that we address the numerous existing barriers to the recruitment and retention of minority clinical researchers.

One of the largest barriers is the lack of minority representation in medicine overall. Despite a 30-year attempt by U.S. medical schools to increase the presence of underrepresented minorities in medicine, certain groups remain underrepresented; of particular note are those designated "underrepresented minorities" by the American Association of Medical Colleges: African–Americans, Mexican-Americans, mainland Puerto Ricans, and American-Indians (Nickens, Ready, & Petersdorf, 1994). Initial successes in boosting minority enrollment have been dampened by anti-affirmative action rulings and policies while the number of minorities in the population has increased (Terrell & Beaudreau, 2003). In addition, of those minority candidates who enter medicine, few choose research careers. Cregler, Clark, and Jackson (1994) found that barriers to choosing a career in clinical research for these candidates include lack of awareness of academic career opportunities, lack of appropriate role models, and a variety of socioeconomic factors.

Although several medical schools offer summer prematriculation programs designed to improve academic performance of minorities in medical school (Tekian, 1997), critics argue that these programs are inadequate to raise student preparedness to the required levels due to earlier barriers in education that minority youth face (see Nickens et al., 1994). Recent reports indicate the need for focused efforts to increase the candidate pool of minority applicants to medical school. The 2004 Sullivan Commission Report, "Missing Persons: Minorities in the Health Professions," urges academic medical centers to identify potential minority candidates early, and to prepare minority students for the rigor of medical school by helping them acquire skills and behaviors necessary for success well before they apply. To accomplish this, many authors (see Cavazos, 1990; Petersdorf, 1992; Ready & Nickens, 1991) suggest that academic medical centers form relationships with community school systems, including primary, secondary, and undergraduate programs, to foster student interest in medicine. The goal of such early outreach programming is (1) to prepare, motivate, and educate junior high or high school students from underrepresented and/or disadvantaged groups to gain the necessary academic qualifications to pursue a career in health professions (Carline, Patterson, Davis, Irby, & Oakes-Borremo, 1998); and (2) to socialize these students to realistically commit to the long-term rigorous programs demanded by health professions (Lourenco, 1983; Thomson & Denk, 1999). However, too few programs have been rigorously designed based on theories of adolescent career development or have tested those theories so that their insights can be used in the development of future programs. TEACH Research was developed based on the theory of aligned ambition, which examines the influence of adolescents' knowledge, attitudes, and behaviors on their career development.

The Role of Aligned Ambition in Fostering Adolescent Career Development

The likelihood that a high school student may ultimately be excited by and prepared for a career in clinical research can be understood in the context of a broader body of knowledge concerning adolescent career planning. Research by Schneider and Stevenson (1990), Csikszentmihalyi and Snyder (2000), and Mortimer (2003) indicates that most young people in high school are unclear about their occupational futures and have a limited knowledge of the world of work. They tend to over- or underestimate the amount of education they will need for the type of work they wish to pursue and to lack a strategic plan for accomplishing their goals. The theory of aligned ambition, developed by sociologist Barbara Schneider, posits three related factors that constitute a realistic and systematic approach to career goals by adolescents. These factors are (1) career-specific knowledge, (2) realistic attitudes about career options and requirements, and (3) behaviors commensurate with success in the classroom and in the workplace. Taken together, these elements make up *aligned ambition.*

An adolescent with aligned ambitions has a clear sense of the relationship between educational expectations and occupational aspirations (Schneider & Stevenson, 1999). For example, a student with aligned ambitions who aspires to be a neonatologist knows she has to go to medical school and then receive additional training. Academically talented students with aligned ambitions are more likely to imbue their daily routines with a broader purpose of career preparation. As alignment of ambition increases, teenagers are more likely to place their lives within a historical context, to be aware of the changing technological demands of the labor force, and to note the increasing demand for specialized training and educational credentials. They demonstrate knowledge of how the adult world works and incorporate that knowledge into their plans for the future, which often reveal an understanding of the institutional rules governing who is admitted to college, who is considered qualified for specific jobs, and who is likely to be hired. For example, a teenager with aligned ambitions who wants to become a physician is more likely to take advanced science courses in high school and thus increase her chances of admission to a competitive college. She may seek after-school employment in a local hospital, rather than a fast-food restaurant, because she wants to learn more about what it is like to work in a medical setting. Overall, students with aligned ambition strive to achieve their occupational goals in a coherent, detailed, and realistic way.

For minority students, the situation may be quite different. The Alfred P. Sloan Study of Youth and Social Development, one of the few longitudinal studies of career development, tracked more than 8,000 students—including 1,000 who were followed longitudinally over 5 years—with the purpose of exploring teenagers' attitudes and experiences while in class, at school activities, with friends, at home, and on the job. Dr. Barbara Schneider found that, although minority students tend to enjoy school more than their White peers do, they are not as engaged in their activities or as likely to view certain activities as significant to their future careers. Based on data collected using the experience sampling method (ESM; described in detail later), it appears that teenagers from minority backgrounds are less likely than White students to work for pay; they also spend a larger fraction of their free time at home alone or in unstructured activities, rather than in class or participating in extracurricular activities. Furthermore, minority students reported that they did not view school as being relevant to their future, and were often unaware of the implications of poor performance.

That these findings are in contrast to the characteristics associated with aligned ambition should not suggest that minority students—or their parents—have low aspirations for the future. Rather, minority students and their parents disproportionately lack access to information about the world of work, the courses needed for acceptance by more competitive colleges, and the preparation needed for specific occupations. As a result, they may not know how to navigate through an educational system in which their choices can have real consequences that are hard to reverse (Schneider, 2002). For example, not taking advanced courses in high school, such as physics and calculus, or not getting good grades in these subjects, makes it harder to be admitted to a highly selective college, as Schneider, Swanson, and Crumb (1998) observe, and, eventually, to get into medical school (Association of American Medical Colleges, 2002). Given that high performance in math and science, even at the high school level, is an essential prerequisite on the career path of a clinical researcher, the early acquisition of this knowledge is essential.

Students with better knowledge of the sequential steps necessary on a given career path may be in a better position to use their time and effort strategically (e.g., deciding between an advanced placement biology course with its more demanding workload and its more rigorous grading standards, or an honors biology course with a lighter workload and increased chances of earning a good grade). Realistically informed students with aligned ambitions are more likely to choose challenging activities that engage them, that they are good at, and for which there is a reasonable probability of success. In addition, they are more likely to view their activities as related to their ultimate goal.

The picture is very different for underrepresented minority students. They are less likely than their White counterparts to be realistically informed, and more likely to spend a larger fraction of their free time in unstructured activities that are not related to their future goals. In short, students from underrepresented minority backgrounds often lack the requisite knowledge, attitudes, and behaviors that comprise aligned ambition. This gap suggests that structured academic programs tailored to minority youth could provide them with direction, a sense of empowerment, and a feeling of connection to the future. The TEACH Research program is designed to maximize aligned ambition among talented minority students with an interest in clinical research. In the discussion that follows we illustrate some of the mechanisms by which we seek to foster aligned ambition in these adolescents.

Mechanisms for Cultivating Aligned Ambition

Engagement. Teenagers interested in careers in medicine often begin high school taking advanced courses in mathematics and science and by the beginning of their junior year in high school are taking subjects such as trigonometry, calculus, chemistry, and physics. Examining the experiences of these students in high school science classes, Shernoff and Hoogstra (2001) found that student interest and engagement in these classes predicted their decision to major in science in college. Students who are academically engaged and motivated are also more likely to seek advice from knowledgeable peers and adults on course selections or tutoring, if needed. Such students are also more willing to dedicate additional time to mastering course-related materials, including seeking any needed additional academic help. Many of these students have been assisted by their parents throughout their schooling careers in developing these life skills and their knowledge of the world of work.

Minority students, however, are less likely to be engaged in activities significant to their future, less likely to view these activities as significant to their future careers, and less likely to be aware of the implications of poor performance (Csikszentmihalyi & Schneider, 2000). This suggests that in developing activities that are relevant to future careers, educators and mentors must make a concerted effort to engage minority students. Increased engagement may be of particular value in motivating these students to enter a given career.

Role models. Career-specific role models also play a critical role in adolescent career development: They can inspire students to enter a career, and actively guide students to make informed decisions during this process. Minority students, who may be the first in their families to attend college or aspire to a professional career, may have fewer contacts through family or friends to professional career role models. As a result, they may underestimate the amount of education they needed to pursue particular careers, misinterpret the actual work required to achieve a specific occupational goal, or base their perceptions of careers on media images rather than specific role models (Csikszentmihalyi & Schneider, 2000; Schneider & Stevenson, 1999).

This is particularly true in medicine. Studies (Basco & Reigart, 2001; Wright, Wong, & Newill, 1997) suggest that the lack of appropriate mentorship is a major reason that minority high school students who have been exposed to medicine through formal programs without strong mentorship components may not follow through with a career in medicine (Thurmond & Cregler, 1999). However, due to the time mentoring requires and sense of social comfort a high school student may need to ask questions, traditional forms of mentorship (i.e., one-on-one partnerships of high school student with faculty members) may not be successful. Because of the multiple steps required to become a clinical researcher (college student, medical student, resident, fellow, faculty), a structure of mentorship that allows access to potential role models at these different stages can enable minority youth to better envision this process than traditional forms of mentorship. It is suggested that medical students prefer mentors who are culturally similar to themselves because of the level of empathy needed to address racially sensitive issues (Parker, 2002). The concentration of minority practitioners in technical fields, as opposed to primary care specialties (Babbott et al., 1994; Lieu et al., 1989), makes this a challenge for the recruitment of potential clinical research mentors, many of whom are drawn from specialties like internal medicine. For more on the role of racial diversity in mentoring, see Cregler et al. (1994), Parker (2002), and Thomas (2001); for a fuller discussion of the matching of mentorship dyads along racial lines, see Blake-Beard, Bayne, Crosby, and Muller (2011).

University–community partnerships are one way to expose students to career-specific role models outside their communities. Educational institutions have the potential to play a pivotal role in developing the career ambitions of urban youth whose parents have limited economic and social resources. Hill (in preparation) has found that minority adolescents in urban schools—primarily African–American and Hispanic in families with limited economic resources—succeed when the school helps with many of the activities and values that adolescents in suburban schools receive from their parents or communities. Some of these activities include guidance on course selections, preparation to take college admissions tests, meeting college representatives who visit the high school, and visiting college campuses. Recognizing the limited resources of these students, a number of educational institutions have engaged in community partnerships designed to increase the college-going rates of these underrepresented minorities and low-income youth, and to assist them in achieving their career goals.

As a result of initial evaluation of the university–community partnerships studied by Hill (see also National Center for Education Statistics, 2001), several factors have emerged as necessary for effectively promoting minority student entry into health professions (Association of American Medical Colleges, 2004; Carline & Patterson, 2003). Successful partnerships depend on prior experience, institutional commitments and resources, clear and common goals, community support, and shared governance. In addition, other characteristics that predict a successful partnership are a pre-existing relationship between partners either through institutions or an individual personal connection, strategic responsiveness, and communication and coordination between members. In designing the TEACH Research Program, we looked to this research to provide a blueprint for a successful career development partnership that would provide strong role models.

Using These Theories to Design the TEACH Program

Based on the research outlined above, we hypothesize that early introduction of a highly structured real-life career experience, including interaction with mentors at various stages of career development, may result in more informed and realistic career development among minority adolescents. From this hypothesis, we have developed the intervention TEACH Research. We are currently evaluating this program with a group of academically talented urban high school students to test a specific theoretical model of how best to support and inspire talented minority youth to enter careers in clinical research.

Participants

TEACH participants are drawn from a pool of approximately 60 rising high school juniors, participants in the University of Chicago's Collegiate Scholars Program, an intensive 3-year enrichment program designed to prepare talented Chicago Public Schools high school students for academic success at the best colleges and universities. Starting in the summer after ninth grade, collegiate scholars select classes in literature, math, science, social sciences, and writing taught by University of Chicago faculty. During the school year, they participate in a series of Saturday seminars in mathematics, laboratory science, social sciences, and humanities, as well as social activities such as playing sports or taking trips to museums.

Selection into this program is highly competitive. In addition to attracting academic high achievers (85% have a 4.0 grade point average or higher, and 60% are ranked in the top 10 of their freshman class), the program targets students from ethnically and demographically underrepresented groups. Over 50% of collegiate scholars are underrepresented minorities (41% African–American and 24% Latino/Hispanic), and 47.4% qualify to receive free or reduced lunch. Moreover, 41.56% of collegiate scholars will be first-generation college students. For the past 4 years, interested juniors from the Collegiate Scholars Program have been randomized either to participate in the TEACH Research program or to continue with didactic science courses (similar to more traditional programs such as the Johns Hopkins Center for Talented Youth and the Harvard Summer Secondary School Program) through funding from NIGMS R01 Effectiveness of TEACH Research.

Structure of the Intervention

The conceptual framework underlying the TEACH Research program is based on the need to cultivate aligned ambition (the combination of career-specific knowledge, career-oriented attitudes, and goal-oriented behavior) to influence

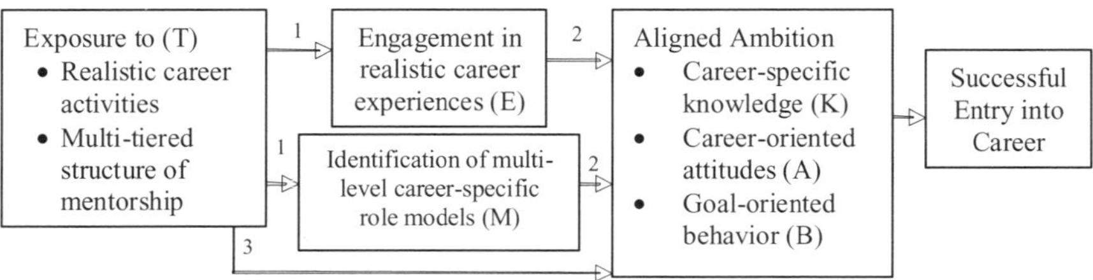

Fig. 1. Conceptual framework for TEACH Research.

adolescent career choice (see Figure 1). The factors responsible for influencing career choice that form the foundation for the career development program, as discussed above, are: (1) students' participation in realistic career activities that actively challenge and engage them and (2) exposure to multitiered structure of mentorship that aids identification of multilevel career-specific role models that can enable career choice (see Schneider & Stevenson, 1999; Shernoff & Hoogstra, 2001; Wright et al., 1997).

Student engagement in realistic career activities. To foster student engagement and build aligned ambition, we have incorporated two distinct career-focused activities into the TEACH experience. Realistic career activities in TEACH Research include (1) a hands-on clinical research experience through an internship with the University of Chicago Hospitalist Project (described in detail below), and (2) observation of clinical rounds with physicians.

The University of Chicago Hospitalist Project. The training context for TEACH Research is the Hospital Medicine Research Program (Hospitalist Project), a large clinical research program that assesses quality of care and resource allocation for hospitalized patients on the general medicine service at the University of Chicago. (For more information on the Hospitalist Project, see also Chung et al., 2002; Meltzer, 2003; Meltzer et al., 2002; Shah, Schmit, Croley, & Meltzer, 2003.) The program, funded since 1997, includes a diverse set of studies examining determinants of the quality and outcomes of hospital care. The program has studied over 80,000 patients at the University of Chicago since 1997 and has completed a multicenter trial involving over 34,000 patients at six hospitals. Undergraduate work-study students do a substantial part of the work required for these massive studies. As a result, in addition to the project's primary contributions to understanding the determinants of the quality of hospital care, the Hospitalist Project has had an unexpected benefit from a training perspective by providing valuable clinical research exposure for University of Chicago undergraduate and medical students. For example, first-year medical students in the Pritzker School of

Medicine Summer Research Program participate in a 12-week experience to complete a mentored research project that culminates in preparation of a manuscript and presentation. Two of us (Dr. Meltzer and Dr. Arora) serve each year as mentors for these medical students and for many of the undergraduate students who work on the Hospitalist Project as paid research assistants. The rich network of student and faculty involvement on this project and its history of inspiring trainees to pursue research careers provides an excellent foundation for TEACH Research.

TEACH students are fully trained in compliance with HIPAA (the Health Insurance Portability and Accountability Act of 1996, which dictates national privacy standards in regard to identifiable health information), and are expected to work alongside full-time Hospitalist Project research assistants during their summer experience. They assume many of the same duties: reviewing patient charts to assess quality of care, conducting follow-up phone interviews with discharged patients, and interviewing patients at the bedside. Students rotate through these activities according to a set schedule, to ensure that each student has the chance to experience the full cross-section of work necessary for a successful large-scale clinical research study. Expectations are high: Students are integrated into the Hospitalist Project staff for the 6-week duration of TEACH, and it is assumed that they will be able to function independently in completing complex and sequential tasks (e.g., chart abstraction, long-form phone interviews). Because virtually every morning of the TEACH program is devoted to work on the Hospitalist Project, students gain significant perspective and experience with the project's methods and goals. Many TEACH students stay on during the school year to work as paid part-time research assistants. This structured, research-oriented experience provides students with a concrete idea of many of the facets of clinical research, and gives them a chance to involve themselves with this work at a high level of engagement.

Observation of clinical rounds. The second mechanism by which TEACH students can engage themselves with a realistic career-oriented activity is the shadowing component of the program. At the start of the program, students are divided into pairs, and approximately once a week each pair of students has the opportunity to follow a doctor on his/her rounds, or to observe his/her clinical practice. This provides an opportunity for students to observe a clinical professional in action, and to gain a realistic sense of a doctor's duties. Students are able not only to witness life inside the hospital, but also, to a degree, to participate in it; they must internalize some of the requirements and sacrifices inherent in a clinical career. For example, students know that to participate in clinical rounds they must arrive early at the hospital, dress professionally, and follow established protocol at all times. In this way, they are able not only to acquire a realistic notion of what the work of a clinical professional consists of, but also to immerse themselves in some of its day-to-day challenges.

Multi-tiered mentorship. To exhibit aligned ambition, it is crucial that adolescents acquire a realistic sense of the requirements of a given career. As shown above, this can be accomplished through engagement with highly structured career-oriented activities. However, more fully aligned ambition also requires that adolescents be exposed to career-specific mentors and role models. Exposure to a multi-tiered structure of mentors occurs in the TEACH Research program in two settings: (1) a series of discussions led by undergraduates, medical students, and faculty members that will facilitate acquisition of knowledge of clinical research and career strategies to enable entry into a career in clinical research; and (2) participation in a research team consisting of a clinical research faculty member, one medical student, two undergraduate students, and four high school students. This exposure provides high school students an opportunity to interact with mentors from all levels of career development, strengthening their own understanding of the process of clinical research training, and enabling the formation of relationships with career-specific role models. As Phinney, Torres Campos, Padilla Kallemeyn, and Kim (2011) find in their study of mentorship interventions for Latino college freshmen, mentorship by student peers can provide meaningful gains in what they term "the psychosocial factors that underlie academic performance"—including the knowledge, attitudes, and behaviors necessary for navigating academic and career pathways successfully.

Lectures and discussions. Every afternoon, TEACH students attend a lecture or panel discussion designed to address a variety of career questions. These sessions are designed to strengthen knowledge of clinical research, and to build strategies for entry into a career in clinical research. Students hear from active clinical professionals on subjects both personal and professional: they participate in a talk focused on "The Life of a Clinical Researcher" that relates the sequential career path through personal stories, as well as engaging with such topics as human subjects research, study methods and design, and racial disparities in health care. (See Table 1 for more examples.)

TEACH students also hear from panels of medical students, residents, fellows, and undergraduates, who discuss topics such as choosing a college, securing financial aid, and looking ahead to medical school. All of these talks have a conversational structure, with students encouraged to participate through questions and/or workshop-type exercises. The wide variety of topics, as well as the varying backgrounds of the speakers—drawn from across stages of the career path—ensure that TEACH students will hear a broad range of perspectives. Through these talks, clinicians and students alike are able to model appropriate attitudes and behaviors for TEACH students, as well as to enhance the students' knowledge of various technical aspects of clinical research.

Table 1. TEACH Research Talks

Education and training	Topics in clinical research
Choosing a college	The importance of clinical research
Medical school	Human subjects research and informed consent
Residency training	Racial disparities in healthcare
Fellowship training	Methods: Study design
Inpatient clinical rounds introduction	Methods: Qualitative research methods
Introduction to clinic	Methods: Literature search and review
Physician-Scientist: MD/PhD programs	Community-based participatory research
Funding an education	Quality improvement and medical error
The life of a clinical researcher	

TEACH Research teams. At the start of the program, TEACH students are divided into three groups of four and assigned to research teams. These teams are composed of four high school students, two college students, one medical student, and one clinical faculty member. Each team has its own research question—usually focused on the faculty member's own current research—and is responsible for formulating a collaborative project based on that question over the course of the summer. (Recent research topics include methods for pain measurement, spirituality in hospitalized patients, patient care transitions among hospitalists, and smoking cessation programming.) The TEACH experience culminates in a poster session, attended by doctors and clinical researchers, Collegiate Scholars Program staff, community members, and parents, in which students present their findings formally before an audience.

Through the research teams, TEACH students are able not only to work alongside clinical professionals to address important research problems, but also to engage with mentors and role models at varying stages of career development. Students thus gain a realistic appreciation for the different steps of the clinical research career path, from undergraduate work through faculty scholarship. Moreover, we believe it is crucial to provide the students with access to younger mentors, who are closer to the students' developmental stage, who have more time to work with them directly, and with whom they more easily identify, so that students will learn the skills to be better able to engage with career-specific role models at more advanced stages.

Efficacy of TEACH Research

While TEACH has not been in existence long enough to evaluate its effect on entry into clinical research, we are exploring the effect of realistic career experiences and a multitiered network of mentors on elements of aligned ambition,

Table 2. Methods for Evaluation of TEACH Research

Element of model	Instrument
Career-specific knowledge (K)	Tests—knowledge, careers in health research
Career-oriented attitudes (A)	Career orientation survey
Goal-oriented behavior (B)	Career orientation survey
Engagement (E)	Experience sampling method (ESM)
Mentors and Role Models (M)	ESM

which has been shown to be an important predictor of successful entry into a career. To test the efficacy of TEACH Research in promoting the development of aligned ambition in minority youth, we are using multimodal methods, including tests and surveys are used to evaluate career-specific knowledge, appropriate attitudes, and goal-oriented behaviors, and assessing the engagement of students within TEACH and whether TEACH helps the students to identify mentors and role models (Table 2).

To assess the development of career-specific knowledge, students take pre- and posttests designed to solicit whether students understand basics of clinical research in addition to how to become a researcher. For example, students are asked to answer items regarding trial design and to report the types of classes that are included in pre-medical requirements. Pre- and postvideo interviews are also administered asking students to report responses to open-ended questions such as "How do you become a researcher?" Video interviews are also used to determine if students have acquired a career-specific role model by asking them to "Tell me about someone who is helping you in your decisions about college or the future." While most students list parents and teachers, we are specifically interested in whether students who participate in the TEACH Research program are more likely to name one of the students or faculty they encountered through the multitiered mentoring system.

To measure changes in career-oriented attitudes, students are administered a pre- and post-Career Orientation Survey that assesses values and attitudes consistent with a career in clinical research. For example, students are asked if they envision a career in which they will be leading a team, presenting information, and synthesizing or evaluating data.

To assess goal-oriented behaviors, we use the ESM, originally developed and applied for the study of occupational satisfaction at the University of Chicago by Mihaly Czikszentmihalyi, to collect detailed, real-time data on participants' subjective interpretations of their experiences. ESM is a method for recording cognitive processes, experienced emotions, and physiologic states in naturalistic settings (outside the lab or field situations) as they occur in real time

(Csikszentmihalyi & Larson, 1987). Concretely, ESM accomplishes this by providing the respondent with an electronic pager, watch, or other device that is programmed to provide a random signal at varying intervals throughout the day and then ask the respondent to report how they are feeling at the moment (Palen & Salzman, 2002). By capturing the representativeness of experiences from the natural environment, the method facilitates the acquisition of ecologically valid research. This innovative methodology can provide greater insight than usual retrospective approaches to assessment of satisfaction or engagement (via surveys or interviews, for example). First, data collection occurs in real time. Because the subjects respond to questions that are directed primarily to what they are experiencing concurrently, there is a minimum of difficulty with recall bias. Secondly, the responses will provide a subject-centered context: For example, using ESM surveys, adequate information can be obtained about what experiential factors or activities may drive changes in the outcome (emotion or feeling being studied). Third, this method allows the survey to be given without the presence of any interviewer, which may alter subjects' responses.

To evaluate engagement in TEACH Research, ESM data are collected using preprogrammed wristwatch alerts that prompt students to rate their activity. Because students' levels of engagement are likely to increase as they become more skilled in program activities, students are surveyed using the ESM at two distinct periods during the study period: Week 1 and week 3 of the program. During ESM periods, students wear digital watches programmed to provide random alerts eight times a day between the hours of 8 a.m. and 10 p.m. At the time of the prompt, students are asked to report their activity, rate their engagement in the activity (on a scale from 0 to 9), and also to rate their feelings about the activity. To date, ESM data have been used to compare the overall engagement of TEACH Research students versus the control group at various periods of program participation.

While evaluation of TEACH has not yet been completed, preliminary findings offer a snapshot of how a highly structured program focused on cultivating aligned ambition can impact career development. Initial ESM findings suggest that TEACH students react strongly to the challenges and high expectations presented by the hospital environment, but that by week 3 they grow accustomed to their surroundings and rise to the challenge of the program. One year after completion of the program, TEACH students' career ambitions are more likely to reflect a refining and deepening of medical aspirations, as well as an increased interest in research-based careers. Furthermore, follow-up video interviews suggest that TEACH students demonstrate concrete understanding of both the knowledge and the attitudes necessary for entry into a career in research: They grasp both the academic prerequisites and the importance of actively engaging in a search for research opportunities (see Table 3).

When asked about role models, TEACH students list their work in the hospital and through the program as a source of strong role modeling; they frequently cast

Table 3. Sample Findings from Follow-Up Video Interviews

Question	TEACH follow-up	Control follow-up
"How do you become a researcher?"	"Statistics. . .math. . .sociology if you're dealing with people"	"I guess a regular 4-year university. . .I'm not really sure what comes after that"
	"College for one thing. . .And from then on you can get more expertise by doing masters, doctorate"	"I'm guessing work for a company and they ask you to do research"
	"Throughout college, take research opportunities that might be available to you. . .get that experience and then eventually look for a job"	"Depending on what field. . .you need to be able to read a certain subject and be able to understand it"
"Is there someone who is guiding your decisions about the future?"	"Just the people who are around me on a daily basis. . .in school, my teachers, the people in the Hospitalist Project. . .they just influence me for the better"	"My brother the most, because he's two and a half years older and he's going through the experiences I will be going through later"
	"I talk to my parents about college constantly. . .so I'm pretty well informed"	"My mother. . .my counselor"
	"My economics teacher. . .has become my life mentor"	"Collegiate Scholars Program is doing a college countdown"

themselves in an actively participatory role with regard to seeking out role models; and they talk about mentorship as it pertains to their own lives. By contrast, control students tend to list more generic role models such as older siblings or parents (see Table 3).

Limitations of the Intervention

In examining the design of the TEACH Research Program we recognize several limitations, most notably the short duration of the program. At its current length of 6 weeks, the program provides an intensive but brief engagement with the clinical research environment. Mentorship relationships might develop more fully over a longer-term program, and student engagement with career activities might deepen over an extended course of time. Given the scheduling constraints of students' summer enrollment with the Collegiate Scholars Program, however, it is at this time not possible to extend the duration of TEACH Research.

Furthermore, we wish to highlight the fact that TEACH Research is a highly targeted intervention dealing primarily with students' psychosocial orientation to career preparation—knowledge, attitudes, and behaviors—rather than with "root" factors such as family background or socioeconomic status. Additionally, TEACH Research focuses on aligning student ambition rather than cultivating basic study skills, and as such may be better suited to underrepresented minority students who are already proven academic achievers. A program not targeted to the specialized Collegiate Scholars Program population might face very different concerns.

A final consideration is the minimal follow-up currently conducted with student participants. TEACH students are tracked and tested extensively during the course of the program, but follow-up video interviews are conducted only once, at the 1-year mark. To more fully assess the effects of the intervention, we hope to be able to conduct longer-range follow-up interviews and testing with TEACH Research participants in the future.

Conclusion

Encouraging minority youth to enter careers in health research is crucial in addressing what the American Association of Medical Colleges characterizes as "the urgent need for a diverse physician workforce" both as a matter of equality of opportunity and to improve the provision of care for underserved communities (Association of American Medical Colleges, 2002; see also Cohen et al., 2002). TEACH Research is a theoretically grounded intervention designed to promote the entry of talented high school students of diverse racial and socioeconomic backgrounds into these careers by helping them to align their knowledge, attitudes, and behaviors with those needed for successful entry into these careers. Whether the realistic career experience and exposure to multitiered mentorship built into TEACH will produce the engagement and role-specific role models and, in turn, knowledge, attitudes, and behaviors that the theory if aligned ambition suggests are needed to produce entry into careers in health research will be addressed by our current work. If we find that TEACH does produce these effects, then the next step will be larger and longer-term studies to determine whether TEACH can, in fact, increase entry of minority youth into these careers in health research. The duration and needed scale of such studies will necessitate creative thought if they are to be supported through traditional NIH mechanisms. Research such as that described here and additional research to develop and validate intermediate and longer-term outcomes of programs such as TEACH will be important precursors to such studies. It will also be important to assess the potential for programs such as TEACH to be expanded to new research settings. Together, studies such as these will help build the scientific base for the larger and longer-term studies that will likely be needed to determine whether programs such as TEACH should become an important tools in national efforts to promote the entry of minority youth into careers in health research.

References

Association of American Medical Colleges (2002). *Minority students in medical education: Fact and figures XII*. Washington, DC: Association of American Medical Colleges.

Association of American Medical Colleges (2004). *Learning from others: A literature review and how-to guide from the health professions partnership initiative*. Washington, DC: Association of American Medical Colleges.

Babbott, D., Weaver, S. O., & Baldwin, D. C. (1994). Primary care by desire or default? Specialty choices of minority graduates of U.S. medical schools in 1983. *Journal of the National Medical Association, 86*, 509–515.

Basco, W. T. Jr., & Reigart, J. R. (2001). When do medical students identify career-influencing physician role models? *Academic Medicine, 76*(4), 380–382. doi:10.1097/00001888–200104000-00017.

Bierman, A. S., Lurie, N., Collins, K. S., & Eisenberg, J. M. (2002). Addressing racial and ethnic barriers to effective health care: The need for better data. *Health Affairs, 21*(3), 91–102. doi:10.1377/hlthaff.21.3.91.

Blake-Beard, S., Bayne, M. L., Crosby, F. J., & Muller, C. B. (2011). Matching by race and gender in mentoring relationships: Keeping our eyes on the prize. *Journal of Social Issues, 67*(3), 622-643.

Carline, J. D., & Patterson, D. G. (2003). Characteristics of health professions schools, public school systems, and community-based organizations in successful partnerships to increase the numbers of underrepresented minority students entering health professions education. *Academic Medicine, 78*, 467–482. doi:10.1097/00001888–200305000-00008.

Carline, J. D., Patterson, D. G., Davis, L. A., Irby, D. M., & Oakes-Borremo, P. (1998). Precollege enrichment programs intended to increase the representation of minorities in medicine. *Academic Medicine, 73*(3), 288–298. doi:10.1097/00001888–199803000-00018.

Cavazos, L. F. (1990). Restructuring education and its impact on medical education. *Academic Medicine, 65*, 230–233. doi:10.1097/00001888–199004000-00003.

Centers for Disease Control and Prevention. (2011) *CDC Health Disparities and Inequalities Report— United States, 2011. MMWR* 2011(60); Suppl. Atlanta, GA: Centers for Disease Control and Prevention.

Chung, P., Morrison, J., Jin, L., Levinson, W., Humphrey H., & Meltzer, D. (2002). Resident satisfaction on an academic hospitalist service: Time to teach. *American Journal of Medicine, 112*(7), 597–601. doi:10.1016/S0002–9343(02)01155–5.

Cohen, J. J., Gabriel, B. A., & Terrell, C. (2002). The case for diversity in the health care workforce. *Health Affairs, 21*(5), 90–102. doi:10.1377/hlthaff.21.5.90.

Cregler, L. L., Clark, L. T., & Jackson, E. B. Jr. (1994). Careers in academic medicine and clinical practice for minorities: Opportunities and barriers. *Journal of the Association of Academic Minority Physicians, 5*(2), 68–73.

Csikszentmihalyi, M., & Larson, R. (1987). Validity and reliability of the experience-sampling method. *Journal of Mental and Nervous Disease, 175*, 526–535. doi:10.1097/00005053–198709000-00004.

Csikszentmihalyi, M., & Schneider, B. (2000). *Becoming adult: How teenagers prepare for the world of work*. New York: Basic Books.

Freimuth, V. S., Quinn, S. C., Thomas, S. B., Cole, G., Zook, E., & Duncan, T. (2001). African Americans' views on research and the Tuskegee Syphilis Study. *Social Science Medicine, 52*(5), 797–808. doi:10.1016/S0277–9536(00)00178–7.

Hill, L. D. (in preparation). High school resources and post secondary outcomes: Implications for a changing student population. In B. Schneider (Ed.), *Strategies for Success* (forthcoming).

LaVeist, TA. (2005). *Minority populations and health: An introduction to health disparities in the United States*. San Francisco, CA: Jossey-Bass.

Lieu, T. A., Schroeder, S. A., & Altman, D. F. (1989). Specialty choices at one medical school: Recent trends and analysis of predictive facts. *Academic Medicine, 64*, 622–629. doi:10.1097/00001888–198910000-00015.

Lourenco, S. V. (1983). Early outreach: Career awareness for health professions. *Journal of Medical Education, 58*, 39–44. doi:10.1097/00001888–198301000-00008.

Meltzer, D. (2003). David Meltzer, physician and economist, discusses the new hospitalist movement. Interview by Sarah Pressman Lovinger. *JAMA: The Journal of the American Medical Association, 289*(4), 411–413. doi:10.1001/jama.289.4.411.

Meltzer, D., Manning, W., Morrison, J., Shah, M., Jin, L., Guth, T., et al. (2002). Effects of physician experience on costs and outcomes on an academic general medicine service: Results of a trial of hospitalists. *Annals of International Medicine, 137*, 866–874.

Mortimer, J. T. (2003). *Working and growing up in America*. Cambridge, MA: Harvard University Press.

National Center for Education Statistics (2001). *Paving the way to postsecondary education: K-12 intervention programs for underrepresented youth. Report of the National Postsecondary Education Cooperative Working Group on Access to Postsecondary Education*, Washington, DC: National Center for Education Statistics.

NIH Director's Panel on Clinical Research. (1997, December). Executive Summary, Report of the NIH Director's Panel on Clinical Research (CRP). Retrieved October 22, 2004, from http://www.nih.gov/news/crp/97report/.

Nickens, H. W., Ready, T. P., & Petersdorf, P. G. (1994). Sounding board: Project 3000 by 2000—racial and ethnic diversity in U.S. medical schools. *New England Journal of Medicine, 331*, 472–476. doi:10.1056/NEJM199408183310712.

Palen, L., & Salzman, M. (2002). Voice-mail diary studies for naturalistic data capture under mobile conditions, *CSCW*, 87–95. doi:10.1145/587091.587092.

Parker, D. L. (2002). A workshop on mentoring across gender and culture lines. *Academic Medicine, 77*(5), 461. doi:10.1097/00001888–200205000-00034.

Petersdorf, P. G. (1992). Not a choice, an obligation. *Academic Medicine, 67*, 73–79.

Phinney, J. S., Torres Campos, C. M., Kallemeyn, D. M. P., & Kim, C. (2011). Processes and outcomes of a mentoring program for Latino college freshmen. *Journal of Social Issues, 67*(3), 599–621.

Ready, T., & Nickens, H. W. (1991). Black men in the medical education pipeline: Past, present, and future. *Academic Medicine, 66*, 181–187. doi:10.1097/00001888–199104000-00001.

Schneider, B. (2002). Strategies for success: High school and beyond. In D. Ravitch (Ed.) *Brookings papers on educational policy* (pp. 55–93). Washington, DC: Brookings Institution Press.

Schneider, B., & Stevenson, D. (1999). *The ambitious generation: America's teenagers, motivated but directionless*. New Haven, CT: Yale University Press.

Schneider, B., Swanson, C. B., & Crumb, C. R. (1998). Opportunities for learning: Course sequences and positional advantages. *Social Psychology of Education, 2*(1), 25–53.

Shah, M. N., Schmit, J., Croley, W. C., & Meltzer D. (2003). Continuity of antibiotic therapy in patients admitted from the emergency department. *Annals of Emergency Medicine, 42*(1), 117–123. doi:10.1067/mem.2003.257.

Shernoff, D., & Hoogstra, L. (2001). Continuing motivation beyond the high school classroom. In M. Michaelson & J. Nakamura (Eds.) *Supportive frameworks for youth engagement. New Directions for Child and Adolescent Development* (pp. 73–87). San Francisco, CA: Jossey-Bass.

Sullivan Commission. (2004). *Missing persons: Minorities in the health professions. A report of the Sullivan Commission on diversity in the healthcare workforce. Executive summary*. Retrieved from http://www.sullivancommission.org./, accessed on October 22, 2004.

Tekian, A. (1997). A thematic review of the literature of underrepresented minorities and medical training, 1981–1995: Securing the foundations of the bridge to diversity. *Academic Medicine, 72*(10), S140–S146. doi:10.1097/00001888–199710000-00070.

Terrell, C., & Beaudreau, J. (2003). 3000 by 2000 and beyond: Next steps for promoting diversity in the health professions. *Journal of Dental Education, 67*(9), 1048–1052.

Thomas, D. (2001). The truth about mentoring minorities: Race matters. *Harvard Business Review*, 99–107.

Thomson, W. A., & Denk, J. P. (1999). Promoting diversity in the medical school pipeline: A national overview. *Academic Medicine, 74*(4), 312–314. doi:10.1097/00001888–199904000-00010.

Thurmond, V. B., & Cregler, L. L. (1999). Why students drop out of the pipeline to health professions careers: A follow-up of gifted minority high school students. *Academic Medicine, 74*(4), 448–451. doi:10.1097/00001888–199904000-00044

Wright, S., Wong, A., & Newill, C. (1997). The impact of role models on medical students. *Journal of General Internal Medicine, 12*(1), 53–56. doi:10.1007/s11606–006-0007–1.

VINEET ARORA, MD, MAPP is Assistant Dean for Scholarship and Discovery at the Pritzker School of Medicine at the University of Chicago. Her research focuses on incorporating and evaluating interventions to improve medical training and the quality and safety of patient care. She co-directs the NIH-sponsored Pritzker Summer Research Program, which provides 80 first-year medical students the opportunity to participate in mentored research. She also directs the NIH-sponsored Training Early Achievers for Careers in Health (TEACH) Research Program, which prepares talented Chicago high school students to enter research careers.

BARBARA SCHNEIDER, PhD is the John A. Hannah Chair and University Distinguished Professor in the College of Education and Department of Sociology at Michigan State University. She worked for 18 years at the University of Chicago, holding positions as a Professor in Sociology and Human Development and as a senior researcher at NORC. Currently she continues to hold an appointment as a university faculty research associate at the University of Chicago and as senior fellow at NORC, where she is the principal investigator of the NSF funded center on Advancing Research and Communication in STEM. Her research focuses on how the social contexts of schools and families influence the academic and social well-being of adolescents as they move into adulthood. Professor Schneider has published 12 books and over 100 articles and reports on family, social context of schooling, and sociology of knowledge. She received her PhD from Northwestern University.

REBECCA THAL, BA is the Administrator of the Committee on Clinical and Translational Science at the University of Chicago. She served as Lead Research Assistant for the TEACH Research Program from 2008–2009.

David Meltzer, MD, PhD is Director of the Center for Health and the Social Sciences (CHeSS) and Chief of the Section of Hospital Medicine at the University of Chicago. His research focuses on using social science techniques to improve the quality and cost of care, with major foci in the cost and quality of hospital care and the theoretical foundations of medical cost-effectiveness analysis. He serves as Principal Investigator for NIH grants that help support the evaluation of TEACH and the Pritzker Summer Research program, and a Center for Evaluation and Research in Therapeutics (CERT) from AHRQ that provides the Hospital Medicine research infrastructure utilized by many TEACH students.

Journal of Social Issues, Vol. 67, No. 3, 2011, pp. 599–621

Processes and Outcomes of a Mentoring Program for Latino College Freshmen

Jean S. Phinney*
California State University

Cidhinnia M. Torres Campos
University of New Haven

Delia M. Padilla Kallemeyn
Western University of Health Sciences

Chami Kim
California State University

The goals of this research program were to develop, implement, and evaluate a mentoring program for Latino college freshmen and to identify processes that account for the effects of the program. In two longitudinal studies, at-risk Latino freshmen (mentees) were mentored from fall to spring by upper division or graduate students from psychology and counseling majors and compared in the spring to an equivalent sample of nonmentored students (nonmentees). In both studies, mentees showed improvement in psychosocial factors that underlie academic performance. In the second study, mentees decreased in depression and stress and were less likely than nonmentees be classified as being at risk for poor academic outcomes. The amount of mentor–mentee contact and the quality of the relationship contributed to positive outcomes for mentees. Results suggest that mentors are of value in alleviating psychosocial risk factors. Selecting at-risk students and using experienced peers as mentors make the program cost effective.

Latino youth and young adults are the largest and fastest growing racial/ethnic population in the United States (Guzmán, 2001; Perkins & Villaruel, 2000).

---

*Correspondence concerning this article should be addressed to Jean S. Phinney, California State University, 1212 Colusa Ave., Berkeley, CA 94707 [e-mail: jphinne@calstatela.edu].

This research was supported in part by the MBRS SCORE Program of the National Institutes of Health through grant S06 GM08101.

599

However, Latino students have lower levels of educational attainment in high school and college as compared to their African–American and non-Hispanic European-American peers (Meier & Stewart, 1991; U.S. Census Bureau, 2004; U.S. Department of Education, 1992). National educational statistics consistently demonstrate that the gap in educational attainment persists in college and beyond. Only 35% of 18- to 24-year-old Latinos enroll in college compared to 46% of European-Americans (Fry, 2002), and only 11% of Latinos (18–24 years of age) have a bachelor's degree, compared to 34% of European-Americans (U.S. Census Bureau, 2004). These figures suggest that substantial numbers of Latinos are being lost to the pool of students who complete college and might pursue careers in science, technology, engineering, and math (STEM). In recognition of this situation, programs have been developed to improve academic outcomes, and mentoring has become an important component of such programs (e.g., Maldonado, Rhoads, & Buenavista, 2005).

Theoretical bases for mentoring include attachment theory (Ainsworth, 1989), which suggests that a relationship with a nurturing older person can contribute to psychosocial outcomes, and sociocultural theory (Vygotsky, 1978), which proposes that a more experienced individual can contribute to positive developmental outcomes. In addition, group socialization theory highlights the importance of peer mentors (Karcher, 2005). Research on mentoring has focused primarily on adolescents (DuBois & Karcher, 2005). Programs for youth have been developed on the assumption that mentoring can lead to a variety of positive outcomes, particularly for those whose family or community are unable to provide adequate support (Rhodes, 2005). There is growing research evidence that mentoring programs make a valuable contribution to successful youth development (DuBois & Karcher, 2005).

With regard to college students, research has traditionally focused on the development of academic skills through tutoring. However, psychosocial factors may be as important or more important than academics for students from diverse backgrounds (Sedlacek, 2004). For Latinos in particular, there are numerous obstacles to succeeding in college, of which academic skills are only one. Latinos, on average, are of lower socioeconomic status than other ethnic groups and thus have great financial need (Swail, Cabrera, & Lee, 2004). They tend to attend schools with lower academic standards and therefore may be less well prepared for college (Fry, 2005). Proportionally more Latinos have parents who did not attend college (Rodriguez, 1996; Strage, 2000; Wawrzynski & Sedlacek, 2003). These parents generally know less about the American educational system and often are not able to help them with college-related issues (Ceballo, 2004; Fuligni, 1997; Okagaki & Frensch, 1998). Cultural differences, such as parents' prioritizing obligations to help with family chores over studying, may present additional challenges (Fuligni & Tseng, 1999; Phinney, Ong, & Madden, 2000; Tseng, 2004).

These factors suggest that Latinos, compared to other students, may need more help in understanding and negotiating the demands of college, especially in their freshman year. Mentoring programs may be particularly well suited for helping Latinos, because mentors can provide personal support that addresses psychosocial as well as academic needs (Swail et al., 2004). For example, Latino students who reported being mentored reported feeling better adjusted to college life (Bordes & Arredondo, 2005)

A number of psychosocial factors play a role in academic success. Dennis, Phinney, and Chuateco (2005) showed that stronger motivation to attend college for personal satisfaction or career-related reasons predicted better adjustment to college 9 months later. A meta-analytic study of college students (Robbins et al., 2004) reported that students having higher levels of motivation achieved significantly higher grade point averages (GPAs). Research with undergraduate college students has shown that self-efficacy is a positive predictor of academic performance (Pajares & Miller, 1994). The work of Chemers, Zurbriggen, Syed, and Bearman (2011) supports the role of self-efficacy on academic commitment. The ability to handle stress can also affect academic success (Brooks & DuBois, 1995). The same difficulties may be experienced differently by students, depending on their coping ability (Phinney & Haas, 2003). Depression can cause impairment to a person's academic productivity. It tends to increase a student's risk of academic impairment (Heiligenstein & Guenther, 1996) and is related to lower GPAs (Fazio & Palm, 1998).

College students vary in the social support they receive, and the availability of support has been linked with academic adjustment (Astin, 1993; Tinto, 1993), social adjustment (e.g., Solberg, Valdez, & Villarreal, 1994), personal-emotional adjustment (e.g., Kenny & Stryker, 1996), overall adjustment to college (e.g., Solberg et al., 1994), and GPA (Dennis et al., 2005). Similarly, academic support programs have been shown to create a sense of belonging among Latino college students (Hurtado & Ponjuan, 2005).

The current study aimed to enhance college performance through mentoring, by focusing on psychosocial characteristics that influence performance but can be more easily changed than underlying factors such as parental education and income. These characteristics (academic and university motivation, self-efficacy, support, sense of belonging, ability to cope with stress, and depression) were studied in college freshmen to see if and how they changed during the academic year, and determine whether the mentoring program made a difference is any such changes. We also evaluated their relationship to academic outcomes, such as GPA.

Research that has examined the processes that account for the effects of mentoring suggests that the quality of the mentoring relationship is critical (Barrera & Bonds, 2005; Parra, DuBois, Neville, Pugh-Lilly, & Povinelli, 2002). In addition, the type of contact and length of time spent with a mentor can influence outcomes (DuBois & Neville, 1997; Sanchez, Esparza, & Colon, 2008; Smith-Jentsch,

Scielzo, Yarbrough, & Rosopa, 2008). A goal of the current study was to identify processes that may explain positive effects of mentoring in college.

Mentoring programs differ widely in their structure and focus. Such programs have been predominantly directed at adolescents (Dubois & Karcher, 2005). Among programs for college students, the usual mentors have been faculty members, advisors, and counselors (e.g., Hurtado et al., 2011). A cost effective but little explored alternative to faculty mentors is the use of peer mentors. Older peers who have themselves recently experienced being new college students can often relate to beginning students more easily than faculty members, who are not only older but who also generally come from a background different from that of minority students. Peers can also more easily form a relationship based on shared interests outside the classroom. The current studies used senior and graduate level students as mentors of entering college freshmen.

Furthermore, given the limited resources available for academic support programs, targeted interventions, aimed at identifying and intervening with students at the highest levels of risk, can provide help where it is most needed (Torres Campos et al., 2009). Students with little internalized motivation, a low sense of self-efficacy, high stress and poor coping abilities, and little social support are at greater risk for doing poorly in college (Robbins et al., 2004; Torres Campos et al., 2009). Few studies have focused on at-risk students, and there are virtually no evaluations of such programs. In the current studies, the mentoring program was aimed at students who are at greatest risk of doing poorly in college, based on psychosocial variables.

In summary, the goals of the present research were to develop, implement, and evaluate a mentoring program for Latino college freshmen and to identify processes that underlie the effects of the program. The mentoring program was developed to be cost effective, by recruiting students who were identified as being at-risk for academic difficulties and using experienced peers as mentors. The program was implemented in two studies, carried out in consecutive years, at a large urban, predominantly minority university, through the recruitment of entering Latino freshmen who were mentored throughout their first year in college. The program was evaluated by following the mentored students throughout their freshmen year and comparing their outcomes to those of a group of nonmentored students. In the second study, additional measures were used to provide information on the processes that might influence the outcomes.

We focused on psychosocial variables that have been shown to underlie academic performance. On the basis of prior research, we expected that the mentored students would show improvement on these variables during the year and would perform better in the spring than the nonmentored students. In the second study, we obtained GPAs of students at the beginning and end of the year; however, because tutoring was not included in the study, we explored, but did not necessarily expect, differences between the groups in GPA. In the second study, we also explored whether aspects of the mentoring program influenced the outcomes, but did not make specific predictions.

STUDY 1

A survey was given in the fall to incoming freshmen at a predominantly minority urban university, to identify at-risk Latino students. Of these, 25 were recruited as mentees in a mentoring program. An additional 29 at-risk Latino students served as a comparison group of nonmentees. Both groups completed a follow-up survey in the spring. Data were analyzed to identify changes in the mentees and nonmentees during the year and differences between mentees and nonmentees in the spring.

Method

Selection and Description of Participants

A survey of 572 freshman was carried out at a predominantly minority urban university, through the Introduction to Higher Education courses required of all incoming students. Students in these classes were given information on how to complete the survey online via a secure website. After accessing the survey, students read an informed consent form and could continue only after agreeing to participate in the study. Some students were given class credit for completing the survey. Students who completed the survey were entered into a lottery for one of 10 prizes of $50 each. A relatively small number of students did not complete the survey.

Surveys of all self-identified Latino freshmen ($N = 275$) were selected from the completed surveys. A hierarchical cluster analysis was carried out using university and academic motivation, belonging, self-efficacy, support, obstacles, stress, and depression. Results suggested five clusters. Two clusters, although differing in the details, included 127 students whose scores indicated moderate to high levels of risk for poor academic performance. These students scored average to low on university and academic motivation, belonging, self-efficacy, and support, and average to high on stress, depression, and obstacles. These students were combined into a high-risk group. The three other clusters included students whose scores showed little or no risk; these students were not included in the study. Of the 127 high-risk students, 38 were already enrolled one of two support programs, the university based Educational Opportunity Program (a support program aimed at low income students) or a group mentoring program called Pals, and were not considered for the intervention.

The remaining 89 at-risk students were contacted and invited to participate in the mentoring program. Of these, 25 participated in the mentoring program (mentees) and completed a follow-up survey in the spring (5 males, 20 females; mean age = 17.9 years; 87.5% U.S. born). Of the mentees, 2 (8%) majored in STEM, 2 (8%) majored in arts/ humanities, 2 (8%) majored in business, 4 (16%) majored in social science/education, 10 (40%) majored in health and human services (HHS), and 5 (20%) were undecided.

A comparison group of 29 high-risk students did not participate in the program but completed the spring survey and served as a comparison group (nonmentees) (8 males, 21 females; mean age = 18 years; 81.5% U.S. born). Among the non-mentees, six (20.7%) majored in STEM, seven (24.1%) majored in arts/humanities, four (13.8%) majored in business, three majored in social science/education, and seven (24.1%) majored in HHS; two nonmentees (6.9%) were undecided.

The *t*-tests and chi-square analyses showed that mentees and nonmentees did not differ significantly in fall on any demographic variables, including age, gender, socioeconomic status (SES), majors, hours of work, chores, family care, and degree goal. Multivariate analysis of variances (MANOVAs) showed that mentees and nonmentees did not differ in the fall on any of the eight psychosocial variables studied.

Mentoring Program

Twelve mentors from counseling or psychology programs (9 female, 3 male; 10 graduate students; 2 seniors; mean age = 28.42) were recruited in the fall. In November, they were matched with one to three mentees each. Mentor ethnicity was reflective of the diversity on campus: four Latina/o, three Asian-American, three European-American, and two African–American. During the year, mentors attended seven monthly group meetings supervised by a trained psychologist in which they discussed communication and mentoring skills and reviewed their mentoring experiences. Mentors were paid $100 per mentee per quarter.

Mentors were instructed to contact their mentees at least twice a month. They met or contacted them informally in person, by phone, or by email, at mutually agreed upon times, to provide support, answer questions, and make referrals. Generally, mentors and mentees were in contact from late November through early May, but no records were kept of actual contacts.

Measures

Academic motivation. A 21-item, 5-point scale was created to assess the motivation for being involved in an academic environment, based on previous academic motivation scales (Vallerand, Pelletier, & Blais, 1992). Students were asked for their agreement to such statements as "I dedicate myself and pay attention in class," and "I am attending my college classes regularly." Responses ranged from

(1) *strongly disagree* to (5) *strongly agree*. The scale had reliabilities of $\alpha = .91$ (fall) and .87 (spring).

Belonging. A 13-item, 5-point scale was adapted for this study based on the Institutional Integration Scale (French & Oakes, 2004). This scale assesses students' feeling of belonging to the university environment. Responses were rated on a 5-point scale from (1) *not at all true* to (5) *very true*. Students responded to items such as "I feel like I am a part of this college," and "I am happy to be at this college." The reliabilities were .87 (fall) and .83 (spring).

Depression. The 10-item Edinburgh Postnatal Depression Scale (EPDS) was adapted to assess depression level in college students. The EPDS has been extensively validated and identified as one of the best scales of depression (Michigan Families Medicaid Project, n.d.). The EPDS categorizes respondents on a 5-point scale where $4 = critical$, $3 = severe$, $2 = moderate$, $1 = mild$, and $0 = no\ depressive\ symptoms$. The reliabilities of the scale were $\alpha = .80$ (fall) and .85 (spring).

Obstacles. The Obstacles scale was developed for this study based on prior research with minority college students (Kohn, Lafreniere, & Gurevich, 1990). This 17-item, 5-point scale was created to understand how students are affected by obstacles in their lives. Students were asked how much obstacles such as "having responsibilities or chores at home" interfered with their academic progress. Response ranged from (1) *no interference* to (5) *very serious interference*. The reliabilities of the scale were $\alpha = .93$ (fall) and .85 (spring).

Self-efficacy. The 13-item, 5-point scale was adapted from prior research including questions related to life-skills self-efficacy, such as "I am confident about my abilities to accomplish things that I set my mind to" and academic-specific self-efficacy, such as "I believe that I have the capability to learn the materials in my classes" (Sherer et al., 1982; Tipton & Worthington, 1984). Items were rated on a 5-point scale ranging from (1) *strongly disagree* to (5) *strongly agree*. The reliabilities of the scale were $\alpha = .91$ (fall) and .90 (spring).

Stress. A short-form of the Perceived Stress Scale (Cohen, Kamarck, & Mermelstein, 1983) was used to assess students' stress level. The 5-item scale asked students to indicate how often they felt or thought a certain way, such as "nervous and stressed" and "things are going your way." Responses were rated on a 4-point scale from (1) *never* to (4) *very often*. The scale had reliabilities of $\alpha = .75$ (fall) and .83 (spring).

Support. In this 9-item, 5-point scale, participants were asked to rate how certain they felt about being able to get support in various situations, such as "difficulties with a class or class assignment," or "having personal problems." Responses ranged from (1) *not at all certain* to (5) *very certain*. The scale had a reliability of .90 in both fall and spring.

University motivation. This 15-item scale was based on the Student Motivations for Attending University scale (Cote & Levine, 1997), as adapted for ethnic minority and low income students (Phinney, Dennis, & Osorio, 2006). Students were asked for their agreement (from 1, *low*, to 5, *high*) to such statements as "university is satisfying because it gives me the opportunity to study and learn." The scale had reliabilities of $\alpha = .83$ (fall) and .85 (spring).

For all the above scales except depression, the mean of all items was used in analyses.

Results

Repeated measures analyses of variance (ANOVAs) were conducted to examine whether there were significant changes from fall to spring on the eight psychosocial variables and whether there were significant differences between the mentees and nonmentees in spring. Results show that nonmentees declined significantly in academic motivation from fall to spring, $F(1, 46) = 5.39, p = .025$ with a medium effect size, $\eta^2 = .11$. Both mentees and nonmentees had a significant decrease in GPA from fall to spring, $F(1, 52) = 17.67, p < .01$, with a large effect size ($\eta^2 = .25$). There were no significant differences between the mentees and the nonmentees on any of the eight psychosocial variables in the spring.

Because of the small sample size, repeated measures ANOVAs may fail to reveal trends that are of interest. Therefore, paired sample t-tests were conducted to explore the data further. Results showed that mentees improved on self-efficacy from fall ($M = 3.79$) to spring ($M = 4.04$), $t = 2.51, df = 24, p < .02$. Nonmentees decreased in academic motivation, $t = 2.56, df = 28, p < .05$ (fall, $M = 4.03$; spring, $M = 3.79$) and in support, $t = 2.06, df = 28, p < .05$ (fall, $M = 3.36$; spring, $M = 3.07$). Independent sample t-tests in the spring showed that mentees scored higher on sense of belonging (mean $= 3.82$) than nonmentees (mean $= 3.53$), $F(1, 51) = 4.08, p < .048$.

Discussion

The results of Study 1 show that during their freshman year, at-risk Latino students who were mentored maintained their academic motivation, while those who were not mentored declined in motivation. In follow-up analyses, mean scores on some additional psychosocial variables showed changes in the expected direction; there were trends suggesting that the mentees did better and the nonmentees did more poorly. However, only the nonmentee decline in academic motivation was significant in the repeated measures analyses. The results suggest that mentors may be making a difference, but the effects are relatively modest. Several factors may have limited the results. The sample was small; a larger sample might reveal significant findings that were only trends in the study. In addition, although the mentors were from majors in counseling or psychology, they had very limited training in mentoring. Informal feedback from the mentors suggested that they would benefit from more training and guidance in mentoring skills. Furthermore, the study did not provide any information about the processes by which mentors might make a difference; to maximize the value of mentoring programs, it is essential to know in what ways programs bring about change. Study 2 was designed to address these issues.

STUDY 2

Using a fall survey similar to that in Study 1, we identified 133 Latino freshmen as being at risk for poor academic outcomes. Of these, 34 participated as mentees in a mentoring program; they completed surveys during the winter and spring quarters of their freshman year, and their mentors kept contact logs throughout the year, recording contact with each mentee. An additional 37 at-risk students did not participate in the program but completed the spring survey; these nonmentees served as a comparison group. The remaining 62 at-risk Latino students neither participated in the program nor completed the spring survey; they were used as a baseline group to test for selection bias. Data were analyzed to identify changes among the mentees and nonmentees between fall and spring and differences between mentees and nonmentees in the spring. Data from mentee surveys and from the mentor contact logs were used to evaluate the program and identify processes that influenced the mentoring process and outcomes.

Method

Selection and Description of Participants

A survey, similar to that for Study 1, was completed by 613 freshmen in a course required of all incoming students. Of these, 327 were self-identified Latinos. In Study 1 and in a prior pilot study (Torres Campos et al., 2009), cluster analysis had been used to identify at-risk students. This procedure took time and delayed assignment of mentees to mentors. Therefore, using data from at-risk students in the two prior studies, mean scores were calculated for eight psychosocial predictors of risk (academic motivation, belonging, depression, obstacles, self-efficacy, stress, support, and university motivation). Latino students who scored below these means on four or more of the psychosocial variables in the fall survey were deemed at risk.

All at-risk students ($N = 133$) were invited to participate in the mentoring program. Of these, 34 mentees (8 males, 26 females; mean age, 17.9 years; 82.9% U.S. born) participated in the mentoring program and completed surveys in the winter and spring. Eleven (31.4%) reported majors in STEM; 1 (2.9%) was a major in arts/humanities; 2 (5.7%) were majors in business, 7 (20%) were majors in social science/education; 12 (34.3%), HHS; and 2 (5.7%), undecided.

The 37 nonmentees (7 males, 30 females; mean age, 18.2 years; 78.9% U.S. born) did not participate in the program but completed the spring survey. Among the nonmentees, 4 (10.5%) were majors in STEM; 5 (13.2%), in arts/humanities; 2 (5.3%), in business; 9 (23.7%), in social science/education; 14 (36.8%), in HHS; 4 were undecided.

The baseline group (23 males, 39 females; mean age, 18.0 years; 82.3% U.S. born) did not participate in the program or complete the spring survey.

We examined whether there were selection biases, as would be indicated by differences in demographic and psychosocial variables in the fall among mentees, nonmentees, and the baseline group. The t-tests and chi-square analyses showed that mentees, nonmentees, and the baseline group did not differ in fall on any demographic variables, including age, gender, SES, majors, hours of work, chores, family care, and degree goal. MANOVAs showed that mentees, nonmentees, and baseline group did not differ on any of the eight psychosocial variables studied or on self- reported high school GPA and fall quarter GPA.

Mentoring Program

Twelve student mentors from counseling or psychology programs (10 female, 2 male; 3 graduate students; 9 seniors; mean age $= 24.3$) were recruited in the summer. Mentor ethnicity was reflective of the campus population: eight Latinos, two of mixed ethnicity, one Asian-American, one European-American. Mentors received a small stipend ($100 per mentee per quarter) for their participation. During the summer, mentors attended six training sessions (approximately 20 hours total) conducted by a licensed clinical psychologist, to strengthen counseling skills such as active listening, empathizing, and exploring feelings. They learned how to develop rapport and provide support; how to help students set goals, manage time, and develop coping skills; and when to refer students to needed services such as tutoring, counseling, or academic advising.

In the fall, mentors were matched with one to four mentees each. During the academic year, from November to May, mentors met individually with their mentees or contacted them by phone, email, or text message approximately twice a month, at mutually convenient times. Data from the contact logs showed that the following topics were discussed, in order of frequency: academic, personal, financial, career, and other. The following strategies were used by the mentors with their mentees, in order of frequency: listen, encourage, empathize, provide information, make suggestions, explore feelings, and other.

Throughout the academic year mentors met once or twice a month as a group with a licensed clinical psychologist. The meetings provided a forum for the mentors to discuss their interactions with their mentees and receive guidance and feedback from the clinician and their fellow mentors.

Measures: Fall and Spring

The same eight psychosocial factors were assessed as in the fall survey in Study 1. Reliabilities (Cronbach alphas) were as follows in Study 2: academic motivation (fall, .88; spring, .92), belonging (fall, .82; spring, .75), depression (fall, .81; spring, .85), obstacles (fall, .92; spring, .98), self-efficacy (fall, .90; spring, .85), stress (fall, .76; spring, .69), support (fall, .89; spring, .86), and university motivation (fall, .81; spring, .89). The same demographic variables were assessed as in Study 1. In the fall only, participants reported their high school GPA.

Measures: Winter

Relationship quality. At the end of winter quarter, mentees and mentors each rated the quality of their relationship with each other, using 14 items based on previous relationship measures (Ang, 2005; Verhofstadt, Buysse, Rosseel, & Peene, 2006; Walker & Little, 1969), e.g., "I feel comfortable with my mentor (mentee)," "I believe that our time together is valuable," and "Sometimes it is difficult to communicate with my mentor (mentee)" (reversed). Items were rated on a 5-point scale, from (1) *strongly disagree* to (5) *strongly agree* ($\alpha = .93$); higher scores indicate a better relationship. The two measures of relationship quality were significantly related, $r = .53$, $p < .001$. The mean of the two measures was used in the analyses, to provide a balanced assessment of the relationship.

Measures: Spring Only

In addition to the eight psychosocial variables assessed in the fall, two measures of program evaluation were completed by mentees only. Mean scores were used in the analyses.

Satisfaction. This 7-item scale was adapted for the study, based on the Customer Satisfaction Questionnaire (Larsen, Atkisson, Hargreaves, & Nguyen, 1979), regarding satisfaction with the program. Mentees rated level of agreement on a 5-point scale (from 1, *low*, to 5, *high*) on such statements as "My experience in this program has been a positive one" and "I would recommend this program to a friend or fellow student." The scale had a reliability .95.

Benefits of program. This 22-item scale was also created based on the Customer Satisfaction Questionnaire (Larsen et al., 1979). Items reflected participants' feelings of benefiting from the program. Sample items were: "My mentor has helped me to think about what I want to do after college" and "My mentor has helped me to handle problems and obstacles to my academic success". Responses ranged from 1 (*not at all*) to 5 (*very much*). Alpha was .96.

Other Measures

GPA and enrollment status. These data were collected from official university records for mentees and nonmentees in both fall and spring. Enrollment was assessed in two ways: First, the number of units taken in fall and spring were assessed. Second, we created a dummy variable that assessed whether students who were enrolled in fall came back and took any courses in spring, 0 = *no units taken in spring*, 1 = *one or more units taken in spring*.

Contact logs. Throughout the year, mentors recorded details of each contact. Logs were analyzed to yield contact frequency (total number of face-to-face, phone, or electronic contacts) and contact time (total time, in minutes, face-to-face and phone contact only). For descriptive purposes, mentors also reported topics discussed and the strategies used in the interaction.

Results

Repeated measures ANOVAs were conducted to examine whether there were any significant changes from fall to spring in mentees' and nonmentees' scores and any overall differences between mentees' and nonmentees' spring scores on the eight psychosocial variables and GPA (see Table 1). Results showed that depression scores for mentees significantly decreased from fall to spring, while nonmentees had a slight increase in depression, so that the two groups were significantly different in spring, $F(1, 41) = 5.51, p = .029$, with a medium effect size, $\eta^2 = .11$. Similarly, mentees had a significant decrease in stress from fall to spring whereas nonmentees saw a slight increase, $F(1, 71) = 4.36, p = .04$, with a small effect size, $\eta^2 = .06$. There was a significant decrease in GPA from fall to spring for mentees and a smaller decrease for nonmentees, $F = (1, 68) 22.34 \, p = .00$, with a strong effect, $\eta^2 = .25$. For two other variables, the repeated measures analysis showed no significant change, but paired comparisons suggested improvement from fall to spring for mentees (belonging, $t = 2.34, df = 24, p = .03$; self-efficacy, $t = 2.58, df = 24, p = .015$; see Table 1 for means) and no change for nonmentees.

A linear regression examined the effect of units taken in spring on the difference in GPA between mentees and nonmentees in spring. Although units taken in spring was a significant predictor of spring GPA while controlling for fall GPA

Table 1. Mean Scores for Mentees and Nonmentees and Tests for Changes over Time and Group Differences

Variables	Mentees		Nonmentees		Fall to spring				Mentee versus nonmentee			
	Fall	Spring	Fall	Spring	F	df	p	η^2	F	df	p	η^2
Academic motivation	3.95	3.94	3.92	3.64	3.332	1	.073**	.053	3.751	1	.058**	.060
Belonging	3.62	3.90	3.46	3.45	3.313	1	.073**	.050	3.602	1	.062**	.054
Depression	1.91	1.27	1.68	1.86	1.698	1	.200	.040	5.513	1	.029*	.112
Efficacy	3.71	3.91	3.86	3.88	3.541	1	.064**	.052	2.010	1	.161	.030
GPA	2.88	2.31	3.02	2.65	22.338	1	.000*	.247	2.009	1	.161	.029
Obstacles	3.33	3.04	3.27	3.18	2.460	1	.122	.042	.755	1	.389	.013
Support	3.04	3.23	2.97	3.09	1.563	1	.216	.024	.079	1	.780	.001
Stress	2.99	2.73	2.89	2.95	4.258	1	.220	.021	1.534	1	.040*	.058
University motivation	4.01	3.96	3.87	3.82	.281	1	.281	.005	.047	1	.830	.001

Note.*$p < .05$; **$p < .10$.

Table 2. Descriptive Statistics and Correlations among Process and Program Evaluation Variables

	Mean (SD)	Contact time	Contact frequency	Relationship quality	Mentee satisfaction
Contact time (minutes)	196.24 (137.46)				
Contact frequency (number)	10.15 (6.35)	.59***			
Relationship quality	4.3 (.63)	.46**	.35*		
Mentee satisfaction	4.2 (.63)	.51**	.39*	.56*	
Mentee benefits	4.3 (1.21)	.46**	.32	.34	.54**

Note. $^*p < .05$; $^{**}p < .01$.

$(R^2 = .31)$, mentees still had significantly lower GPA scores than nonmentees in spring, with fall GPA and units taken in spring controlled $(R^2 = .35)$.

Further analyses were conducted to determine whether the mentoring program affected the at-risk status of the mentees. The same criteria used in the fall to show both groups to be at risk were applied in the spring. Chi-square analyses showed that significantly fewer mentees, 20 (58.8%), than to nonmentees, 32 (86.5%), were at risk in the spring, $X_2(1, N = 71) = 6.92, p < .01$. However, there were no differences in dropouts in the spring between the two groups.

Process and Evaluation Variables: Interrelationships

To gain a clearer understanding of the mentoring process, we examined factors that underlie and may predict positive outcomes for mentees. The process variables, derived from information gathered independently of the psychosocial variables, were: (1) mentor–mentee contact time and frequency, reported by mentors in the contact logs; (2) quality of the mentor–mentee relationship, reported by mentees and mentors in the winter survey; and (3) program evaluation (mentee satisfaction and benefits of the program), as reported by mentees in the spring survey. Means and standard deviations of these variables are shown in Table 2. *Relationship quality* overall was rated as very good: 4.3 on a 5-point scale. Program evaluation was also high: *satisfaction*, 4.2, and *benefits*, 4.3.

Bivariate correlations among these variables showed them to be highly interrelated (see Table 2). Contact time and frequency were highly correlated, as were the two evaluation measures, satisfaction and benefits. Contact time was more strongly correlated than contact frequency with the other variables, specifically, with relationship quality, mentee satisfaction, and benefits.

Because contact time was related to relationship quality and to satisfaction, and relationship quality was also related to satisfaction (see Table 2), we examined whether relationship quality was a mediator. In a regression analysis carried out with contact time and relationship quality as predictors of satisfaction, relationship quality remained significant (beta = .41, $p < .02$), but contact time was no longer a significant predictor of satisfaction (beta = .32, $p = .06$), indicating that relationship quality completely mediated the effect of contact time on satisfaction.

Process and Evaluation Variables as Predictors

Linear regression analyses were conducted to examine whether the process and evaluation variables significantly predicted the psychosocial outcome variables in spring, controlling for their fall values. Separate regressions were run predicting each spring outcome from process and evaluation variables (contact time, relationship quality, benefits, and satisfaction), with the fall score of the outcome variable included as a control (Table 3).

Three outcome variables were significantly predicted by the models, although the predictors were different in each case. Spring academic motivation was predicted by benefits; belonging was predicted by relationship quality; and efficacy was predicted by satisfaction. Support was also predicted by benefits, although the overall model was not significant. Together these results provide evidence regarding the processes by which the mentoring program contributed to improved psychosocial indicators.

For both efficacy and depression, the fall scores predicted the spring scores, suggesting that these may be fairly stable characteristics of students during their freshman year. However, a trend for contact time to alleviate depression is indicative of the possible role of mentors.

GENERAL DISCUSSION

The purpose of this research was to add to our understanding of mentoring as a means of enhancing university outcomes for Latino students. The two longitudinal studies with Latino freshman provide modest support for our expectation that mentoring of at-risk Latino college freshmen makes a difference in the psychosocial factors that underlie academic performance. In the first study, mentored students showed no decline in academic motivation during the year, while students who were not mentored declined on motivation. The second study, in which the sample was larger and the mentors received training for their role, showed stronger effects. Mentored students decreased in both depression and stress during the year, while nonmentored students increased in both. Students who had been mentored were significantly less likely than nonmentored students

Table 3. Summary of Regression Analyses Predicting Outcome Variables from Process and Evaluation Variables, Controlling for Fall Values of the Outcomes

Outcomes spring variable	Control fall variable (beta)	Process and evaluation variables (beta)				Model
		Contact time	Relationship quality	Help received	Satisfaction	F-value
Academic motivation	1.13	−1.63	1.08	3.04**	−.51	3.60**
Belonging	−.52	−1.95	2.56*	1.86***	.85	3.48*
Efficacy	4.32**	.54	−.97	.69	3.42**	8.97**
Depression	2.66*	−2.08***	.36*	.48	.13	.16
Support	−.06	.08	.07	2.32*	−.19	.32

Notes. Each row in the table presents a separate regression analysis.
*$p < .05$; **$p < .01$; ***$p < .10$.

to be classified at the end of the year as being at-risk for poor academic outcomes, based on scores of eight psychosocial variables that have been shown to influence performance in college.

Although the results are not as strong as expected, they were in the predicted direction. All significant comparisons involving the psychosocial variables showed better performance by the mentees, and all nonsignificant trends also favored the mentees. Prior evidence suggests that these psychosocial factors are likely to contribute to better academic outcomes in the long run (Hurtado & Ponjuan, 2005; Pajares & Miller, 1994; Robbins et al., 2004). Students who are motivated, who feel that they belong in college, and who believe that they are able to succeed are more likely to persist in the face of difficulties (Robbins et al., 2004); and students who are unmotivated or under stress may not persist.

Both mentees and nonmentees received lower GPAs in spring than fall. Unexpectedly, the drop was greater for mentees than nonmentees, and the number of units taken did not account for this difference. The mentoring program focused on psychosocial factors rather than on academic assistance, such as tutoring. As shown by the contact logs, the most frequent interaction strategies of the mentors were listening, encouraging, and empathizing. Although these contacts contributed to psychosocial aspects of the students' lives, they did not make a difference in their academic performance. Mentees may not have considered the mentors to be sources of help with class work or may have been reluctant to discuss poor grades. Mentors had no access to students' grades and may not have known when students were having academic problems. Furthermore, mentors were explicitly asked to refer students to tutors when their mentees were having academic difficulties, rather than tutor the students themselves.

Future mentoring programs could deal with this problem in several ways. As part of the mentoring program, mentees might be asked to agree to providing mentors with grades on tests and papers on a regular basis, so that mentors could more closely monitor academic progress and make referrals. In addition, mentors could be recruited from a wider range of departments and matched to mentees by their major, so that they would be more familiar with course content. Such matching might be particularly effective in the more technical subjects like science, engineering, and mathematics, because mentors would have a better understanding of the particular academic challenges that mentees were facing. The role of mentors could be somewhat expanded with training in tutoring. This role could benefit the mentors as well, because tutoring has been shown to benefit tutors as well as the students tutored (Topping, 1996).

The second study, in addition to examining the impact of mentoring, provided insights into processes by which the mentoring program made a difference. The mentoring process was studied with measures of the frequency and length of time of contact, as reported by mentors, and of the quality of the mentoring relationship, rated by both mentors and mentees. Mentees also evaluated the program by rating overall satisfaction and their sense of benefits received from the program. These independently assessed aspects of the program were highly interrelated, suggesting that they work together in contributing to positive outcomes. Contact time and relationship quality are no doubt reciprocally related; more time spent together is likely to improve the relationship, and a good relationship promotes spending more time together. Both contact time and relationship quality in turn led to satisfaction with the program and, to a lesser extent, with a sense of benefiting from the program.

Having a good mentoring relationship, which was associated with more time with a mentor, predicted a mentee's sense of belonging to the university. This result is similar to results of another study with at-risk students (Soucy & Larose, 2000), which showed better attachment to the institution among students with a secure attachment to their mentor. Although contact time per se may not have a direct effect on outcomes, it provides the opportunity for the development of a positive relationship that can in turn lead to feelings of belonging. Contact time and relationship quality also predict a favorable evaluation of the program. Furthermore, students who evaluate a program more favorably show higher motivation and self-efficacy. Together, the results suggest that mentors who establish rapport with their mentees and spend time with them make a positive impact on psychosocial factors underlying academic performance.

Depression was reduced for mentees in Study 2, and there was a trend for extent of contact to account for this effect. Nevertheless, depression in spring was accounted for largely by depression in the fall, suggesting that depression may be difficult to modify by mentors. In future programs, mentors could be trained to identify depression early and refer students experiencing depression to therapists who could provide professional assistance.

The results of the mentoring program support the theoretical position that attachment is the underlying mechanism for the benefits of mentoring (Ainsworth, 1989). Overall, the mentoring program contributed to psychosocial but not to academic outcomes. Mentors may make a difference because of the personal relationship they form with their mentees. The mentors in this study were advanced students from counseling and psychology backgrounds and thus are likely to be people oriented and focused on psychological factors. The use of mentors from such backgrounds was considered as a cost-effective aspect of the program. Many of the mentors reported that mentoring a student was valuable to them professionally, and several got subsequent internships or jobs based on their mentoring experience. Most indicated that they would be willing to serve as mentors again, without the modest stipend that the current study provided. Furthermore, the clinical psychologist who supervised the mentors noted that the mentoring experience could be part of a formal internship or a class at the university, so that the mentors would get academic credit for their participation. Thus such a program could not only benefit the mentees but also contribute to the professional development of the mentors.

The results provide less support for sociocultural theory (Vygotsky, 1978), which implies more structured, content-oriented interactions, with the mentor (or tutor) scaffolding the learning process. Such structured interactions were not a part of the mentoring program, and their absence may explain in part the lack of impact on GPA. A program that includes more structured interactions is more likely to contribute to academic performance. An interesting question for future research would be whether attachment and sociocultural approaches can be effectively combined, and whether one or the other may be more effective depending on the course content. For example, students in STEM fields might benefit more from more structured interactions. However, when students have clear deficits in areas such as motivation, support, and psychological well-being, a personal relationship may be more important in retaining students. Students are likely to do best if they have access to both types of support.

An important aspect of the mentoring program was its focus on students identified as being at risk. Many college mentoring programs are open to all students and may miss students may not be aware of their own needs or lack the initiative to seek help. Rather than funding general peer mentoring programs, schools might better use limited resources to a focus on those students who are most likely to do poorly. By focusing on the most needy students and using older peers pursuing careers in the helping professions, the program could be less expensive than other types of programs and therefore available in institutions with limited resources.

There are several limitations of the study. The samples were relatively small, so the results should be viewed with caution; larger samples would allow for more detailed analyses of mentoring outcomes and processes. The at-risk students were not randomly assigned as mentees or nonmentees; because the mentees chose to participate, they may have been more receptive to being mentored than nonmentees. The findings, obtained from Latinos at a predominantly minority university, may not generalize to other ethnic groups and settings. Outcomes were assessed at one time point; future studies could use repeated assessments, to allow for tracking changes in the mentoring relationship and mentee characteristics. Mentors were not matched with mentees by ethnicity or gender, a factor which may enhance report of help received, although not academic outcomes (Blake-Beard, Bayne, Crosby, & Muller, 2011).

Nevertheless, these results add to our understanding of the impact of mentoring with minority students who exhibit risk factors for poor academic outcomes. The results show the importance of both the extent and quality of the mentoring relationship. Good mentoring and ample contact lead to satisfaction with the program. Programs such as these could be widely applied at a relatively low cost, using peer mentors for those students most at risk.

References

Ainsworth, M. (1989). Attachment beyond infancy. *American Psychologist, 44,* 709–716. doi:10.1037/0003–066X.44.4.709.

Ang, R. (2005). Development and validation of the Teacher-Student Relationship Inventory using exploratory and confirmatory factor analysis. *The Journal of Experimental Education, 74,* 55–57. doi:10.3200/JEXE.74.1.55–74.

Astin, A. (1993). An empirical typology of college students. *Journal of College Student Development, 34,* 36–46.

Barrera, M., & Bonds, D. (2005). Mentoring relationships and social support. In D. DuBois & M. Karcher (Eds.), *Handbook of youth mentoring* (pp. 133–142). Thousand Oaks, CA: Sate.

Blake-Beard, S., Bayne, M., Crosby, F., & Muller, C. (2011). Matching by race and gender in mentoring relationships: Keeping our eyes on the prize. *Journal of Social Issues, 67*(3), 622–643.

Bordes, V., & Arredondo, P. (2005). Mentoring and 1st year Latina/o college students. *Journal of Hispanic Education, 4*(2), 114–133. doi:10.1177/1538192704273855.

Brooks, J. H., & DuBois, D. L. (1995). Individual and environmental predictors of adjustment during the first year of college. *Journal of College Student Development, 36*(4), 347–360.

Ceballo, R. (2004). From Barrios to Yale: The role of parenting strategies in Latino families. *Hispanic Journal of Behavioral Sciences, 26*(2), 171–186.

Chemers, M., Zurbriggen, E., Syed, M., & Bearman, S. (2011). The role of efficacy and identity in science career commitment among underrepresented minority students. *Journal of Social Issues, 67*(3), 469–491.

Cohen, S., Kamarck, T., & Mermelstein, R. (1983). A global measure of perceived stress. *Journal of Health and Social Behavior, 24,* 385–396. doi:10.2307/2136404.

Cote, J. E., & Levine, C. (1997). Student motivations, learning environments, and human capital acquisition: Toward an integrated paradigm of student development. *Journal of college student development, 38*(3), 229–243.

Dennis, J., Phinney, J. S., & Chuateco, L. I. (2005). The role of motivation, parental support, and peer support in academic success of ethnic minority first-generation college students. *Journal of College Student Development, 46*(3), 223–236. doi:10.1353/csd.2005.0023.

DuBois, D., & Karcher, M. (2005). *Handbook of youth mentoring.* Thousand Oaks, CA: Sage.

DuBois, D., & Neville, H. (1997). Youth mentoring: Investigation of relationship characteristics and perceived benefits. *Journal of Community Psychology, 25,* 227–234. doi:10.1002/(SICI)1520–6629(199705)25:3≤227::AID-JCOP1≥3.0.CO;2-T.

Fazio, N., & Palm, L. J. (1998). Attributional style, depression, and grade point averages of college students. *Psychological Reports, 83*(1), 159–162. doi:10.2466/PR0.83.5.159–162.

French, B. F., & Oakes, W. (2004). Reliability and validity evidence Institutional Integration Scale. *Educational and Psychological Measurement, 64*(1), 88–98. doi:10.1177/0013164403258458.

Fry, R. (2002). *Latinos in higher education: Many enroll, too few graduate.* Washington, DC: Pew Hispanic Center.

Fry, R. (2005). *The high schools Hispanics attend: Size and other key characteristics.* Washington, DC: Pew Hispanic Center.

Fuligni, A. J. (1997). The academic achievement of adolescents from immigrant families: The roles of family background, attitudes, and behavior. *Child Development, 68,* 351–363.

Fuligni, A. J., & Tseng, V. (1999). Family obligation and the academic motivation of adolescents from immigrant and American-born families. *Advances in Motivation and Achievement, 11,* 159–183.

Guzmán, G. (2001). *The Hispanic population.* Washington, DC: U.S. Government Printing Office.

Heiligenstein, E., & Guenther, G. (1996). Depression and academic impairment in college students. *Journal of American College Health, 45*(2), 59–64. doi:10.1080/07448481.1996.9936863.

Hurtado, S., & Ponjuan, L. (2005). Latino educational outcomes and the campus climate. *Journal of Hispanic Higher Education, 4,* 235–251. doi:10.1177/1538192705276548.

Hurtado, S., Eagan, M. K., Tran, M. C., Newman, C. B., Chang, M. J., & Velasco, P. (2011) "We do science here": Underrepresented students interactions with faculty in different college contexts. *Journal of Social Issues, 67*(3), 553–579.

Karcher, M. (2005). Cross-age peer mentoring. In D. DuBois & M. Karcher (Eds.), *Handbook of youth mentoring* (pp. 266–285). Thousand Oaks, CA: Sage.

Kenny, M. E., & Stryker, S. (1996). Social network characteristics and college adjustment among racially and ethnically diverse first-year students. *Journal of College Student Development, 37,* 649–658.

Kohn, P. M., Lafreniere, K., & Gurevich, M. (1990). The Inventory of college students' recent life experiences: A decontaminated hassles scale for a special population. *Journal of Behavioral Medicine, 13*(6), 619–630. doi:10.1007/BF00844738.

Larsen, D. L., Atkisson, C. C., Hargreaves, W. A., & Nguyen, T. D. (1979). Assessment of client/patient satisfaction: Development of a general scale. *Evaluation and Program Planning, 92,* 197–207. doi:10.1016/0149–7189(79)90094–6.

Maldonado, D., Rhoads, R., & Buenavista, T. L. (2005). The Student-Initiated Retention Project: Theoretical contributions and the role of self-empowerment. *American Educational Research Journal, 42,* 605–638. doi:10.3102/00028312042004605.

Meier, K. J., & Stewart, J., Jr. (1991). *The politics of Hispanic education. Un paso pa' lante y dos pa' tras.* Albany, NY: State University of New York.

Okagaki, L., & Frensch, P. A. (1998). Parental support for Mexican-American children's school achievement. In H. I. McCubbin, E. A. Thompson, A. I. Thompson & J. E. Fromer (Eds.), *Resiliency in Native American and immigrant families* (pp. 325–342). Thousand Oaks, CA: Sage.

Pajares, F., & Miller, M. D. (1994). Role of self-efficacy and self-concept in mathematical problem solving: A path analysis. *Journal of Educational Psychology, 86,* 193–203. doi:10.1037/0022–0663.86.2.193.

Parra, G., DuBois, D., Neville, H., Pugh-Lilly, A., & Povinelli, N. (2002). Mentoring relationships for youth: Investigation of a process-oriented model. *Journal of Community Psychology, 30,* 367–388. doi:10.1002/jcop.10016.

Perkins, D. F., & Villaruel, F. A. (2000). An ecological, risk-factor examination of Latino adolescents; engagement in sexual activity. In F. A. Villaruel (Ed.), *Making invisible Latino adolescents visible* (pp. 83–106). Newbury Park, CA: Sage.

Phinney, J. S., & Haas, K. (2003). The process of coping among ethnic minority first-generation freshmen: A narrative approach. *The Journal of Social Psychology, 143*(6), 707–726. doi:10.1080/00224540309600426.

Phinney, J. S., Ong, A., & Madden, T. (2000). Cultural values and intergenerational value discrepancies in immigrant and non-immigrant families. *Child Development, 71,* 528–539. doi:10.1111/1467–8624.00162.

Phinney, J. S., Dennis, J., & Osorio, S. (2006). Reasons to attend college among ethnically diverse college students. *Cultural Diversity & Ethnic Minority Psychology, 12*(2), 347–366. doi:10.1037/1099–9809.12.2.347.

Rhodes, J. (2005). A model of youth mentoring. In D. DuBois & M. Karcher (Eds.), *Handbook of youth mentoring.* Thousand Oaks, CA: Sage.

Robbins, S. B., Lauver, K., Le, H., Davis, D., Langley, R., & Carlstrom, A. (2004). Do psychosocial and study skill factors predict college outcomes? A meta-analysis. *Psychological Bulletin, 130*(2), 261–288. doi:10.1037/0033–2909.130.2.261.

Rodriguez, N. (1996). Predicting the academic success of Mexican American and White college students. *Hispanic Journal of Behavioral Sciences, 18*(3), 329–342. doi:10.1177/07399863960183004.

Sanchez, B., Esparza, P., & Colon, Y. (2008). Natural mentoring under the microscope: An investigation of mentoring relationships and Latino adolescents' academic performance.. *Journal of Community Psychology, 38,* 468–482. doi:10.1002/jcop.20250.

Sedlacek, W. (2004). *Beyond the big test: Non-cognitive assessment in higher education.* San Francisco, CA: Jossey-Bass.

Sherer, M., Maddux, J. E., Mercandante, B., Prentice-Dunn, S., Jacobs, B., & Rogers, R. W. (1982). The self-efficacy scale: Construction and validation. *Psychological Reports, 51,* 663–671.

Smith-Jentsch, K., Scielzo, S., Yarbrough, C., & Rosopa, P. (2008). A comparison of face-to-face and electronic peer-mentoring: Interaction with mentor gender. *Journal of Vocational Behavior, 72,* 193–206.

Solberg, S. V., Valdez, J., & Villarreal, P. (1994). Social support, stress, and Hispanic college adjustment: Test of a diathesis-stress model. *Hispanic Journal of Behavioral Sciences, 16*, 230–239. doi:10.1177/07399863940163002.

Soucy, N., & Larose, S. (2000). Attachment and control in family and mentoring contexts as determinants of adolescent adjustment to college. *Journal of Family Psychology, 14*, 125–142. doi:10.1037/0893–3200.14.1.125.

Strage, A. (2000). Predictors of college adjustment and success: Similarities and differences among Southeast-Asian-American, Hispanic, and White students. *Education, 120*(4), 731–740.

Swail, W. S., Cabrera, A. F., & Lee, C. (2004). *Latino youth and the pathway to college*. Washington DC: Pew Hispanic Center.

Tinto, V. (1993). *Leaving college: Rethinking the causes and cures of student attrition*. Chicago, IL: University of Chicago Press.

Tipton, R. M., & Worthington, J. R. (1984). The measurement of generalized self-efficacy: A study of construct validity. *Journal of Personality Assessment, 48*(5), 545–548. doi:10.1207/s15327752jpa4805_14.

Topping, K. (1996). The effectiveness of peer tutoring in further and higher education: A typology and review of the literature. *Higher Education, 32*, 321–345. doi:10.1007/BF00138870.

Torres Campos, C., Phinney, J., Perez-Brena, N., Kim, C., Ornelas, B., Nemanim, L., et al. (2009). A mentor-based targeted intervention for high-risk Latino college freshmen: A pilot study. *Journal of Hispanic Higher Education, 8*, 158–178. doi:10.1177/1538192708317621.

Tseng, V. (2004). Family interdependence and academic adjustment in college: Youth from immigrant and U.S.-born families. *Child Development, 75*(3), 966–983. doi:10.1111/j.1467–8624.2004.00717.x.

U.S. Census Bureau. (2004). *Educational attainment in the United States: 2003*. Washington, DC: U.S. Census Bureau.

U.S. Department of Education. (1992). *Dropout rates in the United States, 1991*. Washington, DC: U.S. Government Printing Office.

Vallerand, R. J., Pelletier, L G., & Blais, M. R. (1992). The Academic Motivation Scale: A measure of intrinsic, extrinsic, and amotivation in education. *Educational and Psychological Measurement, 52*(4), 1003–1017. doi:10.1177/0013164492052004025.

Verhofstadt, L., Buysse, A., Rosseel, Y., & Peene, O. (2006). Confirming the 3-factor structure of the ORI within couples. *Psychological Assessment, 18*, 15–21. doi:10.1037/1040–3590.18.1.15.

Vygotsky, L. (1978). *Mind in society*. Cambridge, MA: Harvard University Press.

Walker, B., & Little, D. (1969). Factor analysis of the Barrett-Lennard Relationship Inventory. *Journal of Counseling Psychology, 16*, 516–521. doi:10.1037/h0028452.

Wawrzynski, M. R., & Sedlacek, W. E. (2003). Race and gender differences in the transfer student experience. *Journal of College Student Development, 44*(4), 489–501. doi:10.1353/csd.2003.0045.

JEAN PHINNEY is a Professor Emeritus from California State University, Los Angeles. She has conducted extensive research with minority adolescents and adults on ethnic identity and acculturation, and, more recently, on mentoring. She is the author of the widely used Multigroup Ethnic Identity Measure. As a member of an international team, she participated in research on immigrant youth in 13 countries and coedited a book on the topic. She is currently a Visiting Scholar at the Institute of Human Development, University of California, Berkeley.

CIDHINNIA M. TORRES CAMPOS holds master's and doctorate degrees in Ecological/Community Psychology from Michigan State University. She has worked with a wide variety of public and nonprofit organizations on issues related to positive youth development and education and is currently the Director of Academic Assessment at University of New Haven.

DELIA PADILLA KALLEMEYN received her Bachelor of Arts in Psychology and Sociology from the University of California, Riverside and her Master of Arts in Psychology from California State University, Los Angeles. She is currently a Research Analyst at Western University of Health Sciences in Pomona.

CHAMI KIM received her Master's Degrees from Tokyo International University and California State University, Los Angeles. She is currently a Behavior Analyst working with children with behavior problems.

Journal of Social Issues, Vol. 67, No. 3, 2011, pp. 622–643

Matching by Race and Gender in Mentoring Relationships: Keeping our Eyes on the Prize

Stacy Blake-Beard*
Simmons College

Melissa L. Bayne and Faye J. Crosby
University of California

Carol B. Muller
Blue Sky Consulting
Stanford University

This study examined the extent to which science, technology, engineering, and math (STEM) students reported having had mentors of their own race and gender and the extent to which they have adopted the idea that matching by race and gender matters. The study also documented the effects of race and gender matching on three academic outcomes, self-reported grade point average, efficacy, and confidence, based on data collected from 1,013 undergraduate and graduate students and postdoctoral scholars actively participating in MentorNet's online community. Analyses indicated that having a mentor of one's own gender or race was felt to be important by many students, especially women and students of Color. Students who had a mentor of their own gender or race reported receiving more help, but matching by race or gender did not affect academic outcomes. Key findings are discussed in terms of implications for future research and mentoring in the STEM fields.

---

*Correspondence concerning this article should be addressed to Stacy Blake-Beard, Simmons College, School of Management, 300 The Fenway, Boston, MA 02115 [e-mail: stacy.blakebeard@simmons.edu].

The data collection for this analysis was undertaken by MentorNet, and this material is based upon work supported by the National Science Foundation under Grant No. EEC-0639762. Any opinions, findings, and conclusions or recommendations expressed in this material are those of the author(s) and do not necessarily reflect the views of the National Science Foundation. Information about the sample can be found in the following report: http://www.mentornet.net/documents/files/evaluation/studentperceptions.completereport.pdf.

622

Some experts have proposed that mentoring programs can help female and ethnic minority students remain in the science, technology, engineering, and math (STEM) fields (Settles, Cortina, Stewart, & Malley, 2007; Wasburn & Miller, 2004). The basis of the claim is the observation that students who have mentors (usually spontaneously chosen) tend to have better experiences and more academic success than students without mentors (Bearman, Blake-Beard, Hunt, & Crosby, 2007).

Yet, because the positive consequences of mentoring are not universal (Tenenbaum, Crosby, & Gliner, 2001), a number of scholars (e.g., Downing, Crosby, & Blake-Beard, 2005) have sought to document the conditions under which mentoring has its greatest success. One condition that has been proposed by some researchers is matching, on the assumption that protégés will experience the greatest successes when they match with mentors on the basis of race and/or gender (Noe, 1988).

What do students themselves think about matching? Do students believe, like some experts, that they would benefit from having mentors of the same race or gender as themselves? And what is the relationship between the students' beliefs and their experiences? Do female and ethnic minority students match with their mentors in terms of gender and race as often as White students and male students? More importantly, does the matching—when it does occur—make any difference in terms of the experiences and the academic outcomes of the students?

Mentoring

Mentoring relationships have been defined as an interpersonal exchange between an experienced senior colleague (mentor) and a less experienced junior colleague (protégé) in which the mentor provides support along three dimensions: career functions, psychosocial functions, and role modeling functions (Kram, 1988; Scandura, 1992). Career functions encompass activities such as protection, exposure and visibility, coaching and feedback. Psychosocial functions include activities such as acceptance and confirmation, friendship, and counseling. Role modeling, a more passive function (Scandura, 1992), is seen in identification of the protégé with the mentor and also looking to the mentor as a source of guidance in shaping her own behavior, values, and attitudes.

Most of the research on mentoring in education concerns naturally occurring mentoring relationships, interactions that develop without external intervention. Many organizations now supplement naturally occurring mentorships with formal mentoring programs. In such programs, protégés are assigned to mentors. Following the recognition that mentoring helps protégés and the recognition that those already privileged may have greater access to mentors than those who have been traditionally excluded (Moore, Miller, Pitchford, & Jeng, 2008), formal mentoring programs gained increasing popularity in both business and education (Allen, Eby, & Lentz, 2006; Arora, Schneider, Thal, & Meltzer, 2011; Blake-Beard, 2001).

One interesting development in the formalization of mentoring is the establishment of electronic mentoring programs (Kasprisin, Single, Single, Ferrier, & Muller, 2008). Even though the field of electronic mentoring is still nascent (e.g., Kasprisin, Single, Single, & Muller, 2003), at least one large-scale, multi-institutional organization has been established to create and support electronic mentoring relationships for women and others underrepresented in engineering and related sciences. Observing that it is sometimes helpful for students to be linked with someone working professionally based on the student's chosen field of study, outside their home institution, of whom they can ask questions without fear of creating a bad impression, Dr. Carol B. Muller founded MentorNet in 1997. MentorNet's initial intention was to help women undergraduate and graduate students in engineering and related science fields gain helpful mentoring experiences; participation in the organization's programs grew steadily over its initial years (Marasco, 2005). The MentorNet e-mentoring program soon grew into an online community, and by 2003, interest from and participation by male students, particularly those who are underrepresented in these fields led to a formal mission expansion to focus on all those underrepresented in STEM fields. Ten years later, by the time the data were collected that were used in this study, approximately 20,000 students and professionals were active in the MentorNet online community. This community includes both students and professionals and during its first 11 years offered opportunities for them to connect via web-based discussion groups, as well as to participate in MentorNet's signature One-on-One program. The One-on-One program allows students in the sciences, engineering, and a few related business fields of study to be linked to distal mentors through e-mail correspondence and guides them through 8 months of an initial mentoring relationship. At any given point in time, some of the students belonging to the MentorNet community are linked to a specific mentor, while others are not.

Empirical Research on the Effects of Mentoring for Students

Research suggests that participation in mentoring relationships contributes to students' satisfaction with and commitment to their academic programs (Phinney, Campos, Kallemeyn, & Kim, 2011) and to their scholastic performance (Clark, Harden, & Johnson, 2000). Campbell and Campbell's (1997) evaluation compared 339 undergraduate students assigned to mentors with 339 students (matched on gender, ethnicity, and initial grade point average [GPA]) who did not have mentors. After 1 year, results showed that mentored students earned higher GPAs (2.45 vs. 2.29), completed more credit units per semester (9.33 vs. 8.49), and had a lower dropout rate (14.5% vs. 26.3%) than nonmentored students. Similarly, in their study of 194 doctoral psychology students, Hollingsworth and Fassinger (2002) found that students' mentoring experiences served as an important predictor of predoctoral research productivity. For both undergraduate and graduate students, mentoring acted as an important source of support.

Mentoring has been shown to be particularly important for women. In a study of 57 male and female graduate students, Gilbert (1985) found that female students rated the role model relationship as more important to their professional development than did male students. Campbell and Skoog (2004) report that undergraduate women who had access to mentoring were positively affected in terms of their career decisions, received critical support, were stimulated to consider particular areas of research and were assisted in applying for graduate school. Results from their study of 57 undergraduate women who had participated in an undergraduate biological sciences education program indicated that mentoring was related to persistence in science; 90% of the women did seek a career in science. Fortunately, contrary to what one might expect, more than one review of the literature has shown that there are no reliable differences in rates of mentoring or on mentoring outcomes based solely on the sex of the protégé (Clark et al., 2000; Johnson, 2007; O'Neill, Horton, & Crosby, 1999).

Mentoring has also been found to be a potent source of support for ethnic minority students. In their examination of 541 adolescents from diverse ethnic and immigration generational backgrounds, Witkow and Fuligni (2011) found that social support was positively associated with GPA. In a study that included individual interviews with 11 students as well as seven focus group interviews, Davis (2007) found that mentors helped to socialize their protégés. Her study participants reported that benefits from their mentoring experiences included support from mentors through recommendation letters, encouragement to participate in scholarly activities (such as grant writing and publishing) and having access to models of effective professional behavior and interpersonal skills. Again, it is fortunate that minority students report being mentored in graduate school at rates similar to White students (Atkinson, Neville, & Casas, 1991; Johnson, 2007). Surveying a sample of 101 recent racial minority PhDs, Atkinson et al. (1991) found that 50% had a graduate school mentor—73% of which were White.

Matching in Mentoring: Conceptualizations and Empirical Research

Almost since the start of research on mentoring, theorists have speculated about whether protégés benefit by being matched with their mentors (Bowman, Kite, Branscombe, & Williams, 1999; Gonzalez-Figueroa, & Young, 2005). Ragins' (1997) theoretical framework on diversified mentoring relationships proposes that the demographic composition of the mentoring relationship influences the type of assistance provided by the mentor. It is easy to imagine that women might benefit from being mentored by more senior women and that ethnic minorities might benefit from being mentored by more senior ethnic minorities. Syed, Azmitia, and Cooper (2011) discuss research that identifies mentors from similar backgrounds as particularly important to students of Color because they represent prototypes that enable students to gain a sense of academic self-efficacy. At an emotional level, it may feel comforting to have the guidance of someone who has already solved some of the problems confronting one's own demographic group, and it may be less difficult to trust "one's own" than to trust someone who seems to resemble "the other" (Ragins, 1997; Sosik & Godshalk, 2005).

In contrast, one can also imagine that for female and for ethnic minority protégés, there may be significant advantages to being mentored by White men (Dreher & Cox, 1996). As Sosik and Godshalk (2005) note, perceptions of power may play an important role in the choice of mentor. And, in fact, the more the mentor has access to power and the predominant culture and its mores, the greater might be the rewards for the protégé.

What does the empirical literature say about matching? Empirical research on the topic of matching has been more limited than theory (Bozeman & Feeney, 2008), and the results are somewhat contradictory. The findings are inconsistent whether one is looking at gender or race and whether one is looking at feelings toward the relationship (e.g., satisfaction with the amount of support given) or at practical outcomes (e.g., numbers of publications).

Looking first at gender, some researchers have found that female protégés enjoy same-gender mentoring relationships more than cross-gender ones. Lockwood (2006) found that female students, but not male students, are more inspired by an outstanding role model of their own gender than by an outstanding role model of the other gender. Several studies have shown that female students and workers experience greater comfort (Allen, Day, & Lentz, 2005) and more psychosocial support (Ensher & Murphy, 1997; Kark & Shilo-Dubnov, 2007) when they have female mentors than when they have male mentors.

While some studies show greater satisfaction with the mentoring relationship when female protégés are matched with female mentors than when they are matched with male mentors, there are also studies that show other results. Campbell and Campbell's (2007) study comparing 339 students who were mentored with 339 students who were not involved in mentoring relationships did not find any advantages to matching students and mentors based on gender. Contrary to their expectations, Sosik and Godshalk's (2005) study of dyads composed of Master in Business Administration (MBA) students and their mentors found that protégés in cross-gender mentoring dyads reported receiving greater amounts of psychosocial support from their mentors than protégés in same-gender dyads. Ugrin, Odom, and Pearson (2008) studied 35 dyads composed of senior faculty and new junior faculty and looked at Leader-Member Exchange scores, representing the degree to which the exchange relationships are characterized by mutual trust, respect, liking, and reciprocal influence (Scandura & Graen, 1984). In terms of gender, Ugrin et al. (2008) found that mixed gender dyads actually reported higher Leader-Member Exchange scores than same-gender dyads. In their supplemental qualitative analysis, Ugrin and his colleagues noted a common theme voiced by their respondents—they preferred mixed relationships, particularly across gender, to decrease unnecessary activities, focus on important tasks and avoid getting into a competitive relationship that pairs in same-gender dyads may face.

Attitudes and feelings are not the only dependent variables of importance. It is also vital to examine the impact of matching on gender and race on behaviors and on outcomes derived from the mentoring relationship. Again the evidence is inconsistent. On the one hand, Goldstein (1979) found that female graduate students published more if they had a female advisor than a male advisor while male students published more with a male advisor than a female advisor. More recently, in a nationally representative survey of workers, Foley, Linnehan, Greenhaus, and Weer (2006) found that respondents reported their supervisors were supportive of family demands more when the supervisors matched their own race and gender than when they differed on demographic variables. Feeney and Bozeman (2008) found that managers in state government report greater networks if they have mentors of their own gender than if they have cross-sex mentors.

Yet other researchers have found that women benefit most from having male mentors. Downing and her colleagues (2005) found that male guides were rated by female college students as significantly more influential in their pursuit of science than female guides. Tenenbaum et al. (2001) also found that gender was relatively unimportant in their study of graduate student–advisor relationships. From their survey of 189 students across nine departments, their results indicate that women and men students were more similar than different in most regards. One significant difference was that men students published more with their advisors than female counterparts. Advisor gender was also not important; men advisors were as likely to give practical help to their students as women advisors. Also, students selected women and men advisors in proportion to their prevalence as faculty. The relative unimportance of matching on gender lines for the outcomes of protégés has been echoed in a large-scale study of British school children where it was found that the school performance of boys and girls was unrelated to the gender of their teacher (Carrington, Tymms, & Merrell, 2008) and in a study of employed adults' salaries (Kirchmeyer, 2002).

Studies of racial matching show no more consistency than do studies of gender matching. Ortiz-Walters and Gilson's (2005) study on the mentoring experiences of 163 business school doctoral students of Color found that graduate students of Color reported receiving more psychosocial and instrumental support from, and being more comfortable and satisfied with, mentors who were also people of Color. In their study of Black students participating in summer research opportunity program, Frierson, Hargrove, and Lewis (1994) found that respondents with Black mentors reported more positive attitudes than did protégés who worked with

White mentors. In contrast, Smith, Smith, and Markham's (2000) study of 200 faculty members involved in mentoring relationships found no difference in the outcomes of matched or "diversified" pairs. Turban, Dougherty, and Lee's (2002) study of faculty advisor–doctoral student relationships did not find differential levels of support in same-race pairs and cross-race pairs. Their sample was 220 dyads (composed of doctoral students and their faculty advisors from a large Midwestern university) for which they had faculty demographics and student perceptions of the relationship. Nor did Atkinson et al.'s (1991) study of psychologists who had experienced mentoring during graduate school find different ratings in cross-ethnic dyads than in same-ethnic dyads.

Some research by MentorNet also has produced inconsistencies. MentorNet's One-on-One program pairs undergraduate or graduate students, postdoctoral scholars or other early career faculty members in science and engineering fields with professionals from their fields for structured, 8-month-long mentoring relationships, conducted primarily if not exclusively via email. Undergraduate students, graduate students, postdoctoral scholars, and early career faculty in engineering, science, math, and business fields may participate as protégés in the program as long as they are enrolled or employed by academic institutions which have subscribed to the MentorNet "partnership," for which the institutions pay a fee and identify a campus representative responsible for outreach to promote the program to interested participants and to provide in situ trouble-shooting if necessary. Or, if a professional society is a fee-paying MentorNet partner, its members who are students or early career faculty members in these fields are also eligible for participation as protégés in MentorNet's One-on-One program. Aside from the requirement of affiliation with a MentorNet "partner," there are no other eligibility requirements for participation. Once prospective protégés complete a profile providing background information and indicating preferences, if any, for the type of mentor with whom they want to be matched, they can then select a mentor from a list of the top five mentors who are the best fit. The mentors are volunteers and generally are external to the protégés' home institutions. Volunteer mentors may participate regardless of their institutional affiliations or employment status, but are required at least to have an educational or employment background in a science, engineering, or business field; they also are not screened in any particular way based on their ability to mentor, but are asked to provide a reference who can confirm that they are who they say they are. Men and women, as well as those of all racial backgrounds, are encouraged to participate. Both prospective mentors and protégés are offered the opportunity to indicate a preference or a requirement to be matched with an individual of a specific gender or race, among other characteristics. In some years of evaluation, the success of dyads in which male mentors were paired with female protégés was comparable to those in which the protégés were paired with female mentors. That is, participants reported similar frequency of email communications, equivalent satisfaction with the overall quality of their matches, and similar ratings of outcome measures. In other years, however, female protégés with female mentors had higher satisfaction with the program. In all years of evaluation, cross-race pairs were as effective as matched-race pairs, but the analyses depended on data in which there were unfortunately very few ethnic minority mentors (MentorNet, 2007).

The Present Study

Our study documents the extent to which STEM students in a particular sample have had mentors of their own race and gender and the extent to which they have adopted the idea that matching by race and gender matters. The study also documents the effects of race and gender matching in terms of the students' mentoring experiences and academic outcomes. In other words, our data allow us to see the basis in fact (or lack of such) of the student preferences. For ease of exposition, we proceed by addressing four specific and interrelated questions: (1) What do respondents of different ethnicities and genders want in terms of the race or gender of their mentors? (2) Are respondents of different ethnicities and genders equally likely to have a mentor of their own race or gender? (3) Does matching by gender or race affect respondents' mentoring experiences? And (4) Does matching by race or gender affect respondents' academic outcomes?

Method

Procedure

Members of the target population were sent an e-mail invitation to participate in the study. Self-selected respondents completed the questionnaire via an online survey program. Participants were offered a small gift card as an incentive.

Participants

The targeted population for this study consisted of the 7,361 undergraduate and graduate students and postdoctoral scholars actively participating in MentorNet's online community at the time of data collection (February 2007). While a majority of the students and scholars were in STEM fields, there was a minority who were in STEM-related business fields. For historical reasons, some STEM-related business fields were included in the MentorNet community. Individuals from those fields are included in the current sample.

Of those invited to participate in the study, 2,441 individuals completed the survey; rendering a 33% response rate. An additional 300 e-invitations were deemed undeliverable, resulting in a final response rate of 34%. The sample matched the known characteristics of the parent population in most ways. Males were slightly underrepresented in the sample, constituting approximately 29% of the population (subscribers to MentorNet) and 15.6% of the sample. Similarly, self-identified Blacks/African–Americans constituted 10% of the population and 4.4% of the sample (MentorNet, 2008).

Responses included in the present analyses are limited to those from participants who reported being U.S. citizens, who reported having had at least one mentor of any kind (at MentorNet or elsewhere), and who reported being an undergraduate student, graduate student, or post-doctoral scholar (with the latter two groups being combined into the category "post-baccalaureate scholar").

The sample contained 868 women, 142 men, and 3 individuals who declined to disclose their gender. Among the women, 614 self-identified as White; 136 as Asian or Asian-American; 44 as Black; 2 as Native American; 27 as Hispanic, 2 as Hawaiian or Pacific Islander; and 41 bi- or multiracial. Among the men, 83 self-identified as White; 26 as Asian or Asian-American; 11 as Black, 12 as Hispanic, 1 as Hawaiian or Pacific Islander; and 8 as bi- or multiracial. Because of their historical underrepresentation in the sciences, and because of their small numbers in the present sample, Black, Native American, Hispanic, Hawaiian, or other Pacific Islander and bi- or multiracial participants were assigned to a composite variable called targeted minority (116 women and 32 men).

Measures

The questionnaire consisted of a series of 38 questions, many of which had multiple subsections. The data collected included participants' demographic information, amounts and sources of mentoring support; desired mentoring experiences and actual mentoring experiences; and academic outcomes including participants' GPA, sense of confidence, and a sense of fit within their field.

Demographics. Several variables concerned demographic items. Participants were asked to select their own field of from a list of 63 fields of study (e.g., mechanical engineering, engineering management, chemistry). To create our variable field, responses were then recoded to indicate whether the participant was within fields of engineering, business, or science. Participants were asked to indicate the academic degree program in which they were currently enrolled (i.e., associate's, bachelor's, master's, doctoral, or postdoctoral scholar). To create our dichotomous variable status, responses were coded to indicate if the respondent was an undergraduate (coded as 0) or a post-baccalaureate scholar (coded as 1). Gender was treated as a dichotomous variable, with female assigned a 1 and male a 0. Participants were asked to indicate their race by "check[ing] as many of the choices below as are appropriate to describe your ethnicity". To avoid double counting participants, responses from those who selected multiple options were recoded so that they were assigned a score of one for the variable multiracial and a zero on all other options. Participants could be counted in one ethnic group: Asian, White, or targeted minority, with each of these being dummy coded.

Matching. Several variables related to matching. The degree to which participants indicated a preference for having a mentor of the same gender, wants gender match, was assessed by one 5-point Likert-type item asking the question: "How important was it to you that you have a mentor who was the same gender as you?" The degree to which participants wanted a same-race mentor, wants race match, was assessed via one 5-point Likert-type item asking the question: "How important was it to you that you have a mentor who was the same race/ethnicity as you?" For both of these items, response options ranged from 1 (*not at all important*) to 5 (*very important*). To assess actual, as opposed to desired, experiences, we looked at gender matching and race matching. Participants were asked: "Were any of your mentors the same gender as you?" and "Were any of your mentors the same race/ethnicity as you?" (We assumed that some, but not all, of the mentors whom the respondents had in mind were from MentorNet). For the variables gender match and race match, a one was assigned to the answer "yes" (i.e., there was a match) and a zero to the answer "no."

Related to the concept of similarity is the concept of empathy or understanding. Respondents were asked: "In order to complete your academic studies, how important is it (or was it) for you to have someone who understands how your background (e.g., gender, race/ethnicity) may affect your experiences of being a student in your field of study?" (which we labeled wants student background understood) and were also asked the importance of having "someone who understands how your background (e.g., gender, race/ethnicity) may affect your experiences of being a professional in your field of study?" (which we labeled wants prof background understood). For both items, response options ranged from 1 (*not at all important*) to 5 (*very important*). To score actual, as opposed to desired, experiences with empathy, participants were asked to indicate whether they had been helped by individuals who "understand how your background (e.g., gender, race/ethnicity) may affect your experiences of being a student in your field of study?" The resulting variable was called student background understood. The single item used to create the closely related variable, prof background understood was: "understands how your background (e.g., gender, race/ethnicity) may affect your experiences of being a professional in your field of study?" For both variables, scores could vary between 0 (*no one provided the help*) to 9 (*nine different sources of help*).

Mentoring experiences. A grid was used to create three variables concerning participants' subjective assessments of the amount of psychosocial, instrumental, and role-modeling help received. We combined nine items (e.g., "respects you as an individual; "is a consistent source of advice and support") that concerned psychosocial help into one index, labeled psychosocial help received. We also combined nine different items (e.g., "gives you challenging assignments that present opportunities to learn new skills"; "goes out of his/her way to promote your academic interests") that concerned instrumental help into another index, labeled instrumental help received. Both of these variables had a potential range from 0 to 81, as there were nine potential sources of support for nine different functions. Prior analyses of the data set, using averages rather than sum scores, had resulted in quite reliable scales ($\alpha = .88$ for psychosocial help, and $\alpha = .87$ for instrumental help), and so we knew that the items used to create each scale were internally consistent (Bayne, Blake-Beard, Crosby, & Muller, 2009). Because our intended scale for role modeling was unreliable, we used a single item ("serves as a role model") which we labeled Role Modeling Help Received, and it could vary from zero to nine.

Academic outcomes. We scored three measures of what might be considered "outcomes" different from the mentoring experiences. First, we scored respondents' self-reported GPA from 8 (*A*) to 1 (*C–or lower*). Student efficacy was measured by six, 5-point Likert-type ("strongly disagree" to "strongly agree"), scale items. Typical items included: "I feel confident that I can find a good job in my field when I have completed my studies"; "I know I am pursuing the career that is right for me"; and "I often wonder if I made the right choice about my field of study" (reverse coded). The scale proved to be statistically reliable, $\alpha = .78$. Student's confidence was assessed by the single item: "How confident are you that your field of study is the right one for you?" Response options were provided on a 6-point scale ranging from "not at all confident" to "completely confident."

Results

In this study, we addressed four research questions: (1) What do participants of different ethnicities and gender want in terms of the race or gender of their mentors? (2) To what extent do respondents of different ethnicities and gender report they have been mentored by an individual of their own race or gender? (3) Does matching by gender or race affect participants' mentoring experiences? And (4) Does matching by race or gender affect participants' academic outcomes?

Matching: What Participants Want

Our first question was: What do participants of different ethnicities and gender want in terms of the race or gender of their mentors? To answer this research question, we analyzed participants' responses to four items: (1) wants gender match; (2) wants race match; (3) wants student background understood; and

(4) wants prof background understood. We conducted four separate hierarchical multiple regressions, one for each of the items. In each regression, we entered field and status in the first step. In the second step, we included gender, Asian, and targeted minority. Below we report the unadjusted means, rather than the conditional ones implied by the regression models, so that interpretation of significant differences can be made with the original metrics.

In the first regression analysis (concerning wants gender match) we found an effect for gender, $\beta = .28, p < .001$ and for targeted minority, $\beta = .07, p < .05$. Using a 5-point scale in which 5 signifies that a match is very important and 1 signifies that a match is not at all important, women had a mean score of 3.07 ($SD = 1.28$) and men had a mean score of 2.00 ($SD = 1.17$). Thus, on average, men found matching to be "not very important," but women found matching to be "somewhat important." Targeted minorities thought a gender match was more important than did Whites ($M = 3.07, SD = 1.35$, and $M = 2.90, SD = 1.32$, respectively).

The second regression analysis (concerning wants race match) revealed effects for status, $\beta = -.07, p < .05$; gender, $\beta = .09, p < .01$; Asian, $\beta = .16, p < .001$; and targeted minority, $\beta = .26, p < .001$. Undergraduates found race matching to be more important than did older students ($M = 2.20, SD = 1.05$, and $M = 2.05, SD = 1.10$, respectively). Women found matching by race more important than did men ($M = 2.17, SD = 1.07$, and $M = 1.94, SD = 1.07$, respectively); Asian-Americans identified being matched with someone of the same race as more important than did than Whites ($M = 2.42, SD = 1.08$, and $M = 1.95, SD = 0.93$, respectively); targeted minorities also found being matched with someone of the same race more important than did Whites ($M = 2.75, SD = 1.38$, and $M = 1.95, SD = 0.93$, respectively). In a descriptive sense, it is also informative to note that the importance ascribed to gender matching was above the midpoint on the scale, at least for women while the importance ascribed to race matching was less.

What about finding someone who "understands your background?" Results of our third regression analysis (concerning wants student background understood) showed effects for gender, $\beta = .13, p < .001$; Asian, $\beta = .12, p = .001$; and targeted minority, $\beta = .20, p < .001$. Women were more likely to say it was important to have a mentor "who understands how their background effects their experiences as a student in their field" than were men ($M = 3.62, SD = 1.06$, and $M = 3.23, SD = 1.39$, respectively); Asian-Americans ($M = 3.75, SD = .96$) and targeted minorities ($M = 4.03, SD = 1.05$) were both more likely to endorse the item than were Whites ($M = 3.42, SD = 1.14$).

Our fourth regression analysis (concerning wants prof background understood) showed effects for gender, $\beta = .18, p < .001$; Asian, $\beta = .10, p < .01$; and targeted minority, $\beta = .19, p < .001$. Women respondents were more likely to say it was important to have a mentor "who understands how their background effects their experiences as a professional in their field" compared to men ($M = 3.72$, $SD = 1.03$, and $M = 3.18$, $SD = 1.34$, respectively); Asian-Americans ($M = 3.75$, $SD = .95$) and targeted minorities ($M = 4.07$, $SD = .98$) endorsed the item more than Whites ($M = 3.53$, $SD = 1.13$) In all four analyses, the amount of variance explained in the first step (field, status) was not significant.

Matching: What Participants Receive

Our second research question was: To what extent do respondents of different ethnicities and gender report they have been mentored by an individual of their own race or gender? To answer this research question, we analyzed participants' responses to four items: (1) gender match; (2) race match; (3) student background understood; and (4) prof background understood.

Using a chi-square analysis, we looked for differences in the numbers of men and women who had been matched with a mentor of the same gender (i.e., who answered "yes" on gender match). The analysis showed significant gender differences, χ^2 (1) $= 16.72$, $p < .001$. Of female participants, 71% indicated that they had had a female mentor whereas 87% of male respondents indicated that they had had a male mentor.

Our second chi-square analysis (concerning race match) showed significant racial differences, χ^2 (2) $= 255.78$, $p < .001$. Of Asian-American participants, 41% indicated that they had had an Asian-American mentor, whereas 47% of targeted minorities and 90% of Whites reported having had a mentor of their own race.

Multiple regression analyses were performed to test the effects of gender and race on the extent to which the participants felt they had received help from persons who understood how their background would affect their experiences as students (student background understood) or professionals (prof background understood). In both regression analyses, field and status were entered in the first step; and gender, Asian, and targeted minority were entered in the second step. Concerning student background understood, we found effects for gender, $\beta = .13$, $p < .01$; and targeted minority, $\beta = .08$, $p < .05$. Women received more help than did men ($M = 1.71$, $SD = 1.46$ and $M = 1.18$, $SD = 1.50$, respectively); and targeted minorities more than Whites ($M = 1.85$, $SD = 1.60$, and $M = 1.64$, $SD = 1.49$, respectively). Concerning prof background understood, we found effects for gender, $\beta = .12$, $p < .001$; Asian, $\beta = -.07$, $p < .05$, and targeted minority, $\beta = .07$, $p < .05$. Women received more help than did men ($M = 1.63$, $SD = 1.47$, and $M = 1.13$, $SD = 1.51$, respectively); and targeted minorities more than Whites ($M = 1.77$, $SD = 1.62$, and $M = 1.59$, $SD = 1.49$, respectively). In both regression analyses, the amount of variance explained in the first step (field, status) was not significant.

Mentoring Experiences

Our third research question was: Does being paired with an individual of the same gender or race make a difference in terms of the amount of psychosocial, instrumental and role modeling help received? We looked first at the issue of gender matching. In the regressions, we entered field and status in the first step; gender, Asian, and targeted minority in the second step; and gender match in the third step. Concerning the amount of psychosocial support participants received, we found effects for gender match, $\beta = .11, p < .01$; gender, $\beta = .11, p = .001$; and Asian, $\beta = -.11, p < .01$. Participants who had a mentor of their own gender reported they received more psychosocial support than those who did not ($M = 20.86$, $SD = 10.09$, and $M = 19.07$, $SD = 9.06$, respectively); women reported receiving more psychosocial support than did men ($M = 20.68$ $SD = 9.60$, and $M = 18.25$, $SD = 10.82$, respectively); and Asians protégés reported receiving less psychosocial support than did Whites ($M = 17.71$, $SD = 9.58$, and $M = 20.91$, $SD = 9.69$, respectively).

Concerning the amount of instrumental support respondents reported they received from their mentors, we found effects for gender match, $\beta = .11$, $p = .001$; gender, $\beta = .09, p < .05$, and Asian, $\beta = -.12, p = .001$. Participants who had a mentor of their own gender reported they received more instrumental help than those who did not ($M = 17.24$, $SD = 8.52$ and $M = 15.18$, $SD = 7.82$, respectively); women more than men ($M = 16.80$, $SD = 8.15$, and $M = 15.80$, $SD = 9.59$, respectively); and Asians less than Whites ($M = 14.17$, $SD = 8.62$, and $M = 17.14$, $SD = 8.16$, respectively).

Concerning the amount of role modeling support participants received, we found no significant effects of having had a mentor of the same gender (even among those who declared having a gender match was "important" or "very important"); however, effects were found for gender, $\beta = .10, t = 2.86, p < .01$; and Asian, $\beta = -.09, t = -2.70, p < .01$. Women reported they received more role modeling support than did men ($M = 2.82, SD = 1.68$, and $M = 2.45, SD = 1.64$, respectively); while Asians reported less than Whites participants ($M = 2.41, SD = 1.72$, and $M = 2.84, SD = 1.66$, respectively).

We then looked at the mentor–protégé pairings in terms of race. In the regressions, we entered field and status in the first step; gender, Asian, and targeted minority in the second step; and race match in the third step. Concerning the amount of psychosocial support participants received, we found effects for race match, $\beta = .14, p = .001$; gender, $\beta = .10, p = .005$; and targeted minority, $\beta = .08, p < .05$. Participants who had a mentor of their own race felt they received more psychosocial help then those who did not ($M = 21.17, SD = 9.97$, and $M = 17.97, SD = 9.06$, respectively); women more than men ($M = 20.68$, $SD = 9.60$, and $M = 18.25, SD = 10.82$, respectively); and targeted minorities more than Whites ($M = 20.92, SD = 10.54$, and $M = 20.91, SD = 9.69$, respectively).

Concerning the amount of instrumental support participants received, we found significant effects for race match, $\beta = .12, p = .003$; gender, $\beta = .07, p < .05$; and targeted minority, $\beta = .08, p < .05$. Participants who had a mentor of their own race felt they received more instrumental help than those who did not ($M = 17.28$, $SD = 8.28$, and $M = 14.87$, $SD = 8.45$, respectively); women more than men ($M = 16.80$, $SD = 8.14$, and $M = 15.80$, $SD = 9.59$, respectively); and targeted minorities more than Whites ($M = 17.34$, $SD = 8.80$, and $M = 17.14$, $SD = 8.16$, respectively). Concerning the amount of role modeling support participants received, we found significant effects for race match, $\beta = .10, p < .01$, and gender, $\beta = .09, p < .01$. Participants who had a mentor of their own race felt they received more role modeling help then those who did not ($M = 2.87$, $SD = 1.70$, and $M = 2.48$, $SD = 1.60$ respectively); and women more than men ($M = 2.82$, $SD = 1.68$, and $M = 2.45$, $SD = 1.64$, respectively).

Academic Outcomes

Our fourth research question was: Does being matched with a mentor of the same race or gender make a difference in terms of participants' academic outcomes? Again, we looked first at gender matching. In the regressions, we entered field and status in the first step; gender, Asian, and targeted minority in the second step; and gender match in the third step. The regression analyses failed to provide evidence that gender or racial matching affects academic outcomes. Gender matching did not significantly predict participants' GPA, efficacy, or confidence in their own good fit with science even when the sample was limited to those who had declared that a gender match was important or very important to them. Even though gender matching did not produce effects, other predictors did affect academic outcomes. Academic status had a significant effect on GPA, $\beta = .34$, $p < .001$. Post-baccalaureate scholars had higher GPAs than undergraduate students ($M = 6.96$, $SD = 1.10$, and $M = 5.87$, $SD = 1.67$, respectively). Gender had a significant effect on efficacy, $\beta = .09, p < .05$. Women feel more efficacious than men ($M = 2.26$, $SD = .65$, and $M = 2.10$, $SD = .67$, respectively). The Asian dummy variable influenced GPA, $\beta = -.11, p = .001$; efficacy, $\beta = .19, p < .001$; and confidence, $\beta = -.14, p < .001$. The targeted minority variable affected GPA only, $\beta = -.20, p < .001$. The mean GPA scores were 6.01 ($SD = 1.52$), 6.49 ($SD = 1.48$), and 5.66 ($SD = 1.81$) for Asian-Americans, Whites, and targeted minorities, respectively. The mean efficacy score for Asians was 2.52 ($SD = .63$), and it was 2.18 for Whites ($SD = .64$); while confidence scores were 4.12 ($SD = 1.01$) for Asians and 4.56 ($SD = 1.06$) for Whites.

In terms of having a mentor of one's own race, a similar pattern emerged. Racial matching did not significantly predict participants' GPA, efficacy, or confidence in their own good fit with science even when the sample was limited to those students who declared that race matching was important or very important.

Even though gender matching did not produce effects, other predictors did affect academic outcomes. Academic status had a significant effect on GPA, $\beta = .35$, $p < .001$. Post-baccalaureate scholars had higher GPAs than undergraduate students ($M = 6.96, SD = 1.10$, and $M = 5.87, SD = 1.67$, respectively). Gender had a significant effect on efficacy, $\beta = .09$, $p < .05$. Women feel more efficacious than men ($M = 2.26, SD = .65$, and $M = 2.10, SD = .67$, respectively). The Asian dummy variable influenced GPA, $\beta = -.11$, $p < .01$; efficacy, $\beta = .19$, $p < .001$; and confidence, $\beta = -.15$, $p < .001$. The targeted minority variable affected GPA only, $\beta = -.20$, $p < .001$. The mean GPA scores were 6.01 ($SD = 1.52$), 6.49 ($SD = 1.48$), and 5.66 ($SD = 1.81$) for Asian-Americans, Whites, and targeted minorities, respectively. The mean efficacy score for Asians was 2.52 ($SD = .63$), and it was 2.18 for Whites ($SD = .64$); while confidence scores were 4.12 ($SD = 1.01$) for Asians and 4.56 ($SD = 1.06$) for Whites.

Discussion

Having a mentor of one's own gender or race was felt to be somewhat important for success by many of the STEM and business students whom we surveyed, especially the women. In terms of the students' experiences of mentoring relationships, matching certainly did seem to make a difference: those who had had a mentor of their own gender or race reported receiving more help. Yet, in terms of academic outcomes, matching by gender or race made no difference at all. There were no differences in protégés' self-reported GPAs, efficacy, or confidence in their own good fit with science, based on being matched by gender or race, even for those who indicated that same-gender or same-race matching was particularly important to them.

Given that our society remains stratified by gender and race, it may not be surprising to find that many individuals believe that same-gender or same-race mentor–protégé pairs will be most satisfying and will produce the best results. How then, can we account for the findings of this study, and some others, which suggest a much more complex picture? In particular, how can we account for the lack of difference in academic outcomes between protégés who had a mentor of their own gender or other their own race and protégés who had only cross-gender or cross-race mentors?

Three explanations come to mind. The first concerns the particulars of this study and its unusual sample. The second concerns the nature of matching. Finally, expectations and needs may be critically important.

First, the sample in our study was unusual in a number of ways. All the participants were in the STEM fields or business, majoring in science or math, in engineering, or less often in business. Second, all of the participants had joined the community of online mentoring network, likely meaning that they valued mentoring, had access to a computer, and were comfortable with the idea of tapping into internet resources and electronic communication with others at institutions other than their home institution. Maybe such people have such high grades, so strong a sense of efficacy, and so much confidence in themselves and their choices that their academic outcomes are unlikely to be influenced by any factor—including the gender or race of their mentor—outside themselves. Examination of the data did reveal that self-reported GPAs were very high, but for neither efficacy nor self-confidence was there a ceiling effect. Also, the variation in the students' reports of the help they had received indicates that our sample was not impervious to outside influences.

More likely, our findings indicate that matching on the basis of characteristics acquired at birth (gender and race) may only be a poor proxy for other, more meaningful types of matches. It makes sense that other factors are much stronger in predicting successful matching of mentors and protégés than simply race or gender. Race and gender may be indicators of shared background experiences, but experiences of women or ethnic minorities, and their own personality characteristics, are sufficiently varied such that we should not assume individuals will be more empathetic just because they are of the same gender or race as each other.

Harrison, Price, and Bell (1998) distinguish between surface level diversity, which they characterize as demographic dimensions, and deep level diversity, which they characterize as attitudinal. They suggest that especially as work group members continue to interact with one another, similarity in deep-level diversity becomes more important than similarity in surface-level diversity. A number of investigations of varying populations such as African–American, Hispanic-American and Native-American graduate students (Ortiz-Walters & Gibson, 2005), Black MBAs (Brown, Zablah, & Bellenger, 2008), and employees of a newspaper (Ensher, Grant-Vallone, & Marelich, 2002) offer support for the importance attitudinal similarities. Also important is motivational similarity, with satisfaction being highest when the mentor and the protégé have similar levels of commitment to the relationship (Poteat, Shockley, & Allen, 2009)

Perhaps what determines the outcomes of any mentoring relationship is not the match between the protégé and the mentor, either in terms of demographic characteristics or in terms of attitudes, but rather the match between what the protégé needs and what the mentor can provide. Sometimes, a protégé may wish to obtain certain types of instrumental or psychosocial help, and when a mentor can provide the help, great outcomes follow; no matter what the gender, race, or attitudes of the mentor and no matter how well or poorly they match the gender, race, and attitudes of the protégé (Bearman et al., 2007). Of course, if a match on demographic characteristics or on attitudes helps the mentor and protégé to engage in open and trusting discussion with one another, then the mentor may be especially likely to know the needs or desires of the protégé. Future research should seek to untangle all aspects of matching and not stop at looking merely at race and gender.

No matter what future research shows, the present results carry with them strong implications for anyone who wants to use mentoring programs as a pathway to diversity. First, knowing that mentoring can have a positive effect, program administrators should not be hampered by the search for women and minorities as mentors. They should also be open to the possibility that mentoring support may come from a variety of sources, across lines of race, gender and even functional role. Hurtado et al.'s (2011) mixed methods study of aspiring scientists found that faculty involvement with students was a critical source of support in preparing the next generation of scientists. Second, administrators should recognize the lack of strong connection between satisfaction, on the one hand, and outcomes, on the other. Like some previous researchers (Tenenbaum et al., 2001), we found that the factors that produced satisfaction did not necessarily produce results. To the extent that we wish to change the compositions of our institutions, and not just make people in them feel satisfied, we might attend to outcome measures. Furthermore, we must keep in mind that the benefits of mentoring may not materialize simply in the present time but may in fact unfold over time. Only by continuing to conduct empirical research will we be able to keep our eyes on the prize.

References

Allen, T. D., Day, R., & Lentz, E. (2005). The role of interpersonal comfort in mentoring relationships. *Journal of Career Development, 31*, 155–169. doi:10.1007/s10871–004-2224–3.

Allen, T. D., Eby, L. T., & Lentz, E. (2006). The relationship between formal mentoring program characteristics and perceived program effectiveness. *Personnel Psychology, 59*, 125–153. doi:10.1111/j.1744–6570.2006.00747.x.

Arora, V., Schneider, B., Thal, R., & Meltzer, D. (2011). Design of an intervention to promote the entry of minority youth into clinical research careers by aligning ambition: The TEACH (Training Early Achievers for Careers in Health) research program. *Journal of Social Issues, 67*(3), 580–598.

Atkinson, D. R., Neville, H., & Casas, A. (1991). The mentorship of ethnic minorities in professional psychology. *Professional Psychology: Research and Practice, 22*, 336–338. doi:10.1037/0735–7028.22.4.336.

Bayne, M. L., Blake-Beard, S., Crosby, F. J., & Muller, C. (2009, November). *Challenging the common dogma: Does mentoring really matter to women and underrepresented student in the sciences?* Presented at the annual conference of the University of New Mexico Mentoring Institute, Albuquerque, NM.

Bearman, S., Blake-Beard, S., Hunt, L., & Crosby, F. J. (2007). New directions in mentoring. In T. D. Allen & L. T. Eby (Eds.), *Blackwell handbook of mentoring: A multiple perspectives approach* (pp. 275–295). New York: Blackwell.

Blake-Beard, S. D. (2001). Taking a hard look at formal mentoring programs: A consideration of potential challenges facing women. *Journal of Management Development, 20*, 331–345. doi:10.1108/02621710110388983.

Bowman, S. R., Kite, M. E., Branscombe, N. R., & Williams, S. (1999). Developmental relationships of black Americans in the academy. In A. J. Murrell, F. J. Crosby, & R. J. Ely (Eds.),

Mentoring dilemmas: Developmental relationships within multicultural organizations (pp. 21–46). Mahwah, NJ: Lawrence Erlbaum Associates.

Bozeman, B. & Feeney, M. K. (2008). Mentor matching: A "goodness of fit" model. *Administration & Society, 40*(5), 465–482. doi:10.1177/0095399708320184.

Brown, B. P., Zablah, A. R., & Bellenger, D. N. (2008). The role of mentoring in promoting organizational commitment among black managers: An evaluation of the indirect effects of racial similarity and shared racial perspectives. *Journal of Business Research, 61,* 732–738. doi: 10.1016/j.jbusres.2007.08.004.

Campbell, T. A., & Campbell, D. E. (1997). Faculty/student mentor program: Effects on academic performance and retentions. *Research in Higher Education, 38*(6), 727–742.

Campbell, T. A., & Campbell, D. E. (2007). Outcomes of mentoring at-risk college students: Gender and ethnic matching effects. *Mentoring & Tutoring, 15*(2), 135–148. doi:10.1080/13611260601086287.

Campbell, A., & Skoog, G. (2004). Preparing undergraduate women for science careers: Facilitating success in professional research. *Journal of College Science Teaching, 33*(5), 24–26.

Carrington, B., Tymms, P., & Merrell, C. (2008). Role models, school improvement and the 'gender gap'—do men bring out the best in boys and women the best in girls?' *British Educational Research Journal, 34* (3), 315–327. doi:10.1080/01411920701532202.

Clark, R. A., Harden, S. L., & Johnson, W. B. (2000). Mentor relationships in clinical psychology doctoral training: Results of a national survey. *Teaching of Psychology, 27,* 262–268. doi:10.1207/S15328023TOP2704_04.

Davis, D. J. (2007). Access to academe: The importance of mentoring to black students. *The Negro Educational Review, 58*(3/4), 217–231.

Downing, R. A., Crosby, F. J., & Blake-Beard, S. (2005). The perceived importance of developmental relationships on women undergraduates' pursuit of science. *Psychology of Women Quarterly, 29* (4), 419–426. doi:10.1111/j.1471–6402.2005.00242.x.

Dreher, G. F., & Cox, T. H. (1996). Race, gender and opportunity: A study of compensation attainment and the establishment of mentoring relationships. *Journal of Applied Psychology, 81,* 297–308. doi:10.1037/0021–9010.81.3.297.

Ensher, E. E., & Murphy, S. R. (1997). Effects of race, gender, perceived similarity and contact on mentor relationships. *Journal of Vocational Behavior, 50*(3), 399–417. doi:10.1006/jvbe.1996.1547.

Ensher, E. A., Grant-Vallone, E. J., & Marelich, W. D. (2002). Effects of perceived attitudinal and demographic similarity on protégés' support and satisfaction gained from their mentoring relationships. *Journal of Applied Social Psychology, 32,* 1407–1430. doi:10.1111/j.1559–1816.2002.tb01444.x.

Feeney, M. K., & Bozeman, B. (2008). Mentoring and network ties. *Human Relations, 61*(12) 1651–1676. doi:10.1177/0018726708098081.

Foley, S., Linnehan, F., Greenhaus, J. H., & Weer, C. H. (2006). The impact of gender similarity, racial similarity, and work culture on family-supportive supervision. *Group & Organization Management, 31,* 420–441. doi:10.1177/1059601106286884.

Frierson, H. T., Hargrove, B. K., & Lewis, N. R. (1994). Black summer research students' perceptions related to research mentors' race and gender. *Journal of College Student Development, 35,* 475–480.

Gilbert, L. A. (1985). Dimensions of same-gender student-faculty role-model relationships. *Sex Roles, 12,* 111–123. doi:10.1007/BF00288041.

Goldstein, E. (1979). Effect of same-sex and cross-sex role models on the subsequent academic productivity of scholars. *American Psychologist, 34,* 407–410. doi:10.1037/0003–066X.34.5.407.

Gonzáles-Figueroa, E., & Young, A. M. (2005). Ethnic identity and mentoring among Latinas in professional roles. *Cultural Diversity and Ethnic Minority Psychology, 11,* 213–226. doi:10.1037/1099–9809.11.3.213.

Harrison, D. A., Price, K. H., & Bell, M. P. (1998). Beyond relational demography: Time and the effects of surface- and deep-level diversity on work group cohesion. *Academy of Management Journal, 41,* 96–107. doi:10.2307/256901.

Hollingsworth, M. A., & Fassinger, R. E. (2002). The role of faculty mentors in the research training of counseling psychology doctoral students. *Journal of Counseling Psychology, 49*, 324–330. doi:10.1037//0022–0167.49.3.330.

Hurtado, S., Eagan, M. K., Tran, M. C., Newman, C. B., Chang, M. J., & Velasco, P. (2011) "We do science here": Underrepresented students interactions with faculty in different college contexts. *Journal of Social Issues, 67*(3), 553–579.

Johnson, W. B. (2007). *On being a mentor: A guide for higher education faculty*. Mahwah, NJ: Lawrence Erlbaum.

Kark, R., & Shilo-Dubnov, R. (2007). The effects of gender on protégés' perceptions of mentoring relationships in Israeli academia. *Megamot, 44*, 707–735.

Kasprisin, C. A., Single, P. B., Single, R. M., & Muller, C. B. (2003). Building a better bridge: Testing e-training to improve e-mentoring programmes in higher education. *Mentoring & Tutoring, 11*, 67–78. doi:10.1080/1361126032000054817.

Kasprisin, C. A., Single, P. B., Single, R. M., Ferrier, J. L., & Muller, C. B. (2008). Improved mentor satisfaction: Emphasizing protégé training for adult-age mentoring dyads. *Mentoring & Tutoring: Partnership in Learning, 16*, 163–174. doi:10.1080/13611260801916424.

Kirchmeyer, C. (2002). Gender differences in managerial careers: Yesterday, today, and tomorrow. *Journal of Business Ethics, 37*, 5–24. doi:10.1037/0021–9010.87.5.929.

Kram, K. (1988). *Mentoring at work: Developmental relationships in organizational life* (2nd ed.). Lanham, MD: University Press of America.

Lockwood, P. (2006). "Someone like me can be successful": Do college students need same-gender role models? *Psychology of Women Quarterly, 30*, 36–46. doi:10.1111/j.1471–6402.2006.00260.x.

Marasco, C. A. (2005). Employment: MentorNet supports women in science. *Chemical & Engineering News, 83*, 55.

MentorNet. (2007). *Success sustained by study: A documentation of MentorNet's growth and a summary of research findings—October 2007*. Retrieved July 23, 2011, from http://www.mentornet.net/documents/files/evaluation/studentperceptions.completereport.pdf.

MentorNet. (2008). *Students' perceptions of the value and need for mentors as they progress through academic studies in engineering and science, a report to the National Science Foundation concerning a Small Grant for Exploratory Research (SGER) EEC-06397621, March 21, 2008*. Retrieved on August 8, 2009, from http://www.mentornet.net/documents/files/evaluation/studentperceptions.completereport.pdf.

Moore, A. A., Miller, M. J., Pitchford, V. J., & Jeng, L. H. (2008). Mentoring in the millennium: New views, climate and actions. *New Library World, 109*(1/2), 75–86. doi:10.1108/03074800810846029.

Noe, R. (1988). Women and mentoring: A review and research agenda. *Academy of Management Review, 13*(1), 65–78. doi:10.2307/258355.

O'Neill, R. M., Horton, S., & Crosby, F. J. (1999). Gender issues in developmental relationships. In A. J. Murrell, F. J. Crosby, & R. J. Ely (Eds), *Mentoring dilemmas: Developmental relationships within multicultural organizations* (pp. 63–80) Mahwah, NJ: Lawrence Erlbaum.

Ortiz-Walters, R., & Gilson, L. L. (2005). Mentoring in academia: An examination of the experiences of protégés of color. *Journal of Vocational Behavior, 67*, 459–475. doi:10.1016/j.jvb.2004.09.004.

Poteat, L. F., Shockley, K. M., & Allen, T. D. (2009). Mentor-protégé commitment fit and relationship satisfaction in academic mentoring. *Journal of Vocational Behavior, 74*, 332–337. doi:10.1016/j.jvb.2009.02.003.

Phinney, J. S., Campos, C. M. T., Kallemeyn, D. M. P., & Kim, C. (2011). Processes and outcomes of a mentoring program for Latino college freshmen. *Journal of Social Issues, 57*(3), 599–621.

Ragins, B. R. (1997). Diversified mentoring relationships in organizations: A power perspective. *Academy of Management Review, 22*(2), 482–502. doi:10.1006/jvbe.1997.1590.

Scandura, T. A. (1992). Mentorship and career mobility: An empirical investigation. *Journal of Organizational Behavior, 13*(2), 169–174. doi:10.1002/job.4030130206.

Scandura, T. A., & Graen, G. B. (1984). Moderating effects of initial leader-member exchange status on the effects of a leadership intervention. *Journal of Applied Psychology, 69*(3), 428–36. doi:10.1037/0021–9010.69.3.428.

Settles, I. H., Cortina, L. M., Stewart, A. J., & Malley, J. (2007). Voice matters: Buffering the impact of a negative climate for women in science. *Psychology of Women Quarterly, 31*(3), 270–281. doi:10.1111/j.1471–6402.2007.00370.x.

Smith, J. W., Smith, W. J., & Markham, S. E. (2000). Diversity issues in mentoring academic faculty. *Journal of Career Development, 26*(4), 251–262. doi:10.1177/089484530002600402.

Sosik, J. J., & Godshalk, V. M. (2005). Examining gender similarity and mentor's supervisory status in mentoring relationships. *Mentoring and Tutoring, 13*(1), 39–52.

Syed, M., Azmitia, M., & Cooper, C. R. (2011). Identity and academic success among underrepresented ethnic minorities: An interdisciplinary review and integration. *Journal of Social Issues, 67*(3), 442–468.

Tenenbaum, H. R., Crosby, F. J., & Gliner, M. D. (2001). Mentoring relationships in graduate school. *Journal of Vocational Behavior, 59*(3), 326–341. doi:10.1006/jvbe.2001.1804.

Turban, D. B., Dougherty, T. W., & Lee, F. K. (2002). Gender, race, and perceived similarity effects in developmental relationships: The moderating role of relationship duration. *Journal of Vocational Behavior, 61*, 240–262. doi:10.1006/jvbe.2001.1855.

Ugrin, J. C., Odom, M. D., & Pearson, J. M. (2008). Exploring the importance of mentoring for new scholars: A social exchange perspective. *Journal of Information Systems Education, 19*(3), 343–350.

Wasburn, M. H., & Miller, S. G. (2004). Retaining undergraduate women in science, engineering, and technology: A survey of a student organization. *Journal of College Student Retention, 6*(2), 155–168.

Witkow, M. R. & Fuligni, A. J. (2011). Ethnic and generational differences in the relations between social support and academic achievement across the high school years. *Journal of Social Issues, 67*(3), 531–552.

STACY BLAKE-BEARD, PhD is an Associate Professor of Management at the Simmons School of Management and Research Faculty in the Center for Gender in Organizations. She holds a BS in Psychology from the University of Maryland and a MA and PhD in Organizational Psychology from the University of Michigan. Dr. Blake-Beard's research focuses on the impact of changing workforce demographics on mentoring relationships and has been featured in several publications including the *Journal of Career Development*, the *Academy of Management Executive*, *Psychology of Women Quarterly*, and the *Journal of Business Ethics*.

MELISSA BAYNE is a Psychology Graduate Student at the University of California, Santa Cruz. An NIH training fellowship recipient, Bayne has served as a graduate student representative an invited Graduate Forum speaker and Chair of *SPSSI*'s Graduate Student Committee. Her primary research interests include academic mentoring; in particular, relationships among mentors' emotional intelligence and their protégés' self-efficacy and performance.

FAYE CROSBY is Professor of Psychology at the University of California, Santa Cruz. A long-time *SPSSI* member, she was honored to serve as its President of *SPSSI* in 1991–1992. Crosby has published nearly 200 scholarly works, including 14 books, mostly on topics concerning discrimination and remedies to discrimination. Crosby has been awarded several honors including the Carolyn Wood Sherif award from Division 35 of the American Psychological Association and the Kurt Lewin Award from *SPSSI*. Crosby is currently serving as the Provost of Cowell College, the oldest residential college at UC Santa Cruz.

CAROL B. MULLER, PhD, is the founder and former CEO of MentorNet (www.MentorNet.net), *The E-Mentoring Network for Diversity in Engineering and Science*, a nonprofit organization. A former university administrator and occasional consultant and advisor for leaders in education and nonprofit organizations, Muller draws upon expertise in mentoring, educational program design and development, engineering education, and diversity. She has authored numerous papers, has won $10m+ in grants for her work from private foundations, corporations, and the federal government, as well as a variety of national awards.

Journal of Social Issues, Vol. 67, No. 3, 2011, pp. 644–648

Understanding Educational and Occupational Choices

Jacquelynne S. Eccles*

University of Michigan

I am delighted to write the commentary for this very rich set of papers. It is wonderful to have such a diverse set of papers together in one volume. When I began my work on this topic in the mid 1970s, the focus in the field was entirely on the underrepresentation of women in science, technology, engineering, and mathematics, the theoretical tools were quite limited, and the scholars were all of European-American heritage. These papers illustrate how far this area of study has advanced along each of these dimensions.

In 1977, the National Institute of Education put out a call for proposals to study the underrepresentation of women in mathematics based on the findings of Lucy Sells. Dr. Sells had shown that girls in the United States were less likely to take advanced mathematics in high school and that taking advanced mathematics courses was a critical step in the pipeline toward careers in mathematics and science. My colleagues and I put together a theoretical model (the updated version of which is illustrated in Figure 1) as a foundation for our research proposal. We had two goals in developing this model: (1) to focus on choice rather than deficits by asking the question "why were women making the educational and occupational choices they did" rather than the question "why aren't women making the same choices as men"; and (2) to develop a theoretical model that took both personal agency and social/cultural structures into account. The model was grounded in my training as a social-cognitive motivational psychologist, a developmental psychologist, and my growing identification as a feminist psychologist, hence the emphasis both on expectancies and subjective task values as core psychological influences on educational and occupational choices and on social roles and socialization processes as key influences on the ontogeny of individual and group differences in expectancies and task values. My colleagues and I stressed the importance of what we labeled subjective task value, which we proposed is the joint function of several other

---

*Correspondence concerning this article should be addressed to Jacquelynne S. Eccles, Department of Psychology and Education, University of Michigan, 5118 ISR, 426 Thompson Street, Ann Arbor, MI 48197 [e-mail: jeccles@umich.edu].

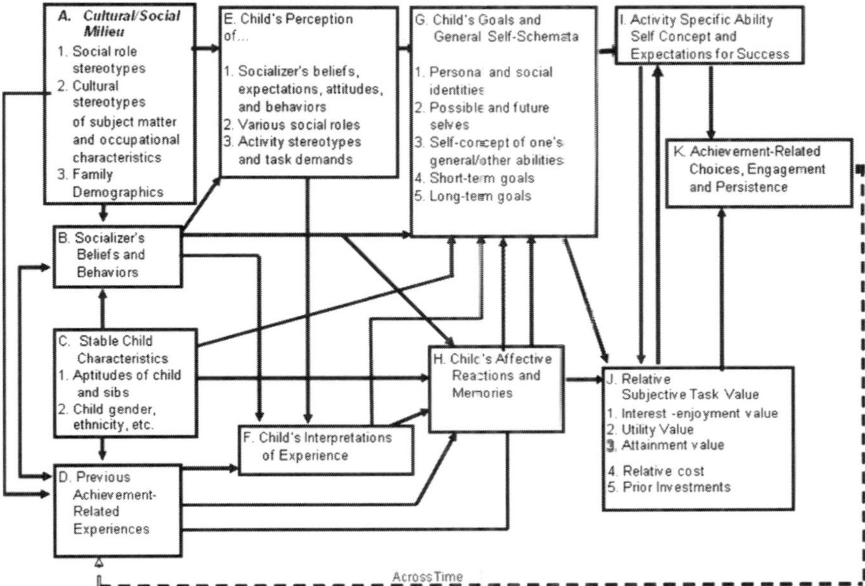

Fig. 1. Updated Eccles et al. socioculturally embedded expectancy value model of achievement choices. (Copyright Jacquelynne S. Eccles.)

motivational beliefs including anticipated interest likely to be experienced in, the attainment and utility value of, and the anticipated psychological, economic and social costs of various possible task or activity choices. We also stressed that each choice is based on the relative subjective task values and expectations for success across the variety of perceived possible options at the time. Third, we stressed the need to take into account the role that social structures/culture/social class play in determining the range of options individuals can and do consider as they make educational and occupational decisions. Finally, we stressed the idea that the hierarchies of the subjective task values of various options are directly influenced by the immediate social context and the developmental stage of the individual making the choice. Thus we stressed the need for a quite general developmental approach to the issue of disparities in science, technology, engineering, and mathematics (STEM). We felt it was critical to understand the "roads taken" to understand the "roads not taken." We stressed that the question of "why women and minorities were less like to aspire to and enter STEM fields than white males and Asians" is best thought of as a subset of the more general question "why does anyone do anything." These same themes are evident in the papers in this issue—most clearly in Syed, Azmitia, and Cooper (2011), Chemers, Zurbriggen, Syed, Goza, and Bearman (2011), Smart Richman, vanDellen, and Wood (2011), London,

Rosenthal, and Gonzalez (2011), Witkow and Fuligni (2011), Arora, Schneider, Thal, and Meltzer (2011), and Phinney, Torres Campos, Kallemeyn, and Kim (this issue).

At the time we developed this model, there was very little interest in developmental and social psychology in any social roles other than gender and that interest focused primarily on very early development. One of the most striking characteristics of the papers in this issue is how much broader and more sophisticated the authors' approach to social identities and sociocultural processes is now than it was then. For example, Smart Richman et al. (2011) discuss the importance of social identity threats to performance and well-being. This paper illustrates how the field has a much better understanding of the links between social identity processes, contextual cues, and actual performance. We would consider these processes as part of the link between social settings and the anticipated cost of task involvement. An even broader view of the many ways in which personal and social identities relate to academic success of underrepresented ethnic minorities is provided by the papers by Syed et al. (2011), Chemers et al. (2011), and Witkow and Fuligni (2011). Equally striking is the progress that has been made in designing well grounded and effective intervention strategies for both high school and college students. This is evident in the all of the papers in Section III, *Institutional Efforts: Barriers and Opportunities*, and Section IV, *Intervention Strategies: Aligning Ambitions and Mentoring*, of the issue.

Finally, these papers provide very concrete evidence of how persistent the problems underlying disparities in participation have been. As noted by Syed and Chemers (2011), although we have seen some increases in the proportion of women in STEM fields, particularly in those linked to the medical, biological, and social sciences, the underrepresentation of women in the physical sciences, engineers, information technology, and other fields of technology persists. There has been even less progress in recruiting students of color into these fields. On the one hand, these articles make it clear that we now have very powerful theoretical and intervention tools to address these disparities at several points in the pipeline. On the other hand, to the extent that both personal and collective or social identities explain group differences in both STEM aspirations and persistence, these papers also make it clear that reducing these disparities will require us to change the stereotypes regarding both the subjective task value and perceived costs of preparing oneself for participation in STEM professions and the stereotypes of STEM professions themselves. The complexity of these transformations is made particularly clear in the articles stressing the role of both personal and contextual social supports in helping URM and women to consider STEM professions as a serious and attainable option and then to support their exploration of and training for STEM careers in both secondary and tertiary educational setting. These points are best illustrated in the articles of Witkow and Fuligni (2011), Hurtado et al. (2011), Arora et al. (2011), Phinney et al. (2011), and Blake-Beard, Bayne,

Crosby, and Muller (2011). We would classify such interventions under the interplay between identity-based processes and the perceived attainment and utility values and perceived costs of aspiring to and then training oneself to enter STEM professions.

The papers also illustrate the methodological gains that have been made in studying the subtle psychological and social processes underlying the association of identities processes with task choice and performance. This is best illustrated in the papers by Smart Richman et al. (2011) and London et al. (2011), both of which provide examples of relative new methods for studying the link between identity processes and both task choice and performance. I particularly like the experience sampling methodology method discussed by London et al. (2011). This method yields a rich set of information on the day-to-day affective experiences related to STEM and non-STEM activities. Coupling this method with developmental changes in aspirations and course choices provides an excellent way to look at the mediating role of affective memories, the perceived interest value of, and the anticipated emotional costs of STEM versus non-STEM activities in task choice.

In closing, I would like to note that each of these papers illustrates the importance of both social and psychological processes in the ontogeny of career development. Although the papers focus most directly on the career selection processes linked to STEM, the processes discussed contribute broadly to our fundamental understanding of career choice. Developmental and social psychologists have paid relatively little attention to ontogeny of career choice, despite the fact that educational and occupational choices have a major influence on all aspects of life-span development. These papers provide a model of how we can study the confluence of both psychological and social process in the ontogeny of such central, life-defining choices. They also illustrate the importance of looking at the social and psychological influences on the subjective task values of various options as carefully as we have looked at the influences on self-efficacy and expectations for success for various options.

References

Arora, V., Schneider, B., Thal, R., & Meltzer, D. (2011). Design of an intervention to promote entry of minority youth into clinical research careers by aligning ambition: The TEACH (Training Early Achievers for Careers in Health) research program. *Journal of Social Issues, 67*(3), 580–598.

Blake-Beard, S., Bayne, M. L., Crosby, F. J., & Muller, C. B. (2011). Matching by race and gender in mentoring relationships: Keeping our eyes on the prize. *Journal of Social Issues, 67*(3), 622–643.

Chemers, M. M., Zurbriggen, E. L., Syed, M., Goza, B. K., & Bearman, S. (2011). The role of efficacy and identity in science career commitment among underrepresented minority students. *Journal of Social Issues, 67*(3), 469–491.

Hurtado, S., Eagan, M. K., Tran, M. C., Newman, C. B., Chang, M. J., & Velasco, P. (2011) "We do science here": Underrepresented students interactions with faculty in different college contexts. *Journal of Social Issues, 67*(3), 553–579.

London, B., Rosenthal, L., & Gonzalez, A. (2011). Assessing the role of gender rejection sensitivity, identity, and support on the academic engagement of women in non-traditional fields using experience sampling methods. *Journal of Social Issues, 67(3)*, 510–530.
Phinney, J. S., Torres Campos, C. M., Kallemeyn, D. M. P., & Kim, C. (2011). Processes and outcomes of a mentoring program for Latino college freshmen. *Journal of Social Issues, 67(3)*, 599–621.
Smart Richman, L., vanDellen, M., & Wood, W. (2011). How women cope: Being a numerical minority in a male-dominated profession. *Journal of Social Issues, 67(3)*, 492–509.
Syed, M. & Chemers, M. M. (2011). Ethnic minorities and women in STEM: Casting a wide net to address a persistent social problem. *Journal of Social Issues, 67(3)*, 435–441.
Syed, M., Azmitia, M., & Cooper, C. R. (2011). Identity and academic success among underrepresented ethnic minorities: An interdisciplinary review and integration. *Journal of Social Issues, 67(3)*, 442–468.
Witkow, M. R., & Fuligni, A. J. (2011). Ethnic and generational differences in the relations between social support and academic achievement across the high school years. *Journal of Social Issues, 67(3)*, 531–552.

JACQUELYNNE S. ECCLES, the McKeachie/Pintrich Distinguished University Professor of Psychology and Education at the University of Michigan, got her PhD at UCLA in 1974. She has taught at Smith College and the universities of Michigan and Colorado. She is Past President of the *Society for Research on Adolescence* and Division 35 of the APA, as well as past editor of the *Journal of Research on Adolescence* and current editor of *Developmental Psychology*. She has received many awards including lifetime career awards from APS, SRA, SSHD, and Division 15 of the APA and has chaired or co-chaired two international graduate and postgraduate training programs and the MacArthur Research Network for Successful Pathways through Middle Childhood. Her research focuses on: (1) the role that social and personal identities play in individual's life defining decisions and (2) the role of social contexts in human development.

Journal of Social Issues, Vol. 67, No. 3, 2011, pp. 649–650

Introduction to Mark Zanna's *SPSSI* Kurt Lewin Award Address

Faye J. Crosby*
University of California

Mark P. Zanna, you are being awarded the Kurt Lewin Memorial Award from the *Society for the Psychological Study of Social Issues* (*SPSSI*) for your sustained leadership in both conducting and enabling research that advances our understanding of the dynamics of attitude formation and change. Through your own rigorous empirical work and the work that you have fostered in the social psychological community over the last four decades, you have helped us understand and foster behaviors in individuals that are healthy and sane for themselves and their communities.

Through your curiosity-driven research, you have made substantial contributions to our understanding of the dynamics of attitude formation and attitude change. From your early work on the connections between commitments and opinions through your work on social comparison to your recent work on persuasion and self-persuasion, you have published work that is both theoretical and applied, and true to the tradition of Kurt Lewin, you have made sure that each side informs the other. Your methodologically sophisticated applications of theory have advanced our ability to help people act in pro-social and healthy ways. You have helped modify theory and concepts in light of the results of your applied work. Nowhere is the synergy of theory, method, and social dedication more apparent than in your work, most vigorous over the last decade, on tobacco use and tobacco policy.

Consistent with the ideals that underlie all of *SPSSI*'s work, you have excelled at fostering community. You have consistently worked for the benefit of the field and all in it. Since 1980, you have served as co-editor of the *Ontario Symposium on Personality and Social Psychology*. And over the last 20 years, you have

---

*Correspondence concerning this article should be addressed to Faye J. Crosby, Psychology Department, UC Santa Cruz, Santa Cruz, CA 95064 [e-mail: fjcrosby@ucsc.edu].

been the editor of one of the most influential organs in our field: the prestigious *Advances in Experimental Social Psychology.* Through your decades of service on editorial boards, review boards, national and international councils—all too numerous to mention—you have worked as a quiet presence, helping us to evolve as a community of scientists and citizens, to move beyond the old strictures and prejudices.

One particularly noteworthy contribution has been your work on behalf of junior scholars. In your official and unofficial editorial roles, you have helped shape the work of countless younger scholars, making sure that they have been able to use methodologically sound research that is the hallmark of contemporary social psychology to realize the lofty ideals that are and long have been the underpinning of true democracy. By helping junior scholars gain prominence in our field, you have also enabled the field to grow and to improve. Brilliant methodologist that you are, you germinated the kind of critical self-appraisal that can flourish only when those who have previously been excluded are now genuinely included.

For your work, you have received many accolades. In 1992, *SPSSI* gave you the Otto Klineberg Intercultural and International Relations Prize. A year later, the Canadian Psychological Association honored you with the Donald O. Hebb Award for Distinguished Contributions to Psychology as a Science. You have also received the Donald T. Campbell Award for Distinguished Research in Social Psychology from the *Society for Personality and Social Psychology* (1997) and the Distinguished Scientist Award (SESP, 2007). Your own university, the University of Waterloo, has named you as a University Professor. Now in bestowing on you with the Kurt Lewin Memorial Award, *SPSSI* adds to the long list of your honors and, at the same time, honors our own aspirations to craft and then to craft anew a psychologically informed science of social issues.

FAYE CROSBY is Professor of Psychology at the University of California (UC) Santa Cruz. A long-time *SPSSI* member, she was honored to serve as its President of *SPSSI* in 1991–1992. Crosby has published nearly 200 scholarly works, including 14 books, mostly on topics concerning discrimination and remedies to discrimination. Crosby has been awarded several honors including the Carolyn Wood Sherif award from Division 35 of the American Psychological Association, the Kurt Lewin Award from *SPSSI*, and the Alice and Clifford Spendlove Prize for Social Justice, Diplomacy, and Tolerance from UC Merced. Crosby is currently serving as the Provost of Cowell College, the oldest residential college at UC Santa Cruz.

Journal of Social Issues, Vol. 67, No. 3, 2011, pp. 651–662

While Waiting for Nature to Take Her Course: There's Nothing So Practical as a Good…Design

Mark P. Zanna*
University of Waterloo

In this essay, I first describe some examples of curiosity-based, basic research inspired by Lewin's famous dictum that there is nothing so practical as a good…theory. Then, I describe several examples of recent intervention studies that leverage basic research to make the world a better place. Next, in the spirit of Lewin, I suggest that there is nothing so practical as a good…design—and describe "state of the art" quasi-experimental designs to evaluate tobacco control policies and suggest the sort of designs one might employ to evaluate smoking prevention programs implemented before kids have even started smoking. Finally, I conclude by suggesting the need to change our academic culture to encourage more emphasis on mobilizing the knowledge we obtain from our research.

First, let me thank the Kurt Lewin Award Selection Committee for bestowing this great honor on me. Needless to say, it was a big surprise to be considered in the same group as past winners—including several of my graduate school heroes, Fritz Heider, Mort Deutsch, Don Campbell, and Hal Kelly, and several of my close professional friends, Jim Jones, Claude Steele, Faye Crosby, and Mark Snyder. Jim, Claude, Faye, Mark, and I go back so far it would be impolite to say how far!

Second, let me acknowledge my professional debt to Kurt Lewin. Of course, I never met Lewin. I was, however, trained by his direct "descendants." At Yale,

---

*Correspondence concerning this article should be addressed to Mark P. Zanna, Department of Psychology, University of Waterloo, Waterloo, Ontario N2L 3G1, Canada [e-mail: mzanna@uwaterloo.ca].

Because virtually all my research is a collaborative effort, the research discussed in the present essay was conducted with several graduate students—and a couple of colleagues. Therefore, I need to acknowledge the following individuals, in their "order of appearance," for their immense contributions to the research: Christian Jordan, Leanne Son Hing, Steve Spencer, Tara MacDonald, Geoff Fong, Sonya Dal Cin, Erin Strahan, Emiko Yoshida, Jennifer Peach, Christine Logel, Danu Stinson, Dave Hammond, and Shelagh Towson. I also thank Gene Borgida, Christine Logel, and Adam Zanna for comments on an earlier draft of this essay. Finally, I thank Steve Spencer for delivering an abridged version of this essay at *Society for the Psychological Study of Social Issues'* 8th Biennial Convention in New Orleans—while I was on the "Disabled List."

Chuck Kiesler was my primary PhD advisor; Dick Nisbett was my secondary advisor. Chuck was supervised by Leon Festinger, who in turn, of course, was supervised by Kurt Lewin. Dick was supervised by Stan Schachter, who in turn, was supervised by Festinger. So, I guess I am either Lewin's great grandson through Kiesler or great, great grandson through Nisbett. At any rate, there is no doubt that my mentors taught me in the Lewinian tradition to conduct high-impact experiments that tested theory relevant to (and often inspired by) social issues. Put simply, when feasible I am inclined to create high-impact psychological states as independent variables and assess consequential behaviors as dependent variables relevant to social issues (see Jordan & Zanna, 2007) for an essay that recommends this strategy for creating "persuasive experiments").

Third, given this background it should not be surprising to learn that I have been a member of the *Society for the Psychological Study of Social Issues* for my entire academic career.

There is Nothing So Practical as a Good…Theory

Curiosity-based, Basic Research

As a "card-carrying" Lewinian, I continue to believe that there is nothing so practical as a good theory. For me, this means (1) doing curiosity-based, basic research that is relevant to the social issues of the day, and (2) as mentioned above, when possible, doing high-impact research with consequential behavioral dependent variables.

For example, recently I have taken advantage of the "loose connection" between explicit and implicit prejudice to identify aversive racists on the left side of the political spectrum by proposing that aversive racists are individuals low on explicit prejudice but high on implicit prejudice. In our first study, we tested this hypothesis in the context of a hypocrisy-induction experiment (Son Hing, Li, & Zanna, 2002). Put simply, when we "rubbed the noses" of our participants in the fact that they do not always practice what they have preached in the context of intergroup relations, aversive racists (so defined), as we expected, felt guilty, and bent over backwards not to discriminate on a consequential budget-reduction ballot (i.e., they voted to minimally reduce the budget of a visible minority club on campus). More recently, we demonstrated that aversive racists only discriminate when there is a subtle excuse to do so (Son Hing, Chung-Yan, Hamilton, & Zanna, 2008). In this follow-up research, we also discovered that not all individuals on the right side of the political spectrum are modern racists. In fact, although modern racists (those high in explicit modern racism and high in implicit prejudice) do discriminate when there is a subtle excuse to do so, principled conservatives (those who score high on the explicit modern racism scale, but low in implicit prejudice) do not —that is, they are indistinguishable from those who are not likely to be prejudiced (those low on both explicit and implicit prejudice). Thus, although not all individuals on either the left or the right are prejudiced, some clearly are and we can now identify them a priori! So, let us get started on studying the similarities and the differences in prejudice both on the right and the left.

I have also taken advantage of the "loose connection" between explicit and implicit self-esteem to identify defensive individuals by proposing that such individuals are high on explicit self-esteem, but low on implicit self-esteem. In our first studies, we tested this hypothesis by demonstrating that defensive individuals (so defined) are more likely to be defensive than other groups, both dispositionally (i.e., they are the most narcissistic, a personality trait related to defensiveness) and situationally (i.e., they reduce dissonance by rationalizing their decisions the most) (Jordan, Spencer, Zanna, Hoshino-Browne, & Correll, 2003). More recently, we demonstrated that following a threat to their self-esteem defensive individuals are also the most likely to discriminate against an out-group member (Jordan, Spencer, & Zanna, 2005).

Intervention Studies

But if there is nothing so practical as a good theory, then we ought to use the theories that curiosity-based, basic research support to design interventions to make the world a better place. I view such intervention studies as both basic and applied. They are basic in the sense that they often test the theory in a new context. And, of course, they are applied in the sense that they are designed to make a difference in the world. Although intervention studies have not always been the focus of my research, they have become more of a focus in recent years.

So, what exactly do I mean by an intervention study? Although the hypocrisy study described above did seem to reduce prejudice for aversive racists, I do not regard it as an intervention study. To be an intervention study, we would have had to create and test the effects of an educational module that induced hypocrisy in students in an actual school context.

Let me now describe a few recent intervention studies that have followed up on curiosity-based, basic research.

Alcohol Myopia and Condom Use

For several years, my colleagues and I have tested Claude Steele's "Alcohol Myopia" Theory (the notion that intoxication reduces cognitive capacity so that individuals are influenced primarily by cues that are momentarily salient) to solve the puzzle of why men who claim to always use condoms do not always do so when intoxicated (Ebel-Lam, MacDonald, Zanna, & Fong, 2009; MacDonald, Fong, Zanna, & Martineau, 2000). In lab studies we have demonstrated that, when impelling cues (such as "she is attractive") are most salient (as they typically are in the real world), intoxicated individuals are more likely to intend to have unsafe sex than their sober counterparts, whereas when restraining cues (such as "she might have a STD") are most salient (as they typically are not in the real world), intoxicated individuals are less likely to intend to have unsafe sex than their sober counterparts. This basic research was exciting for two reasons. First, it supported the alcohol myopia prediction that intoxication does not always lead to risky decisions. Second, it suggested an intervention, namely, to expose intoxicated individuals to restraining cues when they are "in the heat of the moment." So, that is what we did in a field experiment. Put simply, we added a cue to a standard "safe sex" intervention (in the form of a friendship bracelet) designed to remind participants that they should act on their sober intentions to use condoms. To our amazement, we found that the reminder cue worked and did so to a greater extent when our participants reported they had been drinking (Dal Cin, MacDonald, Fong, Zanna, & Elton-Marshall, 2006).

Norms for Ideal Appearance and Contingencies of Self-Esteem

Colleagues and I have also been interested in testing the notion that the cultural norms for women's ideal appearance are problematic for women's satisfaction with their bodies and, ultimately, their eating behavior because the salience of such norms leads women to base their self-worth more strongly on appearance (Strahan, Spencer, & Zanna, 2007). What was interesting (to us) about this research was the fact that we assessed contingencies of self-worth for the first time at the dependent variable (rather than at the independent variable) level. With support for our hypothesis, we decided to conduct an intervention study designed to delegitimize the cultural norms for women's ideal appearance in a middle school, focusing on the notion that one's self-worth ought not to be solely contingent on one's appearance. In one 80-minute session, students discussed the historical changes in "ideal" body types, problem solved solutions to scenarios in which an individual felt pressure to look a certain way, and discussed how unrealistic and unattainable appearance ideals are (e.g., by contrasting the real-life photos of celebrities with their "perfected" media images). In a second 80-minute session, they applied what they had learned in a series of debates and created posters challenging the norms of appearance. Interestingly, we were able to delegitimize the cultural norms for ideal appearance for both girls and boys. And, as a result girls came to feel better about their bodies, mediated by the fact that girls did, indeed, base their self-worth less strongly on appearance (Strahan et al., 2008). Although the delegitimization of cultural norms for ideal appearance did not influence boys' contingencies of self-worth, the fact that they came to believe the cultural norms of appearance were illegitimate for boys and, especially, for girls was probably critical to the effectiveness of the intervention for the girls. At any rate, the presence versus the absence of boys ought to be tested in future interventions designed to delegitimize appearance norms for girls.

A "Chilly Climate" for Female Engineering Students

In recent years, perhaps, the line of research about which I am most excited concerns implicit norms. Following Olson and Fazio's innovation of "personalizing" the traditional Implicit Association Test (IAT) by changing the evaluative category labels from "pleasant" and "unpleasant" to "I like" and "I dislike" (Olson & Fazio, 2004), it was clear to me that the traditional IAT captured two sources of variances: automatic personal evaluative associations (i.e., implicit attitudes) and automatic cultural or normative evaluative associations (i.e., implicit norms). Recognizing that Olson and Fazio had "tweaked" the traditional IAT to capture implicit attitudes, Steve Spencer and I (and, of course, our students), in turn, decided to "tweak" Olson and Fazio's personal IAT to capture implicit norms by changing the evaluative labels to "most people like" and "most people dislike." So far, we have demonstrated that although they are often "loosely connected" to implicit attitudes and explicit norms, implicit norms have different/unique causes and consequences (Yoshida, Peach, Zanna, & Spencer, unpublished data). For example, the amount of time Asian students have spent in North America decreased their implicit normative regard, but not their implicit attitudes, toward the elderly. Situations that elicit stereotype threat in women decreased implicit norms toward women but not implicit attitudes. Hearing an audience laugh at a racist joke about people from the Middle East (vs. hearing the same joke with no laughter) made implicit norms toward people from the Middle East more negative but did not influence implicit attitudes—and, as a consequence, resulted in participants discriminating more against Muslims (i.e., by voting to cut more funds for a Muslim student organization on campus). Implicit norms toward Blacks predicted response times on a shooter bias task (such that those with more negative implicit norms were faster to shoot a Black target holding a gun and slower not to shoot a Black target holding a cell phone, cf., Correll, Park, Judd, & Winterbrink, 2002), whereas implicit attitudes, explicit attitudes, and explicit norms did not (Yoshida, Peach, Spencer, & Zanna, 2008).

Most important for the present essay, we also successfully "bottled" the chilly climate for female engineering students by assessing implicit normative evaluations of women in engineering at the beginning and end of their first year. We found not only that these implicit norms became more negative over the year—that is, students came to automatically associate exemplars of "female engineering students" more strongly with exemplars of what "most people dislike"—especially in engineering departments in which females comprised less than 20% of the class, but also that the more negative these female students' implicit normative evaluations of female engineers became, the more likely they were to be considering dropping out of engineering (Spencer, Peach, Yoshida, & Zanna, 2010). These findings are exciting because we now have an implicit "thermometer" of the engineering culture—and, thus, can begin to study exactly what (presumably) subtle cues actually create a chilly climate. These findings are also exciting because they led to a logical, follow-up intervention study in which we created a "belongingness" intervention (patterned after Walton & Cohen, 2007) designed to convey the message that female students do, in fact, "belong" in engineering (i.e., we employed audio-taped interviews with several upper-year male and female students that conveyed the message that although most students worry during their first year about whether they belong in engineering, these worries lessen with time). This intervention was delivered at the beginning of the fall semester. So far, after 3 years of data collection, we have discovered that the belongingness intervention increases female engineering students' grades, prevents their implicit norms of women in engineering from becoming negative, and increases their intentions to remain in engineering (Logel, Walton, Peach, Spencer, & Zanna, unpublished data)! Interestingly, it also prevented male students' implicit norms of women in engineering from becoming negative over time. In future interventions, it might make sense to "beef up" the belongingness intervention to make the normative belief even more clear that both female and male engineering students not only discover that they personally belong in engineering, but also come to recognize that all admitted students, both male and female, belong in engineering.

Self-Esteem and Health

Another recent line of research in which I am currently interested concerns the negative relation between self-esteem and health. Put simply, individuals low in self-esteem experience poorer health. Danu Stinson, Christine Logel, and I thought this might be so because individuals with low self-esteem experience poorer close relationships (i.e., they incorrectly believe their relationship partners do not like/respect them) and that poorer close relationships are likely to relate to poorer health. So far, in two longitudinal studies, we have demonstrated that self-esteem assessed early in the term negatively predicts health outcomes later in the term, and that this effect is mediated by the perceived quality of relationships assessed at a time half-way between the assessments of self-esteem and health outcomes. In one of the studies we even found that change in self-esteem predicted change in health outcomes mediated by change in the perceived quality of close relationships (Stinson et al., 2008).

Having demonstrated that low self-esteem individuals experience poorer health because they erroneously perceive their relationships to be problematic, we next created an intervention, a "psychological flu shot" if you will, designed to improve their perceptions of their relationships and, thereby, their health outcomes—and, ultimately, their self-esteem. Specifically, we employed a standard self-affirmation manipulation (in which participants select the value that is most important for themselves and explain why this value is so important). Preliminary results suggest that the self-affirmation manipulation entirely eliminated the negative relation between self-esteem and health by improving the health outcomes among low self-esteem participants who reported high levels of stress— and that this effect seemed to be mediated by decreasing the perception of stress in their relationships (Logel, Stinson, Shepherd, & Zanna, unpublished data).

Scaled-Up Interventions in Appropriate Settings

Are the sort of intervention studies described above sufficient to change the world? Obviously, they are not. This implies that, if we "bottle" a theoretically based intervention in either a laboratory or field experiment, we ought to consider the next step of disseminating the intervention more widely, perhaps with more than a little help from colleagues who have, at present, more expertise in disseminating such interventions. For example (and to be clear about what I am suggesting), once we discover (and replicate the findings) that female engineering students come to implicitly feel they do not belong in engineering and once we discover that a belongingness intervention works to prevent this from happening, we (with the help of others) should try to make this intervention an integral part of freshmen orientation week in our university, then in all universities in Canada, and then in all universities in North America, etc. For quality control, we should also continue to evaluate the effectiveness of the intervention as it is disseminated more widely. Of course, this is more than any individual faculty member can accomplish, but it is something for the field to contemplate and something to work toward in the future—in the service of making the world a better place.

There is Nothing So Practical as a Good ... Design

I also believe that, as experts in research methodology, we can also improve the quality of assessing intervention experiments and, more generally, of policy-relevant research by creating better research designs. Put simply, designs that capture the applied question at hand can be incredibly useful and practical. Let me now turn to two examples: one ongoing and one from the distant past.

Evaluating Tobacco Control Policies with Quasi-Experimental Designs

Just as we now believe that medical, and even clinical, treatments ought to be evidence based, so should we expect health policy to be evidence based. In recent years, Geoff Fong and his many colleagues (including me) have been evaluating the national tobacco control policies (such as banning "light/mild" brand labels, creating more effective warning labels, banning cigarette advertising, increasing cigarette taxes) mandated by the Framework Convention on Tobacco Control, the first international treaty devoted to health. Because governments, not researchers, control the implementation of such policies, we obviously cannot randomly assign one or more countries to "roll out" a particular policy. Thus, we have to use a quasi-experimental design that best approximates a true experiment. Following Campbell and Stanley (1963), we are tracking a panel of smokers in several countries, including Canada, United States, United Kingdom, and Australia. When one country (e.g., United Kingdom) initiates a national tobacco control policy (e.g., bans light/mild brand labels, or mandates new, more effective warning labels) between waves of data collection, it becomes the "experimental" country and the other countries (i.e., Canada, United States, and Australia) become the "control" countries with respect to that particular tobacco control policy. Thus, we have designed a pretest–posttest, longitudinal panel study with a comparison between the country that initiates a new, national tobacco-control policy and the countries that do not (Borland et al., 2008).

So far, this quasi-experimental design comes as close as possible to the sort of experimental designs that existed in the 1960s when Campbell and Stanley wrote their classic article on quasi-experimental designs. But, interestingly and importantly, we do not design experiments nowadays like we did in 1960s. What is new? Put simply, there is much more emphasis on testing mediation hypotheses. That is, nowadays we want to know the mechanisms/processes by which the independent variable influences downstream dependent variables. In the present context, for example, how can we be sure that, if smokers in the United Kingdom (compared to the smokers in the three control countries) are more likely to intend to quit smoking following the initiation of new, improved warning labels, this "effect" is actually due to the warning labels—and not something else?

Our solution to this problem was to create a quasi-experimental design (circa 2000) in which we attempted to assess mediation variables uniquely relevant to each of the potential tobacco-control policies under investigation. So, notwithstanding our critique of the standard way mediation hypotheses are tested in experimental research (Spencer, Zanna, & Fong, 2005), we believe that, if the downstream effects of a given policy are mediated by processes uniquely relevant to the policy and, importantly, not by processes uniquely relevant to other policies, we have strong, discriminative evidence that the initiated policy was, indeed, the variable responsible for producing the downstream effects (Fong, Hammond, & Zanna, 2006).

Evaluating Smoking Prevention Programs. . .While Waiting for Nature to Take Her Course

So far, I have discussed relatively recent research conducted within the last decade. Let me now close by going "back to the future" to talk about research I conducted over 25 years ago—and, in the process, finally explain the title of this essay.

The story begins when I was invited to collaborate on an ongoing smoking prevention program with colleagues in the Health Studies Department at the University of Waterloo. My colleagues in Health Studies had initiated a second-generation smoking prevention program in several school districts in Ontario. In addition to "beefing up" the intervention itself, the main change from the first-generation smoking prevention programs was that the Waterloo intervention was delivered earlier (in the sixth grade) before kids were likely to have started smoking in the first place. The logic was simple: If you want to prevent smoking, intervene before kids start smoking.

OK, but why did these colleagues want me to collaborate with them, given the facts that their intervention was, if anything, likely to be an improvement, that their logic was entirely reasonable and, importantly, that they had just finished collecting a posttest wave of data at the end of the school year? It took me some time (perhaps, a half dozen research meetings over a 2-month period) to figure out not only that my colleagues' logic did, in fact, result in a design problem that put their future funding at risk, but also that, although they needed some help to solve the problem, they were reticent to explicitly ask for advice. Put simply, if you deliver the intervention early—when few kids are already smoking in the control schools—you will not be able to detect an effect of your intervention in the experimental schools. I came to realize that I was being asked to help design a "quick fix" to this problem in the face of an imminent site visit from the funding source!

So, while waiting for nature to take her course (which in this context means, while waiting for kids to start smoking in the control schools), what did we do to convince the funding source to continue funding the project because the intervention was, in fact, making a difference (or, at least, was likely to make a difference)? To answer this question I came up with two design solutions: A correlational ("at risk") design and an experimental (social psychological) design. (Because we did not have time to conduct the experimental design before the site visit, let me first describe the at-risk design.)

The at-risk design recognizes the fact that although most kids have not started smoking by the end of the sixth grade, some may have. In this situation, the question becomes: Can we identify these kids a priori? Although this was not my area of research, I did not have to be a "rocket scientist" to suggest that the kids who were most at-risk to start smoking were probably those whose parents, siblings, and/or friends smoked. And, because my colleagues had collected this pretest data, we were able to create an at-risk index. Two relatively straightforward questions followed this insight: (1) Are the at-risk kids (even if only 10–15% of the sample) randomly assigned to the control schools, in fact, smoking by the end of the sixth grade?, and (2) If so, are the at-risk kids who were randomly assigned to the experimental schools smoking, too, or (hopefully) not? Well, it turns out that the at-risk kids in the control schools had started to smoke and did so to a significantly greater extent than the at-risk kids in the experimental schools. So, it looked like the intervention was working—and, happily, was working for the kids for whom we most wanted it to work, i.e., those who were the most at-risk (see Flay et al., 1985, for a report of the completed study).

A couple of years later my colleagues conducted a follow-up smoking prevention intervention (in which they manipulated whether researchers, teachers, or school nurses delivered the intervention) that allowed us to carry out an experimental design in the tradition of social psychology. The cover story for the experiment was that, because summer was around the corner and summer camp directors were in the process of hiring summer camp counselors, we were interested in seeing whether camp directors would recommend hiring the same or different camp counselors than prospective campers, such as our participants. So, students were led to believe we were evaluating several applicants for the job of camp counselor. In the critical videotaped job interview the applicant either smoked a cigarette or not. Thus, in a 2 × 2 design, students from experimental versus control schools evaluated a smoking versus nonsmoking applicant for a summer camp counselor job. Interestingly—and importantly—before kids had started to smoke (and, thus, before we could detect whether the intervention had prevented kids from smoking) we found that sixth graders evaluated the smoking job applicant more negatively, but only if they had attended an intervention school (Towson, Pepperall, & Zanna, 1984).

Although nowadays we could (and probably would) assess students' implicit attitudes toward smoking (as a way to rule out demand characteristics as an alternative explanation), I still believe it is important to consider the sort of experiment we conducted "while waiting for nature to take her course." In fact, if I had to do it all over again, I'd make the dependent variable more consequential by convincing participants that their evaluations of the camp counselors would actually influence who would be hired!

In conclusion, in the spirit of Kurt Lewin, although I truly hope we never stray too far from doing curiosity-based, basic experimental research in the lab and in the field that is inspired by social issues, I also hope that we begin to change our academic culture to become a whole lot more serious about mobilizing our knowledge—by creating and testing theory-based interventions that we eventually disseminate—to make the world a better place—and, at least, to make our granting agencies happy, and, more importantly, to inspire our graduate students! And while we are at it, when we evaluate social policies, let us make sure we use "state of the art" designs.

References

Borland, R., Fong, G. T., Yong, H-H., Cummings, K. M., Hammond, D., King, B., et al. (2008). What happens to smokers' beliefs about light cigarettes when 'light/mild' brand descriptors were banned in the UK? Findings from the International Tobacco Control (ITC) Four Country Survey. *Tobacco Control, 17*, 256–262. doi:10.1136/tc.2007.023812.

Campbell, D. T., & Stanley, J. C. (1963). *Experimental and quasi-experimental designs for research.* Chicago, IL: Rand McNally & Company.

Correll, J., Park, B., Judd, C. M., & Wittenbrink, B. (2002). The police officer's dilemma: Using ethnicity to disambiguate potentially threatening individuals. *Journal of Personality and Social Psychology, 83*, 1314–1329. doi:10.1037/0022–3514.83.6.1314.

Dal Cin, S., MacDonald, T. K., Fong, G. T., Zanna, M. P., & Elton-Marshall, T. E. (2006). Remembering the message: Using a reminder cue to increase condom use following a safer sex intervention. *Health Psychology, 25*, 438–443. doi:10.1037/0278–6133.25.3.438.

Ebel-Lam, A. P., MacDonald, T. K., Zanna, M. P., & Fong, G. T. (2009). An experimental investigation of the interactive effects of alcohol and sexual arousal on intentions to have unprotected sex. *Basic and Applied Social Psychology, 31*, 226–233. doi:10.1080/01973530903058383.

Flay, B. R., Ryan, K. B., Best, J. A., Brown, S., Kersell, M. W., d'Avernas, J. R., et al. (1985). Are social-psychological smoking prevention programs effective? The Waterloo Study. *Journal of Behavioral Medicine, 8*, 37–59. doi:10.1007/BF00845511.

Fong, G. T., Hammond, D., & Zanna, M. P. (2006). Bridging to evidence-based public health policy. In P. A. M. Van Lange (Ed.), *Bridging social psychology: Benefits of transdisciplinary approaches* (pp. 267–280). Mahwah, NJ: Lawrence Erlbaum Associates.

Jordan, C. H., & Zanna, M. P. (2007). Not all experiments are created equal: On conducting and reporting persuasive experiments. In R. J Sternberg, D. Halpern, & H. L. Roediger III (Ed.), *Critical Thinking in Psychology* (pp. 160–176). New York: Cambridge University Press. doi:10.1177/0146167204271580.

Jordan, C. H., Spencer, S. J., Zanna, M. P., Hoshino-Browne E., & Correll, J. (2003). Secure and defensive self-esteem. *Journal of Personality and Social Psychology, 85*, 969–978. doi:10.1037/0022–3514.85.5.969.

Jordan, C. H., Spencer, S. J., & Zanna, M. P. (2005). Types of high self-esteem and prejudice: How implicit self-esteem relates to racial discrimination among his explicit self-esteem individuals. *Personality and Social Psychology Bulletin, 31*, 693–702

MacDonald, T. K., Fong, G. T., Zanna, M. P., & Martineau, A. M. (2000). Alcohol myopia and condom use: Can alcohol intoxication be associated with more prudent behavior? *Journal of Personality and Social Psychology, 78*, 605–619. doi:10.1037/0022–3514.78.4.605.

Olson, M. A., & Fazio, R. H. (2004). Reducing the influence of extrapersonal associations on the Implicit Association Test: Personalizing the IAT. *Journal of Personality and Social Psychology, 86*, 653–667. doi:10.1037/0022–3514.86.5.653.

Son Hing, L. S., Li, W., & Zanna, M. P. (2002). Inducing hypocrisy to reduce prejudicial responses among aversive racists. *Journal of Experimental Social Psychology, 38*, 71–78. doi:10.1006/jesp.2001.1484.

Son Hing, L. S., Chung-Yan, G. A., Hamilton, L. K., & Zanna, M. P. (2008). A two-dimensional model that employs explicit and implicit attitudes to characterize prejudice. *Journal of Personality and Social Psychology, 94*, 971–987. doi:10.1037/0022–3514.94.6.971.

Spencer, S. J., Zanna, M. P., & Fong, G. T. (2005). Establishing a causal chain: Why experiments are often more effective in examining psychological process than meditational analyses. *Journal of Personality and Social Psychology, 89*, 845–851. doi:10.1037/0022–3514.89.6.845.

Spencer, S. J., Peach, J., Yoshida, E., & Zanna, M. P. (2010). Learning what most people like: How implicit attitudes and normative evaluations are shaped by motivation and influence meaningful behavior. In J. Forgas, J. Cooper, & W. Crano (Eds.), *The Social Psychology of Attitudes and Attitude Change* (pp. 155–169). New York: Psychology Press.

Stinson, D. A., Logel, C., Zanna, M. P., Holmes, J. G., Cameron, J., Wood, J. V., & Spencer, S. J. (2008). The cost of lower self-esteem: Testing a self-and-social bonds model of health. *Journal of Personality and Social Psychology, 94*, 412–428. doi:10.1037/0022–3514.94.3.412.

Strahan, E. J., Spencer, S. J., & Zanna, M. P. (2007). Don't take another bite: How sociocultural norms of appearance affect women's behavior. *Body Image, 4*, 331–342. doi:10.1016/j.bodyim.207.06.003.

Strahan, E. J., Lafrance, A., Wilson, A. E., Ethier, N., Spencer, S. J., & Zanna, M. P. (2008). Victoria's dirty secret: How sociocultural norms influence adolescent girls and women. *Personality and Social Psychology Bulletin, 34*, 288–301. doi:10.1177/0146167207310457.

Towson, S. M. J., Pepperall, G., & Zanna, M. P. (June 1984). *The impact of a smoking prevention programme on the evaluation of smokers and non-smokers.* Paper presented at the annual meeting of the Canadian Psychological Association, Ottawa, Canada (Abstract published in *Canadian Psychology, 25* (2a), no. 487).

Walton, G. M., & Cohen, G. L. (2007). A question of belonging: Race, social fit, and achievement. *Journal of Personality and Social Psychology, 92*, 82–96. doi:10.1037/0022–3514.92.1.82.

Yoshida, E., Peach, J. M., Spencer, S. J., & Zanna, M. P. (January 2008). *The influence of implicit norms on discrimination.* Symposium presentation at the 9th annual conference of the Society of Personality and Social Psychology, Albuquerque, NM.

MARK P. ZANNA is a University Professor and Chair of Psychology at the University of Waterloo. He received his bachelor's and doctoral degrees from Yale University. His area of research is the psychology of attitudes. Currently, he is studying self-esteem and prejudice at both the explicit and implicit levels. A former President of the *Society of Experimental Social Psychology* (1985) and the *Society of Personality and Social Psychology* (1997), he currently edits *Advances in Experimental Social Psychology* (since 1991) and the *Ontario Symposium on Personality and Social Psychology* (since 1981). A Fellow of the *Royal Society of Canada*, he is the recipient of Distinguished Scientific Contribution Awards from the Canadian Psychological Association (D. O. Hebb Award in 1993), the *Society of Personality and Social Psychology* (D. T. Campbell Award in 1997), the *Society of Experimental Social Psychology* (in 2007), and the *Society for the Psychological Study of Social Issues* (K. Lewin Award in 2010).